# LENSES ON READING

# Lenses on
# Reading

## AN INTRODUCTION TO
## THEORIES AND MODELS

Diane H. Tracey
Lesley Mandel Morrow

**THE GUILFORD PRESS**
New York      London

© 2006 The Guilford Press
A Division of Guilford Publications, Inc.
72 Spring Street, New York, NY 10012
www.guilford.com

Printed in the United States of America

This book is printed on acid-free paper.

Last digit is print number:   9   8   7   6   5   4   3

**Library of Congress Cataloging-in-Publication Data**
Tracey, Diane H.
   Lenses on reading : an introduction to theories and models / Diane H.
Tracey, Lesley Mandel Morrow.
      p. cm.
   Includes bibliographical references (p. ) and index.
   ISBN-10: 1-59385-296-7      ISBN-13: 978-1-59385-296-2 (paper)
   ISBN-10: 1-59385-297-5      ISBN-13: 978-1-59385-297-9 (cloth)
   1. Reading—Philosophy—History.   2. Reading—Research—
Methodology—History.   3. Reading, Psychology of—History.   I. Morrow,
Lesley Mandel.   II. Title.
   LB1050.T69 2006
   428.4—dc22

                                                    2005035105

*To my husband, Stephen,*
*who centers the most important part of my life;*
*and to our daughters, Katie and Julia,*
*who light up our world*

—DHT

*To my daughter and son-in-law, Stephanie and Doug; and*
*to my grandchildren, James and Natalie,*
*who have made the theories in this book come alive*

—LMM

# About the Authors

**Diane H. Tracey, EdD,** is Associate Professor of Education at Kean University, where she teaches graduate classes to students planning to become reading specialists. She has written widely on topics related to literacy achievement, received numerous grant awards, and is an active presenter at national conferences. She has served on editorial review boards for the *Journal of Literacy Research, The Reading Teacher,* and the *National Conference Yearbook,* and is a past chair of the International Reading Association's Technology Committee. In addition to university teaching, Dr. Tracey is a literacy consultant for school districts and educational software companies. Prior to her work at the university level, she was an early childhood educator and a research assistant on a large, federally funded grant project studying children's reading disabilities.

**Lesley Mandel Morrow, PhD,** holds the rank of Professor II at the Graduate School of Education at Rutgers University, where she is Chair of the Department of Learning and Teaching. She began her career as a classroom teacher, then became a reading specialist, and later received her PhD from Fordham University in New York City. Her research deals with early literacy development and the organization and management of language arts programs, and is carried out with children and families from diverse backgrounds.

Dr. Morrow has written more than 250 publications, including journal articles, chapters in books, monographs, and books. She has received numerous grants for her research from the federal government and has served as a principal research investigator for several research centers. She received Excellence in Research, Teaching and Service Awards from Rutgers University and was the recipient of the International Reading Association's Outstanding Teacher Educator of Reading Award and Fordham University's Alumni Award for Outstanding Achievement. Dr. Morrow was an elected member of the board of directors of the International Reading Association, and served as President of the organization from 2003 to 2004.

# Acknowledgments

As authors of this volume, we gratefully acknowledge the support and help of our colleagues, students, families, and friends during the writing of this book. We would especially like to note the outstanding contributions of our editor and friend, Chris Jennison of The Guilford Press. Chris nurtured this project from its infancy with patience, kindness, and a tremendous amount of professional knowledge. He contacted many reviewers on our behalf as we wrestled with which theories to include in the manuscript and the ways in which they should be organized. After the structure of the text was complete, he regularly secured feedback to ensure that we were meeting our readers' needs. He also enlisted the capable hands of Craig Thomas, Jeannie Tang, and Robin Lenowitz to provide the finishing touches to the book. Chris—we thank you and your staff for the significant additions to this endeavor that make it yours as well as ours.

We would also like to thank our colleagues, the academic community of literacy educators, for their exceptional camaraderie. Many members of our fellowship generously lent their minds to this project and we are truly indebted to them. Of special note are the contributions of Michael Pressley, who met with us dutifully for 5 years at the NRC and IRA conferences to share his personal insights on the nature and content of this work. We also gratefully acknowledge the support of our university colleagues, especially Dr. Roberta Karstadt of Kean University, who graciously offered to use this text with her class when it was still in its draft form. We thank our wonderful students who heard and responded to this material before it was printed, and contributed anecdotes that linked the theories with their real-life classroom successes and challenges.

I, Diane H. Tracey, thank my family and friends for their support and love during the writing of this work. I thank my husband, Stephen, and daughters, Katie and Julia, for many things but, at this moment, most especially for the years of Sunday dinners they made joyful at the end of writing days. I would also like to thank my closest friends of heart and spirit: Barbara Hirschmann, Nancy Wolf, Janet Esposito, Stephanie Solaris, and Martin Gliserman. I thank my parents, Bridgewater friends, yoga friends, and Temple Beth-El community. Last, and perhaps most of all, I thank my dear friend, mentor, and writing partner Lesley Mandel Morrow, an inspiration to us all.

I, Lesley Mandel Morrow, would like to thank my family for their support: my husband, Frank Morrow; daughter, Stephanie; and son-in-law, Doug Bushell, for their interest in my work; and most of all my grandchildren, James, age 3, and Natalie, age 5 months. James and Natalie have been modeling the theories before my very eyes. I thank Diane Tracey for asking me to write with her, for doing the major portion of the work, and for being such a good friend.

# Preface

*Lenses on Reading: An Introduction to Theories and Models* is an introductory text that offers an overview of the major theories and models regarding the reading component of literacy learning. The objectives of the text are to summarize the key theories and models related to reading processes and instruction, and to provide readers with implications and ideas for both practice and research. The ultimate goals of the text are to help educators enhance their instruction through better understanding of theories and models, and to assist researchers and graduate students in situating their research within theoretical frameworks. The book is designed for use as a text in graduate courses such as Foundations of Reading, Psychology of Reading, and Reading Research Seminars. The volume should also prove useful as a reference and resource tool for personal and professional libraries.

## PRINCIPAL THEMES AND UNIQUE FEATURES

The principal theme of the book is that there are myriad perspectives and viewpoints (lenses) that can be used to examine all of life's circumstances. It is suggested that the more lenses through which individuals are able to see the world, the more flexible, and ultimately capable, they can be in responding to and discussing it with others. Narrowing these ideas to the realm of literacy learning, the text suggests that the more lenses educators possess for examining the reading process and instruction, the better equipped they will be to understand, facilitate, and articulate literacy development. Knowledge of theories and models, along with their implications for practice and research, will contribute to educators becoming informed decision makers. The conceptualization of teachers as informed decision makers is consistent with exemplary literacy instruction practice (Pressley, Allington, Wharton-McDonald, Block, & Morrow, 2001). With regard to framing research, knowledgeable use of models and theories significantly strengthens the value of reading investigations (Creswell, 2002). In short, the first unique feature of this text is its philosophical orientation regarding the importance of multiple lenses on reading for both instructional application and for framing research.

The second distinctive feature of the text is its design as an introduction to theories and models relevant to reading. As an introductory text, the book assumes little, if any, theoretical background knowledge on the part of the reader. Care is taken to define unique vocabulary terms and to provide opportunities to link subject matter areas within the text to each other. While it is hoped that advanced literacy researchers and practitioners will find the book useful, it is the beginning professionals for whom the work is crafted.

The third distinctive feature of the book is its sections on "Classroom Applications" and "Research Applications" for each chapter. The section on "Classroom Applications" offers discussions and anecdotes that illustrate the use of each theory or model as a lens for actual classroom practice. Many of the reflections are written by practicing teachers who were enrolled in graduate classes on the book's topic. The section on "Research Applications" offers suggestions for the use of each of the theories or models for particular topics of research. Additionally, sample research studies illustrating the application of many of the theories and/or models are included in this section.

## SEQUENCE AND SCOPE OF THE TEXT

The present text has adopted a semihistorical approach to the examination of theories and models with the greatest implications for reading instruction and research. The approach is "semihistorical" rather than completely historical because, despite the clear-cut chapter titles and accompanying dates, in reality the emergence of the theories and models has been neither straightforward with regard to category, nor linear with regard to chronology. Rather, the theories and models presented in this volume have evolved from strands of research and writing that often overlap and affect each other. Furthermore, the strands have grown from a variety of disciplines, including psychology, general education, and sociology, all of which have influenced thinking and research regarding the reading process and reading instruction. Despite the overlap and ultimate influence that the ideas presented here have upon one another, the text has attempted to identify and organize, from a semihistorical perspective, the major theoretical strands that have had the greatest impact for understanding reading practice and research. The chapters are sequenced in the approximate time frames in which the strand emerged. We hope that this organization will allow readers to appreciate not only the multiple theoretical lenses from which reading has been examined throughout the past centuries, but also the approximate chronology of the appearance of these varying perspectives. Two appendices are included at the end of the book for easy reference. Appendix A offers a chronological summary of all the theories and models discussed in the text; Appendix B presents an outline of these theories and models with examples of instructional practices that are representative of each.

The topic of reading is one that is situated within multiple contexts. It is impossible, however, to present an exhaustive examination of all the theories and models relevant to these contexts. Rather than trying to create an all-inclusive volume, we have sought to present those theories and models that we believe have the greatest relevance for informing graduate students, practitioners, and reading researchers of the 21st century. In defining our scope we have not used hard-and-fast rules with regard to what and what not to include. In contrast, prior to our writing we examined as many different theories and models as possible and then carefully selected those that we believed would be most meaningful for our intended audience. In making our inclusion decisions we continually kept the importance of a particular theory or model for classroom practice as a discriminator, but also included those theories and models with great significance for framing reading research. Our decisions regarding inclusion have not been made easily, nor have they been made in isolation. As with any published work, the completed text reflects the continuous effort of our editor, rounds of reviews by committed colleagues, and many discussions by the authors. Despite the best efforts of all of these parties, we acknowledge that important theories or models relevant to this topic may have been excluded. We apologize for any oversights in this realm and encourage our readers to contact us with any thoughts and ideas for strengthening future editions of this work.

Each of the theories and models in this text is illustrated by classroom application activities, teaching anecdotes, and ideas for related research investigations. Importantly, many of these illustrations can be used to describe multiple theories. For example, the popular practice of brainstorming a web with students prior to reading can be used to illustrate a classroom application activity reflective of Associationism, Connectionism, and/or Schema Theory. Thus, the reader is urged to maintain an open and flexible stance when reading this volume. The ability to see the ways in which classroom practices are reflective of many theories strengthens the mind of the reader and underscores the primary premise of the text: the value of multiple perspectives in improving literacy education.

Given the broad scope of this text, the book aims to provide an introduction and overview of the major theories and models that influence reading instruction and research. As such, to use the words of R. Murray Thomas (1996) in his excellent book on theories of general education, "This book serves the same purpose in the world of theories that a three-week guided tour of Europe has in the world of travel" (p. xv). Readers should expect an introduction and overview when reading this work, and are encouraged to read additional information on all of the topics to gain greater depth and insight. Indeed, most, if not all, of the topics presented in this volume are the subjects of books in and of themselves.

In sum, this text aims to tell a story: the semihistorical story of the major strands of thinking that have come to be known as theories and models, and their influences on our understanding of the reading process, reading instruction, and reading research. It is hoped that this story extends and enriches the minds of all who read it.

# Contents

1. **Introduction to Theories and Models**      1

    *What Is a Theory?: A General Definition 2*
    *Are People Aware of the Theories That They Possess? 3*
    *What Is a Theory?: A Definition for Education 4*
    *The Importance of Theories to Educational Practice 4*
    *Are Teachers Aware of the Theories That They Possess? 5*
    *The Importance of Theories to Educational Research 6*
    *Is a Model Different from a Theory? 9*
    *Why Is It Important to Understand Models? 10*
    *The Value of Multiple Lenses 10*
    *Theories and Models Included in This Text 12*
    *Summary 13*

2. **Early Roots: Early Theories and Models Applicable**      15
   **to Reading (400 B.C.–1899)**

    *Mental Discipline Theory 16*
    *Associationism 17*
    *Unfoldment Theory 19*
    *Structuralism and Early Scientific Foundations of Reading 22*
    *Classroom Applications 24*
    *Research Applications 28*
    *Summary 30*

3. Behaviorism: The Dominant Educational Theory          32
   for 50 Years (1900–1950s)

   *What Is Behaviorism?  33*
   *Classical Conditioning Theory  33*
   *Connectionism  34*
   *Operant Conditioning Theory  36*
   *Classroom Applications  38*
   *Research Applications  43*
   *Summary  45*


4. Constructivism (1920s–Present)                         47

   *Constructivism: The General Concept  47*
   *Inquiry Learning  48*
   *Schema Theory  51*
   *Transactional/Reader Response Theory  54*
   *Psycholinguistic Theory and Whole Language Theory  57*
   *Metacognition  61*
   *Engagement Theory  64*
   *Classroom Applications  65*
   *Research Applications  71*
   *Summary  74*


5. Theories of Literacy Development (1930s–Present)       76

   *Theory of Cognitive Development  77*
   *Maturation Theory  79*
   *Theory of Literacy Development  80*
   *Stage Models of Reading  82*
   *Emergent Literacy Theory  84*
   *Family Literacy Theory  87*
   *Classroom Applications  90*
   *Research Applications  95*
   *Summary  98*


6. Social Learning Perspectives (1960s–Present)          100

   *Sociolinguistic Theory  101*
   *Socio-Cultural Theory  104*
   *Social Constructivism  108*
   *Social Learning Theory  111*
   *Critical Literacy Theory  113*
   *Classroom Applications  115*
   *Research Applications  121*
   *Summary  123*

7. **Information/Cognitive Processing Perspectives**      **125**
   **(1950s–1970s)**

   *General Characteristics of the Cognitive Processing View   126*
   *Information Processing Theories   126*
   *Substrata-Factor Theory of Reading   129*
   *Rauding Theory   131*
   *Gough's Model   132*
   *Automatic Information Processing Model   134*
   *Interactive Model   138*
   *Classroom Applications   140*
   *Research Applications   143*
   *Summary   146*


8. **Information/Cognitive Processing Perspectives,**      **148**
   **Continued (1980s)**

   *Interactive–Compensatory Model   149*
   *Orthographic Processing Perspective   151*
   *Verbal Efficiency Theory   152*
   *Construction–Integration Model   153*
   *Phonological–Core Variable Difference Model   155*
   *Classroom Applications   157*
   *Research Applications   159*
   *Summary   162*


9. **Information/Cognitive Processing Perspectives:**      **164**
   **State of the Art (1989–Present)**

   *Parallel Distributed Processing Model   164*
   *Dual-Route Cascaded Model   169*
   *Double-Deficit Hypothesis   171*
   *Neuroscience and Education   173*
   *Classroom Applications   175*
   *Research Applications   178*
   *Summary   181*


10. **Putting It All Together**      **183**

   *Early Roots   183*
   *Behaviorism   185*
   *Constructivism and Reading   187*
   *Theories of Literacy Development   191*
   *Social Learning Perspectives   195*
   *Information/Cognitive Processing Perspectives   198*

*Information/Cognitive Processing Perspectives,*
    *Continued   201*
*Information/Cognitive Processing Perspectives:*
    *State of the Art   202*
*Final Thoughts   204*

## APPENDICES

APPENDIX A.  Summary Chart: Onset of Presented Theoretical          208
                 Perspectives Affecting Literacy Education
APPENDIX B.  Summary of Theories Presented and Sample              210
                 Representative Instructional Practices


**References**                                                    **213**

**Author Index**                                                  **227**

**Subject Index**                                                 **232**

# CHAPTER 1

# Introduction to Theories
# and Models

Sara, a pretty but quiet 8-year-old, squirms uncomfortably in her chair, aware that all eyes are upon her. She stares at the words on the page, unable to utter a sound. At first, her classmates are courteous as they wait for her to respond, but then they grow impatient as her silence persists. The students themselves begin to squirm as they exchange knowing glances with each other: "Here we go again, waiting for Sara to read." Ms. Brown, the classroom teacher, grows uncomfortable too. Was she wrong to call on Sara to read? Why hasn't this child been able to keep up with her peers in reading? How can she, Ms. Brown, help Sara learn to read?

This scene, all too common in the United States and throughout the world, depicts a fundamental concern of reading educators: how to help a child experiencing reading difficulties in the classroom. Even teachers of students not experiencing difficulties struggle with how best to promote their students' literacy growth. Most classroom teachers use all of the materials and strategies at their disposal to help their students achieve. These include reading programs purchased by the school district, supplemental materials they personally collect, ideas adapted from conferences and workshops, approaches borrowed from professional development books, projects downloaded from the Internet, suggestions from their colleagues, and the like. As most educators will attest, a good classroom teacher will try almost anything to help a student succeed in reading. If, after all of a teacher's best efforts, a student is still making insufficient progress, the teacher will turn to a reading specialist or a child study team in his or her school for help. At this point, increased diagnosis and a wider range of interventions are implemented. So goes the approach to most reading instruction in this country.

The link between typical approaches to reading instruction and the content of this text lies in the ways in which classroom teachers, reading specialists, child study team professionals, and reading researchers think about which instructional approaches and assessments should be used in helping students progress in reading. What may not be immediately apparent to these professionals, however, is that the ways in which they approach reading instruction and research are, to a large degree, driven by the theories that they hold regarding the ways in which children learn to read. Many educators are not consciously aware of the theories that drive their practices. Few classroom teachers can tell you which theories contribute to their instruction; even fewer would tell you that they care. For decades, the term "theory" has been associated with something only scholars who live and work in ivory towers need to know.

This text seeks to convince educators that understanding the theories that are related to reading instruction, and learning to link these theories to classroom practice, will strengthen both classroom instruction and research. As a result of reading this text, educators will better understand the full range of perspectives (i.e., theories) from which the reading process can be understood. A greater understanding of the reading process will enable educators to use a wider range of approaches when working with students, and help them to more selectively decide which approaches should be used when helping individual students. Collectively, this knowledge can lead to a greater ability to help students learn to read.

## WHAT IS A THEORY?: A GENERAL DEFINITION

According to the *American Heritage Dictionary* (2001), a *theory* is "a set of statements or principles devised to explain a group of facts or phenomena, especially one that has been repeatedly tested or is widely accepted" (p. 848). Theories are explanations that are grounded in belief systems usually supported by extensive research and databases, and often held by large groups of people. Competing theories are often studied, tested, and debated over long periods of time. Thomas (1996) writes:

Theory is *an explanation of how the facts fit together.* More precisely, theorizing about [a topic] means the act of proposing (1) which facts are most important for understanding [that topic] and (2) what sorts of relationships among the facts are most significant for producing this understanding. Theory is what makes sense out of facts. Theory gives facts their meaning. Without theory, facts remain a clutter of disorganized specks on the canvas, unconnected spots that form no picture of how and why children grow up as they do. (p. 4)

There are theories to describe almost every phenomenon in life. One example of a phenomenon that can be examined theoretically is the question of life's very beginning. One theory of the beginning of human life is the biblical version that God created man in an instant in the form of Adam and Eve. This theory is known as "creationism." A contrasting theory for explaining the beginning of human life is evolution, which posits that man evolved biologically in a gradual process over a very long period of time from lower ordered species. Large numbers of people subscribe to one or the other of these theories.

With regard to daily life, theories are explanations that people turn to when they are trying to understand what has happened to them in the present or the past, or what might happen to them in the future. When individuals become ill, for example, some attribute the event to a spiritual theory ("it was meant to happen" or "it happened for a reason"), while others attribute the occurrence to a medical theory such as genetic predisposition, exposure to a particular germ, a relationship with nutrition, or a mind–body connection. In general, people adopt particular theories and use them repeatedly throughout their lives to explain a wide variety of experiences. The theories then become the *lenses* through which individuals view the world.

## ARE PEOPLE AWARE OF THE THEORIES THAT THEY POSSESS?

People may be conscious or unconscious of the theories that they use in daily living. When individuals are conscious of their theories, or belief systems, they are able to label them, think about them, talk about them with others, and compare their own theories with alternative ones. For example, a psychologist who applies a treatment based on a specific theory, such as Behaviorism, should be able to explain why he or she is using that treatment and theory instead of alternative ones. In contrast, when individuals are unconscious of their theories, they are unable to reflect on or talk about them. A mother who gives her child a treat when the child is well behaved but punishes the child when the child is poorly behaved is applying Behaviorism theory, even though she is unaware of it. Importantly, regardless of whether or not individuals are conscious of the theories they use, the theories still operate and affect the ways in which all human beings see, think about, and respond to the world. In short, in all areas of life, people perceive the world through their theoretical lenses, whether or not they are aware that these lenses exist.

## WHAT IS A THEORY?: A DEFINITION
## FOR EDUCATION

In many scientific fields, including that of education, the concept of "theory" is frequently used. When the term "theory" is used in the field of education, it refers to a well-documented explanation for a phenomenon related to teaching and/or learning. This explanation (i.e., theory) then becomes part of the body of content knowledge that constitutes the field.

Educators have a multitude of theories that they can use to explain a wide variety of learning and teaching phenomena. In the field of education, theories are used to explain learning, motivation, memory, achievement, and intelligence, among others things. When a child has difficulty learning to read, for example, one theory (i.e., explanation) is that the cause is related to a cognitive problem. Other theories that might be used to explain the reading problem include theories of motivation, language, behavior, and/or social differences.

## THE IMPORTANCE OF THEORIES
## TO EDUCATIONAL PRACTICE

As explained above, one of the most important reasons for understanding theories is that individuals' theories are closely linked to their behaviors and practices. Let's return to the example above regarding ill health. An individual with a nutritional theory of health and illness would most likely seek healing differently than would an individual with a spiritual theory regarding health and illness. Similarly, in the example of Sara, the child with a reading difficulty, a teacher who theorizes that the child's reading problem is caused by auditory- and or visual-processing deficits would create different educational interventions for Sara than would a teacher whose theory of reading is centered in the concept of motivation. Thus the link between theory and behavior is the central reason that knowledge of theories is essential for optimal classroom instruction. When teachers become aware of the full range of theories from which their educational practices can radiate, their repertoire of teaching skills can greatly expand. Similarly, when teachers understand the full range of theories from which instructional strategies stem, they can select those interventions that best suit the particular teaching situation, thus optimizing the effectiveness of their instruction. A broad understanding of theories also allows educators to coordinate and provide complementary instructional interventions from a wide variety of theoretical orientations. Hayes (1997), who conducts research with teachers, confirms that thinking related to educational theories does affect teachers' practices. Hayes writes:

> During instruction, teachers continually interpret the events surrounding their interactions with learners. . . . Their thinking concerns several variables always present during instruction: learners, subject matter, materials, procedures, and time. . . . How teachers think about and deal with these matters ultimately depends on their overall orientation to teaching, as well as the structures of thinking and acting suggested for achieving their goals. . . . Thus, . . . classroom practice is never entirely neutral, but carries with it its own implicit theory of instruction. (p. 50)

In short, as Hayes states, "Teachers bring in their theories and beliefs when they plan for teaching and when they attempt to understand and interpret classroom events" (p. 51).

## ARE TEACHERS AWARE OF THE THEORIES THAT THEY POSSESS?

Although the link between theory and behavior is always present, educators, like members of the general public, are not always consciously aware of the theories that guide their behaviors (Bigge & Shermis, 1992). While all teachers possess theories that drive their teaching, they may or may not be able to explicitly describe them. Bigge and Shermis (1992) state that, "the important question is not whether a teacher has a theory of learning but, rather, how tenable it is" (p. 3).

Teachers with a firm grasp of educational and psychological theories have a clear basis for making instructional decisions. Their understanding of educational theory provides them with a foundation for understanding *why* they are choosing the instructional practices that they use. Such theoretically based instructional decisions are linked to exemplary literacy instruction and improved literacy learning (Pressley, Allington, Wharton-McDonald, Block, & Morrow, 2001). Indeed, as Pressley et al. (2001) have found, highly effective, exemplary educators are able to articulate the relationships between what they do in the classroom and their theoretical reasons for doing so. In other words, highly effective teachers align their educational practices with their theoretical beliefs. Additionally, when teachers such as Pressley et al.'s exemplary educators are able to make their instructional theories conscious, they are then able to discuss and reflect upon them. These discussions and reflections provide avenues for greater understanding of the relationships between educational theory and practice, and thus further facilitate instructional effectiveness.

In contrast, teachers who are unaware of the theories that drive their instruction are often unable to provide a coherent explanation for why they choose one set of instructional procedures or materials over another. Bigge and Shermis (1992) write that teachers lacking a conscious awareness of theories often provide instruction based on "a hodge-podge of methods without theoretical orientation" (p. 5). Along this line, Bigge and Shermis emphasize that psychological and educational theories are not all complementary, and describe the problems that teachers may encounter when using incompatible theoretically based practices. "Many teachers, from time to time, have adopted conflicting features from a variety of learning theories without ever realizing that they were basically contradicting in nature and could not be brought into harmony with each other" (p. 3).

## THE IMPORTANCE OF THEORIES
## TO EDUCATIONAL RESEARCH

Knowledge of educational theories is central to the work of educational researchers as well as to the work of educational practitioners (Brumbaugh & Lawrence, 1985). Ideally, all research studies have theoretical foundations. Theoretical perspectives are required for the publication of articles in high-quality research journals, and for most doctoral dissertations and master's theses. The reason that theories are central to educational research is that they are the concepts by which scholars explain their research. Researchers use theories as explanations for *why they expect something will happen* (their hypotheses) in their studies as well as *why they believe something did happen* (their discussion) in their studies. Creswell (2002) states that "a theoretical lens in narrative research is a guiding perspective or ideology that provides structure for advocating for groups or individuals writing the report" (p. 524). Pemberton (1993) notes that "all forms of inquiry depend upon the existence of an interrelated set of conceptual frameworks to guide and direct research" (p. 53). Theories provide the philosophical grounding for research studies.

Theories also provide the frameworks through which various research studies can be linked both within and between fields of study. As stated previously, by definition, theories provide explanations that can be used to describe a variety of phenomena. Therefore, if a theory can be used to explain the research findings in study "A," it may also be used to explain the findings in study "B," thus linking the two studies. Research that is theoretically linked to other research makes a more substantial contribution toward extending a knowledge base in any field than that which is not linked (Creswell, 2002). In contrast, research that is not theory-based does not offer a cohesive, meaningful explanation of what is already known about any single subject area. Since it is theoretically disconnected, it has far less of an opportunity to make a meaningful contribution to the current knowledge base.

In addition to providing a basis for hypotheses, explaining research findings, and linking research studies to each other, theories allow variables to be generated and evaluated. *Variables* are "the conditions or characteristics that the experimenter manipulates, controls, or observes" (Best & Kahn, 1998, p. 160). Creswell (2002) notes that researchers often turn to theories to identify variables to be investigated and the possible relationships between them. He states that "a theory explains and predicts the relationship between independent and dependent variables. . . . You might think about a theory as a bridge that connects the independent and dependent variables. Theories are no more than broad explanations for what we would expect to find when we relate variables" (p. 137). He continues:

> In quantitative research, investigators locate a theory in the literature, examine predicted relationships among variables, and then test the relationships with new participants or at new sites. To test a theory, researchers write purpose statements, research questions, and hypoth-

eses that advance the predicted relationships. . . . The use of a theory provides a sophisticated approach to research. (p. 137)

One example of the use of a theory to generate variables and possible relationships between them is documented in the work of Tracey and Young (2002). These authors were interested in studying the ways in which mothers assist their children during their children's oral reading practice at home. They knew that their research should be framed in a theoretical context. They decided to choose the Social Constructivism Theory to frame their work. In this theoretical perspective learning is viewed as a result of social interactions between individuals, and oral language patterns are often studied as a way of illustrating these interactions. Tracey and Young then examined other studies that used a social constructivist perspective to see which specific variables had been previously found to be significant in similar parent–child research projects. The search yielded the identification of a number of variables including a mother's educational level, the sex of the child, and the child's reading ability. Tracey and Young proceeded to use these variables to study mothers and children during children's at-home oral reading practice. When their study was finished, their research not only extended the current knowledge base regarding mothers' helping behaviors during children's reading, it helped affirm that the social constructivist theoretical perspective, and variables generated from it, were useful tools in understanding parent–child dynamics in this specific reading situation.

Ruddell, Ruddell, and Singer (1994) note that researchers vary in the degree to which they may or may not be aware of the theoretical bases of their research. They write, "In effect, researchers who study literacy development operate from a theory of the reading or literacy process, whether they state this explicitly or not. . . . Nevertheless, being as explicit as possible about the theory allows us to explore and evaluate the explanatory power of our conceptual frameworks" (p. 53). Venezky (1984) comments on the problem that results from research investigations that are not grounded in theory. He dismisses them as "fishing expeditions, that is, almost random searches for relationships, unanchored by any theoretical frameworks" (p. 17).

Just as there is no single correct theory or model for practitioners to use when engaging in classroom practice, there is no correct single theory or model for a researcher to use when framing his or her research. Researchers can choose from a wide variety of theoretical perspectives when situating their studies, and in fact, though this is rarely done, they can simultaneously present their research from multiple theoretical viewpoints. The important point here is that like practitioners, researchers benefit from an awareness of the broad and diverse choice of theories that are available to them. Just as theories provide orienting frameworks for teachers' practices, theories provide orienting frameworks for researchers' investigations. The more aware researchers are of the value of theoretical orientations to high-quality research, the more likely they will be to learn about and use theories in their work.

## IS A MODEL DIFFERENT FROM A THEORY?

There appears to be disagreement in the field of education with regard to whether or not the terms "theories" and "models" can be used interchangeably (Thomas, 1996). Ruddell, Ruddell, and Singer (1994) clearly differentiate between theories and models. They state:

> Remember that a theory is an explanation of a phenomenon (such as the reading process), while a model serves as a metaphor to explain and represent a theory. This representation often takes the form of a depiction of the interrelationships among a theory's variables and may even make provisions for connecting the theory to observations. The theory is thus more dynamic in nature than the model but describes the way the model operates; the model is frequently static and represents a snapshot of a dynamic process. (p. 812)

For example, researchers who are in favor of making a distinction between theories and models would suggest that Social Constructivism (described above; also see Chapter 6) is a theory because its conceptualization has always been limited to a verbal description; there are no graphic depictions or flow charts to illustrate the general concept of Social Constructivism. Similarly, researchers who are in favor of making a distinction between theories and models would suggest that Gough's description of the reading process (see Chapter 7) is a model because the central ideas are presented in a graphic, flow-chart diagram.

Many researchers, however, do not distinguish between the concepts of theories and models, and in fact use the terms interchangeably. In Rosenblatt's (1994) writing, for example, this distinction is not clear. She states that "a theoretical model by definition is an abstraction, or generalized pattern devised in order to think about a subject" (p. 1057). Here, the difference between the concept of a model and the concept of a theory is not discernible. Tierney's (1994) writings also use the term "model" as interchangeable with the term "theory." He writes that "[models] pursue explanations that account for a host of variables and the variables' relationships to one another" (p. 1165). Regarding use of the term "model," Thomas (1996) states that "the term has caused some confusion because one writer will use it in a broad sense while another will limit its meaning" (p. 12). In the end, Thomas decides to use the terms "model" and "theory" interchangeably in his text to compare theories of child development.

Given the inconsistency in our discipline regarding the terms "theories" and "models," in this book we have decided to adhere to authors' own practices in descriptions of their work. When authors present their thoughts using the term "theory," we too use that term. When authors present their thoughts using the term "model," we likewise use that word. When authors use both terms interchangeably to describe their work, we do the same. Finally, in some cases the term "perspective" is used (e.g., the social constructivist perspective). This term is a general phrase used interchangeably with the terms "model" and "theory," and sometimes to encapsulate both of them (Hiebert & Raphael, 1994).

## WHY IS IT IMPORTANT
## TO UNDERSTAND MODELS?

In Tierney's (1994) description of the importance of models we can see how he views the concept of a model as similar to that of a theory. Tierney attributes the importance of models to their explanatory and predictive properties, the identical value attributed to theories by other writers (Bernard, 2000; Best & Kahn, 1998; Stanovich, 1992) Tierney writes, "Each [model] provides suggestions for research and offers implications for teaching and learning" (p. 1165). He concludes, however, "Indeed, I want models to do more than describe or predict; I want them to spur thinking. To me, this function should be viewed as the intent of models and the nature of reading" (p. 1179).

## THE VALUE OF MULTIPLE LENSES

As early as 1994, Tierney noted that the field of literacy learning seemed to have passed beyond the search for a single theory or model of reading that could comprehensively explain *all* the phenomena (e.g., reading process, reading development, reading disability, and reading instruction) observed in our field. Rather, he suggested that "the search for a single model of reading has been supplanted by recognition of the worth of multiple models of different reading and writing experiences" (p. 1163). Many authors concur with this perspective. Pressley and McCormick (1995) state that "we believe that none of [these theories] offers a conception that can stand alone, but that all of them offer perspectives that complement one another" (p. 181). Similarly, Woolfolk (1999) writes, "Few theories explain and predict perfectly.... Because no one theory offers all the answers, it makes sense to consider what each has to offer" (p. 16).

Authors who believe in the importance of multiple lenses assert that each theory makes a unique and valuable contribution to understanding the phenomena under examination. A metaphor of a group of artists all painting the same scene can be used to explain the value of using multiple theories to understand an educational issue. In the painting metaphor, each piece of artwork will be different—for example, with some painted in a realistic style, others in an impressionist or an abstract style. Yet each artist will provide a unique way of viewing the scene at hand. The same is true regarding educational theories and models that aim to explain an educational issue: each of the theories and models provides a unique and valuable perspective on the topic.

It is important to note that the value of multiple lenses has different implications for classroom practitioners versus educational researchers. As stated above, a wide array of theories and models are available to classroom practitioners. Good practice can be grounded in multiple theoretical frameworks. For example, an effective teacher may sometimes use practices grounded in a behavioral perspective, and other times use practices from constructivist, cognitive, or motivational frameworks. For the classroom teacher, multiple lenses often coexist and complement each other in his or her teaching. In contrast, a researcher who needs to situate her or his study in a theoretical framework typically chooses a single perspective from the many perspectives that are available. Although it is possible for researchers to use multiple theoretical perspectives in their work, most often they do not. As Brumbaugh and Lawrence (1985) write, researchers typically choose the theory or model "that is most relevant to the problems and aims at hand" (p. 22). Additionally, many researchers have a particular affinity for one theory as an explanation of their work rather than another. Indeed, as Thomas (1996) states, "data can assume quite different meanings when different theories are used for organizing the facts" (p. 11).

The use of multiple lenses is also seen in the classroom application activities and teaching anecdotes used to illustrate each of the theories discussed in this book. Importantly, many of these teaching ideas can be used to reflect multiple theories. For example, the popular practice of brainstorming a web with students prior to reading can be used to illustrate a classroom application activity reflective of Associationism, Connectionism, and/or Schema Theory. Thus the reader is urged to maintain an open and flexible stance when reading this volume. The ability to see the ways in which classroom practices are reflective of many theories strengthens the mind of the reader and underscores the primary premise of this text: the value of multiple perspectives in improving literacy education.

## THEORIES AND MODELS INCLUDED
## IN THIS TEXT

Adding to the already described complexity of the landscape of theories and models relevant to reading instruction and research is the diversity of the fields that have generated information related to this topic. As described in this book's preface, theories and models with implications for reading instruction and research do not have their own unique history. Rather, the theories and models that have impacted our field originated in diverse content areas including general education, psychology, sociology, linguistics, and neuroscience, to name a few. Additionally, there are many variations to basic theories that then yield new theories (Thomas, 1996).

In this text we have sought to identify the theories and models that have been most influential in the field of reading. Using some of the criteria listed above, these include theories that have attracted much scholarly attention throughout time, those that have most impacted instruction and/or research, and those that have steered the field in a new direction. As stated in the preface, a great deal of thought has been given to which theories and models to include in the text and how they should be organized. The result of this work is a text that is organized semihistorically according to the authors' perceptions of the major strands of theories and models that have influenced the study of reading, and when these strands chronologically emerged. It is important to emphasize that, following a great deal of deliberation, the authors, the editor, and the reviewers of this volume have concluded that there is no single correct or incorrect way to organize the theories that have impacted the study of reading, nor is there a black-and-white line dividing those theories that should be included in a volume such as this and those that should be omitted. Finally, even the dates attached to the emergence of the theories in this work are approximate. Despite the chapter titles and accompanying dates used to organize this text, readers should be aware that the emergence and development of the actual theories and models that have influenced the field of reading have been greatly affected by each other. Thus the lines drawn between the chapters of this text are primarily abstract, and are presented for the purposes of illuminating the differences between each of the theoretical perspectives. In reality, all of the theories are influenced by those that came before them, and also by those that coexist with them. The lines of separation and distinction are not nearly as clear as the organization of this text suggests. As the Buddhists would say, In reality all is one.

## SUMMARY

A *theory* is an explanation for a phenomenon that is widely held by a large group of people. In the field of education, the use of the term "theory" refers to explanations of learning and teaching phenomena that have been developed over long periods of time, following intensive research and writing efforts. While some writers use the terms "theories" and "models" interchangeably, others suggest that models serve as a metaphors to explain and represent theories. Theories and models are held consciously and unconsciously by all individuals. Whether held consciously or unconsciously, theories shape individuals' behavior in all areas of life, including teaching and research.

Knowledge of theories and models provides a necessary foundation for coordinated and cohesive instructional activities. In the absence of a strong theoretical basis, educators use teaching techniques without a clear understanding of how or why they may be effective. With a conscious knowledge of theories, teachers can make more clearly informed decisions regarding how and why their literacy instruction is choreographed. The better that educators understand the variety of theories and models that can be applied to literacy learning situations, the more effectively they can design and implement high-quality literacy instruction.

Researchers need to understand theories to provide theoretical foundations for their studies. For researchers, theories and models provide explanations for research hypotheses and findings. Furthermore, theories provide a way of understanding the links between research studies and a basis for generating research variables. Just as there is no single correct theory or model for practitioners, there is no single correct theory or model for a researcher. The use of multiple theoretical lenses for examining the reading process, reading instruction, and reading research is presented as ideal.

# CHAPTER 2

# Early Roots

*Early Theories and Models Applicable*
*to Reading (400 B.C.–1899)*

The history of theories and models related to reading is embedded and entwined within the history of general theories that have affected education and psychology. Multiple sources on the topic suggest that the following theories and models have been central in providing the earliest foundation (prior to the 20th century) for current thinking in education: Mental Discipline Theory, Associationism, Unfoldment Theory, and Structuralism (Bigge & Shermis, 1992; Brumbaugh & Lawrence, 1985; Gutek, 1972; Schwartz & Robbins, 1995; Sternberg, 1996). In this chapter, as in all the other chapters this book, many of the theories are illustrated by discussions of current literacy instructional practices associated with them. Additionally, many of the theories are linked to a classroom anecdote written by a practicing teacher. The purpose of the anecdotes is to illustrate the use of the theory in current, real-life classroom experiences. Finally, each theory is discussed in relation to current literacy research topics and studies. The goal of the present chapter is to provide information to readers regarding the earliest theoretical foundations related to education, and to examine the role of those theories in modern-day literacy instruction and research.

## MENTAL DISCIPLINE THEORY

Mental Discipline Theory was the first major historical theory to provide a foundation for the field of education. The roots of Mental Discipline Theory can be traced to the writings of the philosophers Plato (ca. 428–347 B.C.) and Aristotle (384–322 B.C.). Both Plato and Aristotle lived in ancient Greece, which is usually referred to by historians as "the birthplace of Western civilization." Although Homer and many other early thinkers of ancient Greece used myths to understand the universe, philosophers such as Plato and Aristotle (as well as Socrates and Isocrates) sought to explain the universe in rational terms (Gutek, 1972). Among his many writings on a variety of subjects, Plato developed a theory, later elaborated by Aristotle, that the mind is like a muscle—its various parts, or faculties, need to be exercised regularly (e.g., through the repetitive reciting of texts) in order to become strong and function optimally. This is now known as Mental Discipline Theory. Bigge and Shermis (1992) summarize the highlights of this early learning theory:

> The central idea in mental discipline is that the mind, envisioned as a nonphysical substance, lies dormant until it is exercised. Faculties of the mind such as memory, will, reason, and perseverance are the "muscles of the mind"; like physiological muscles, they are strengthened only through exercise, and subsequent to their adequate exercise they operate automatically. Thus, learning is a matter of strengthening, or disciplining, the faculties of the mind, which combine to produce intelligent behavior. (p. 21)

Brumbaugh and Lawrence (1963), historians of educational theory, write that "Plato's dialogues, because of their extraordinary quality of raising the right questions and identifying the important ideas relevant to their answers, have had more impact and influence on Western philosophy and Western educational theory than any other writings in these fields" (p. 10). As Brumbaugh and Lawrence suggest, Mental Discipline Theory is an example of Plato and Aristotle's work that has widely permeated the educational and psychological literature for approximately 2,500 years. Most educators will readily agree with the notion that students' minds are like muscles that need to be exercised and strengthened in order to develop and grow. Below, one classroom teacher describes how she relates Mental Discipline Theory to her current classroom teaching.

## TEACHER'S ANECDOTE:
## MENTAL DISCIPLINE THEORY

In listening in class and writing this paper I began to think of how some of these theories relate to my classroom experiences. Mental Discipline, the theory of exercising the mind, jumped right out at me. I was immediately brought back to the first day of school in September. I teach first grade, but those first few weeks of school in September are like teaching kindergarten again! I have to reteach many of the children how to write their letters and names again. It is as if their minds have been asleep, or have not exercised at all, during the 2 months of summer vacation. Probably for the same reason, I find myself having to reteach other concepts after long vacations such as Christmas and Easter. It is amazing to think that an educational theory from more than 2,000 years ago can still be applicable in my classroom.

—JOHANNAH ROGERS, first-grade teacher

## ASSOCIATIONISM

A second educational and psychological theory that dates back to ancient times but which is still reflected in current educational practice is *Associationism*. Associationism is a theory of psychology and education that is devoted to the study of how learning occurs. Sternberg (1996) writes, "Associationism examines how events or ideas can become associated with one another in the mind, to result in a form of learning" (p. 9).

The earliest observations related to Associationism are attributed to Aristotle, who in the fourth century B.C. speculated about three kinds of connections that would aid memory and learning. The first type of association that Aristotle identified as increasing learning is *contiguity*, the idea that things that occur together in time or space tend to become associated in the mind. For example, brushing one's teeth, taking a shower, getting dressed, and having breakfast are all ideas that are associated with things we do early in the morning. The second type of association that Aristotle said facilitated learning is *similarity*, the idea that people tend to associate things that have similar features and properties. For example, if a person were trying to remember a list of grocery items one good approach would be to organize the items according to similar categories, such as dairy, produce, breads, and meats. The third type of association that Aristotle postulated to be facilitative of learning is *contrast*. Contrast is association by opposition, such as the associations that exist between the words light–dark, high–low, and happy–sad (Sternberg, 1996).

Mental Discipline Theory and Associationism retained their prominence in educational thought for an unprecedented, and still unequaled, period of time. These were the reigning educational theories throughout the Hellenistic Age, the Age of the Roman Empire, and the Middle Ages (Gutek, 1972). They retained their prominence throughout the period of the European Renaissance, an historical era often called the beginning of modern thought, and the period of the Protestant Reformation in the 16th century (Bigge & Shermis, 1992; Gutek, 1972; Sternberg, 1996). Although alternative philosophies regarding general living were put forth during these times (for additional information on this topic, see Gutek, 1972), Mental Discipline Theory and Associationism remained premier regarding education and learning. In retrospect, these two theories persisted as the predominant theories of education and learning for approximately 2,000 years, from the time of Plato (ca. 428 B.C.) and Aristotle (384–322 B.C.) until the period of the Enlightenment in the 18th century.

One of the most well-known, and relatively modern, associationists was John Locke (1632–1704). Locke directly challenged Mental Discipline Theory with his *Tabula Rasa—"Blank Tablet"—Theory*. This theory suggests that people are born without any internal, innate knowledge. In the Tabula Rasa Theory view, all learning results as a consequence of the individual's interactions with the environment. Locke's work has been credited as a turning point in professional thinking about learning in that, as a result of his theory, attention was turned away from an emphasis regarding the importance of innate knowledge (e.g. the faculties of the mind that needed to be strengthened), and toward an emphasis on the importance of external influences on learning (Brumbaugh & Lawrence, 1985). Although Aristotle's thinking focused on internal connections that needed to be made for learning to occur, and Locke's writings focused on the importance of external information in learning, both philosophers are considered associationists because their primary interest was the way by which knowledge is constructed. In emphasizing Locke's contributions to this theory, Brumbaugh and Lawrence write, "Locke's work may be fairly regarded as a foundation block, if not the cornerstone, of associationist psychology" (p. 16).

Commenting on the importance of Associationism in general, Sternberg (1996) writes, "traveling forward in time, Associationism laid the groundwork for behaviorism and for models of cognition based on mental connections" (p. 9). Below, a teacher comments on the way she sees Associationism reflected in her high school English instruction.

---

### TEACHER'S ANECDOTE: ASSOCIATIONISM

Building on or retrieving prior knowledge is very important in many of my classes because so many students do not have many real-life experiences they can connect to in order to understand the texts we read. For example, several years ago I was going to read a story about a family that was involved in an avalanche on a skiing trip. I first asked students if anyone had ever been skiing. No one had. I then asked if they knew anything about avalanches; they did not. I proceeded to photocopy some newspaper articles about skiing and avalanches to share with the class. We also talked about being stuck in the house during a snowstorm. Although being stuck in one's house during a snowstorm is not the same as being caught in a house at a ski resort during an avalanche, I felt they could make the connection because in both instances the house is surrounded by snow and the same items are needed to survive. . . . I believe that making connections is one of the most important concepts in reading because a text is meaningful only when students can relate to it.

—MELISSA A. HUDANISH, high school English teacher

---

## UNFOLDMENT THEORY

In the realm of educational theory, the first serious challenge to Mental Discipline Theory and Associationism came with Unfoldment Theory (Dupuis, 1985; Gutek, 1972). In contrast to Mental Discipline Theory, in which the attributes of the mind must be strengthened through disciplined efforts, and to Associationism, which attempts to explain how learning occurs through connections, beginning in the 18th century several theorists suggested that learning was most facilitated through a natural unfolding of the mind based on individual curiosity and interest. This shift in educational philosophy mirrored the shift in social philosophy occurring at the same time (Gutek, 1972). Although the dominant approach in the Age of the Enlightenment continued to be the cultivation of rational thought through mental discipline, some thinkers in this period began to advocate cultivating feeling and passion through the development of a natural unfolding of personal interests. This pointed the way to a new period now called Romanticism (Gutek, 1972).

Rousseau (1712–1778), one of the earliest educational theorists to hold the Unfoldment perspective, postulated that children's learning would evolve naturally as a result of their innate curiosity. Rousseau is best known for his educational novel, *Emile* (1762). In his book, Emile, a young boy, is raised in nature, away from the evils of society, and allowed to follow his own curiosities and interests. Emile develops into an adult of high moral character and goodness as a result of his unique upbringing. In accordance with Unfoldment Theory, first presented in this popular novel, Rousseau advocated that educators should follow children's leads regarding what and when they wanted to learn. If children were forced to learn information about which they were not interested, Rousseau argued, their learning would be impeded. Rousseau also argued that adults should intervene as little as possible in children's education and instead just let children "unfold" (Morrow, 2001). He firmly believed that children's verbal abilities would be developed as a result of extended and enriched experiences with manipulatives (Brumburgh & Lawrence, 1963). Shannon (1990) notes that Rousseau believed so strongly in the idea that nature should be at the center of children's learning that he recommended postponing reading and writing instruction until they were 10–15 years old. With regard to Rousseau's ultimate influence on modern-day education, Gutek (1972) writes that "it is no exaggeration to state that Rousseau had an impact on some of the twentieth-century progressive educators who asserted that educations should be based on the interests and inclinations of the child" (p. 146).

Pestalozzi (1746–1827) a Swiss educational reformer, was greatly influenced by Rousseau's beliefs concerning natural learning, but felt that in addition to "natural unfolding" children needed informal instruction from adults to facilitate their learning. Using these ideas, Pestalozzi, created a philosophy of child-centered learning, and built a school to implement his ideas. Central to his version of Unfoldment Theory was his belief that for an educational environment to be effective it must also be warm and nurturing. In Pestalozzi's school the positive affective climate and the engaging physical environment were designed to stimulate children's natural curiosity for learning. In addition, teachers provided instruction based on children's learning interests. Pestalozzi's school was also recognized for its heavy emphasis on sensory manipulative experiences as foundational for educational growth (Seefeldt & Barbour, 1994). According to Smith (1986), author of the seminal text *American Reading Instruction,* which traces the historical development of reading instruction in the United States, Pestalozzi's influence most likely contributed to the use of familiar objects, pictures, and storylines in early reading materials.

After Pestalozzi's death in 1827 his ideas and methods were carried on and developed by disciples in both North America and Europe. Froebel (1782–1852), one of these disciples, emphasized the importance of play in the development of young children's learning. Froebel's version of Unfoldment Theory both evolved from, and differed from, those of his predecessors Rousseau and Pestalozzi. Morrow (2001) explains:

> Like Rousseau, Froebel believed that the adult responsible for the education of a child needs to be concerned with the child's natural unfolding. He also followed Pestalozzi's ideas and provided plans for instructing young children. But he is best known for emphasizing the importance of play in learning. He specified, however, that realizing the fullest benefits of playing-to-learn required adult guidance and direction and a planned environment. Froebel saw the teacher as a designer of activities and experiences that facilitate learning. . . . It was Froebel who coined the word *kindergarten* which means children's garden. (p. 4)

The contributions of the major Unfoldment theorists Rousseau, Pestalozzi, and Froebel laid the groundwork for John Dewey's work (see Chapter 4) that came to the forefront of U.S. education in the early 1900s. Furthermore, this theoretical orientation influenced many U.S. schools during the early 1900s to build their reading instruction programs based on children's interests and the use of activities and problem solving as instruments for learning (Smith, 1986).

Below, a special education teacher responds to an assignment to reflect on the ways in which she sees Unfoldment Theory present in her classroom.

## TEACHER'S ANECDOTE: UNFOLDMENT THEORY

Rousseau, Pestalozzi, and Froebel developed the Unfoldment Theory in the 1700s and early 1800s. I strongly agree with their beliefs of having children be interested in what they are learning as well as having a stimulating environment. As a special education teacher, my first year of teaching was very difficult for me. I had students with three to four levels of abilities in my classroom, and some of my students had severe behavior problems. I quickly found out that one of the things that my students loved to do was to eat. I then created an environment that built on this interest. One weekend I went to 10 different restaurants in the neighborhood and gathered menus. With the help of my students, I used the back of the classroom to create a restaurant atmosphere including a table, chairs, plastic silverware, and paper products. During class we learned to read the menus including appetizers, entrees, sandwiches, and desserts. At center time the students were able to "play" in the restaurant area using all of the props. They would read the menus and take orders on small pads. Monopoly money was used to pay for meals. On special occasions I would bring some of the items from the menus to class. I found that my students were engaged while working/playing in this environment. I think it is because of the components of the Unfoldment Theory—creating an exciting environment and focusing on play and natural development—that my students were happy and well behaved during this time of the day. I am quite sure that they were learning during this time as well.

—AMY SMITH, seventh-grade special education teacher

## STRUCTURALISM AND EARLY SCIENTIFIC FOUNDATIONS OF READING

The previously discussed Mental Discipline Theory, Associationism, and Unfoldment Theory were developed as nonexperimental, general philosophies that would apply to all areas of education. In contrast, the historical roots of the specific study of reading were embedded within the early history of cognitive psychology, which was situated within an experimental, structuralist theoretical framework. *Structuralism,* which is usually thought of as the first major school in psychology, sought to explain the structure of the mind through the study of perception (Sternberg, 1996). Thus reading was first studied through perception research designed to explain general psychological functioning rather than to explain reading in and of itself (Venezky, 1984).

Venezsky (1984) has summarized the early history of reading research. Early studies of reading took place within the world's first experimental psychology laboratory, established in the late 1870s in

Leipzig, Germany by Wilhelm Wundt (1832–1920), a German psychologist associated with the structuralist perspective. J. M. Cattell, an American student and Wundt's assistant, pursued the study of perceptual processes by investigating aspects of the reading process such as letter and word recognition, legibility of print, and span of attention. According to Venezky, two seminal research findings, based on work conducted in Wundt's laboratory, were reported by Cattell (1886, 1890). In his research Cattell demonstrated that subjects' speed for reading words connected in sentences was faster than their speed for reading disconnected words, and that, similarly, subjects' speed for reading letters connected in words were faster than their speed for reading disconnected letters. Unfortunately, these findings were not investigated or fully understood until the 1950s.

At the same time that Wundt and Cattell were investigating perceptual processes in Germany in the late 1870s and early 1880s, Javal was conducting early reading research by studying eye movements at the University of Paris (Venezky, 1984). Javal's major research contribution was identifying and naming the "saccade," the phenomenon that eye movements during reading occur in small jumps that are often not completely smooth, progressive, or linear. Prior to Javal's research, eye movements were presumed to be steady, continuous, and flowing during the reading process.

Early contributions to the beginnings of a cognitive processing theoretical orientation to reading continued in the late 1800s and early 1900s. According to Venezky (1984), three major summaries in cognitive processing theory, often referred to as psychology of reading, were published during this period. Quantz (1897) was the first to identify the concept of "eye–voice span," the time lapse between the eyes' exposure to print and the subjects' enunciation of what he or she is reading. Dearborn's (1906) doctoral dissertation examined eye movements during reading. Huey's (1908) book *The Psychology and Pedagogy of Reading* examined perception, reading rate, subvocalization, the nature of meaning, and the history of reading and reading instruction. Hiebert and Raphael (1996) summarize the advances made (and also discuss what was missed) during the structuralist period of reading research:

> From the late 1800s through the early 1900s, psychologists focused on reading as a perceptual process, primarily measuring perception of print (i.e., single letters, words) through reaction time studies, or focused on areas such as eye–voice span, speed of reading, and lip movements during silent reading (see Venezky, 1984, for a review of

this research). Within these lines of research, virtually no attention was paid to whether or not the readers had comprehended the text—either because connected text was not used or because meaning construction was beyond the purview of the study. Thus, despite research reflecting what Venezky termed "the golden years" (1984, p. 7), in hindsight, psychology had little to say about the complex processes of literacy that must be understood to influence the development of literate youngsters through formal education. . . . (p. 553)

Below, one teacher explains the way in which she sees Structuralism reflected in her literacy instruction.

---

### TEACHER'S ANECDOTE: STRUCTURALISM

Structuralism, the theory that focuses on print perception as a critical component of the reading process, is evident in the special arrangements I make for one of my fourth-grade students. Michael is a mainstreamed, learning-disabled reader whose listening comprehension is much better than his decoding skills. Many times I am able to scan the text that the class is reading into one of our computers that is equipped with the software, Intellitalk. Using this software, I am able to enlarge the size of the font for Michael, which seems to help him with his speed of decoding. Additionally, Michael is able to click on any words that he doesn't know and the computer will read and/or define them for him. If the text is especially hard, Michael or I can adjust the software so that the computer actually reads the text. This software, which uses many of the concepts inherent in Structuralism, has given Michael much support in helping him to keep up with his peers.

—HEATHER CANNON, fourth-grade teacher

---

## CLASSROOM APPLICATIONS

Whether or not educators are aware of it, many of the teaching practices that they currently use are grounded in educational and psychological theories that were originally created more than 2,000 years ago. For example, Mental Discipline Theory is still a foundational theoretical orientation of many current classroom instructional practices. Every time teachers engage in activities in which their intention is to strengthen students' skills through the use of practice, Mental Discipline Theory is present. Thus this theory permeates almost every aspect of literacy instructional practices from the earliest skills of letter and sound identification to the advanced skills of metacognitive control. Mental Discipline Theory is highly visible in spelling and vocabulary instruction, sight word identification, and the use of context clues.

One current practice in literacy instruction that is highly reflective of Mental Discipline Theory is *repeated reading*. During repeated reading students read passages aloud to their teachers multiple times. Throughout each reading, teachers provide feedback to the students and guidance for further improvement. Teachers' feedback and guidance are directed to such areas as pronunciation, expression, and pace. Repeated reading has been linked to improvements in word recognition, speed, accuracy, and fluency (Armbruster, Lehr, & Osborn, 2001). Repeated reading is reflective of Mental Disciple Theory because it is built on the basic premise that reading skill, like a muscle, needs to be exercised to be strengthened.

The historic theory of Associationism has also spawned instructional practices that can be seen in modern-day literacy classrooms. For example, learning experiences that build and activate students' background knowledge are reflective of Associationism because of their emphasis on using connections as a foundation of learning. In literacy education, teachers build students' background knowledge in particular subject areas prior to reading because it is believed that increased background information is positively correlated with increased reading comprehension. For example, if a class will be reading a story about going to the beach, the teacher can build students' knowledge by showing them beach pictures; asking children to think about times they have gone to the beach; sharing audio, video, and/or virtual renditions of the beach; and even sharing other beach stories with the students. Specific activities designed to increase students' awareness of these types of connections are usually referred to as "brainstorming" or "webbing activities." These activities are further discussed in Chapter 4 because they are most reflective of Schema Theory.

Unfoldment Theory, originally generated in the 18th century, is also the basis for several of our contemporary practices in literacy education. One of the most effective approaches to promoting children's literacy development in the classroom is the use of literacy centers (Morrow, 2002). A *literacy center* is an area of the classroom designed to facilitate children's authentic engagement with a wide variety of literacy materials and activities. In addition to promoting engagement with reading activities, literacy centers are designed to increase children's social collaboration during these experiences, which subsequently leads to increased motivation for literacy learning (Morrow, 2002). The use of literacy centers in the classroom is a practice that is consistent with Unfoldment Theory because literacy centers are designed to capture and build on children's natural curiosity about their surroundings. The use of literacy centers in the classroom is also consistent with Social Learning Theories, Emergent Literacy Theory, and Motivation Theory, all of which are discussed in later chapters of this text.

Establishing a classroom literacy center requires both materials and plans for children's activities. In the second edition of *The Literacy Center: Contexts for Reading and Writing*, Morrow (2002) describes all of the aspects necessary for implementing literacy centers in the classroom. Although an in-depth description of the entirety of this information is beyond the scope of the present text, a brief description based on Morrow's guidelines is presented here.

The creation of the classroom literacy center begins with the construction of the physical environment. The literacy center is most often located in a corner of the classroom, set off by bookshelves and a colorful rug to establish its boundaries. In addition to an abundance of meaningfully organized books (five to eight per child), other materials frequently found in the reading center include a rocking chair; throw pillows; beanbag chairs; stuffed animals; a spot for private reading (such as a large cardboard box); a check-out/check-in system for borrowing books; tape recorders, headsets, and audiotaped stories; and story retelling materials (see Morrow, 2002). Frequently, the writing center, or author's spot, is located within or next to the classroom literacy center. Materials used for this area include a table with chairs, an assortment of writing implements (pencils, pens, markers, crayons), an assortment of paper items (different sizes and colors of paper, notebooks, and pads), and folders for each child's writing. Additional items for the literacy center include bulletin boards for sharing students' work, posters for sharing messages such as ideas for completing literacy center activities, rules for engaging in literacy center work, and information related to reading, writing, thematic units, and authors. In short, and consistent with Unfoldment Theory, the physical environment of the literacy center is designed to stimulate children's curiosity to engage with its materials.

In addition to preparing the physical classroom environment, teachers need the classroom management skills to enable literacy center time to be both productive and enjoyable for the students. Morrow (2002) recommends that literacy center time be used at least two to three times a week for 30–45 minutes per session. Literacy center time should begin with teachers modeling a new activity that is being added to the literacy center, such as a new flannel board story, a new word game, or a new writing activity. Following the teacher's demonstration, students should choose the peers whom they want to work with that day (or decide to work alone) and the activity in which they are going to engage. Furthermore, students can also decide what their jobs within their groups will be that day. For example, if students are going to retell a story with a set of flannel board materials, they will need to determine which student will assume the role of which character. Additionally, one student should be the group leader and another the recorder of everyone's accomplishments. Students may also choose to just observe other students during literacy center time. Providing students with all of these choices is a cornerstone of the literacy center experience and is positively related to increasing students' motivation for literacy learning (Morrow, 2001). During literacy center time the teacher is a facilitator and an observer in the classroom. He or she can take anecdotal notes on students' activities and interact with students on a small-group or an individual basis as is needed. Additional information on designing and managing classroom literacy centers can be found in Morrow (2002).

Structuralism is also reflected in current literacy instructional practices. Classroom instructional practices that support students' increased accuracy regarding print perception are consistent with this theory. Many techniques are available to support students' reading in this way. When teachers are working with whole-class instruction, they may use a pointer to help students follow the print as they read. A fancier and fun version of the pointer is a wand with a star at its end. Some teachers use a version of this activity with a flashlight and a word wall. In this educational experience teachers turn off the lights in the classroom and then use a flashlight to point to words on the wall. Students read the words aloud as the flashlight illuminates them. Other approaches to facilitating print perception include using sentence strips for class instruction, and using different colors to draw students' attention to varying aspects of print. When teachers work with students individually and in small groups they can also teach students to use line markers and their own fingers as pointers, which may also improve print perception.

Much educational software is available to enhance students' print perception. Software easily changes print size, font, and color. Students with special needs can sometimes read words more easily when these features of print are altered. Software that contains print-talking features, such as Intellitalk, highlights words on a computer screen for students, and uses computerized technology to "read" the words to students as they are identified. Another way for students to use the software is to read the text independently and then have the computer "read" any word identified as difficult by the student. All of these teaching techniques that focus on improving text perception are consistent with Structuralism and have their roots in work that was completed in the late 1800s and early 1900s in Europe and the United States.

## RESEARCH APPLICATIONS

Just as the early historical theories of Mental Discipline Theory, Associationism, Unfoldment Theory, and Structuralism are still reflected in current classroom practices, so too are they reflected in current literacy research.

Researchers and graduate students who are conducting studies in the areas of practice and repetition effects on students' achievement may want to link the theoretical context of their work back to the ideas of Plato, Aristotle, and Mental Discipline Theory. Practice effects are seen in research studies in a wide variety of areas affecting children's reading achievement such as oral language development, phonemic awareness, exposure to print, and experience with storybook reading (Snow, Burns, & Griffin, 1998). Any contemporary research study that includes skill practice as a research component is using a theoretical frame that was originally grounded in Mental Discipline Theory.

In one such study, Smith (1986) examined the effects of a variety of forms of reading practice on adults' literacy achievement. Smith's study was comprised of two applications of the concept of practice: the *type* of reading practice in which adults engaged and the *amount* of reading practice in which adults engaged. Using data from a nationally representative sample of approximately 26,000 adults, the study demonstrated that newspaper reading was the most frequent practice in which adults engaged. With regard to the effects of the amount of reading practice, the study showed that practice at reading, particularly when practice involved a variety of types of reading activities, was associated with higher literacy achievement in adults. This finding is consistent with Plato's Mental Discipline Theory.

Associationism provides the foundation for two branches of psychology that eventually emerged in the 1950s: cognitive psychology and Behaviorism. As a result, any educational or psychological research conducted within these two very broad areas could ultimately link its theoretical framework back to that of Associationism. Among many areas of study in reading that could conceivably be situated in an associationist theoretical context are those of metacognition, reading think-alouds, schema building, schema activation, and comprehension activities such as Venn diagrams, KWL charts, and story mapping.

Research related to Schema Theory is one contemporary application of Associationism. *Schema Theory* proposes that knowledge is organized in the brain in complex, interrelated structures in which everything that is known about a particular topic is connected (for additional information on Schema Theory, see Chapter 4). Schema theory is rooted in Associationism. Indeed, its central concepts regarding the ways in which information is organized to promote learning were originally established in Associationism. Pressley (2000) reports a study by Bauer and Fivush (1992) that demonstrated that even very young children create schemas to help them understand the world. Similarly, Hudson and Nelson (1983) have shown that preschoolers use their existing schemas to interpret and respond to stories.

Researchers and graduate students who are conducting studies on the effects of the learning environment on students' performance may want to link the theoretical framework of their studies back to the ideas of Unfoldment Theory and the work of Rousseau, Pestalozzi, and Froebel. Unfoldment Theory would also be a suitable context for studies of motivation linked to children's natural interests.

Studies regarding the effects of classroom literacy centers on students' learning have often used Unfoldment Theory as the theoretical lens (Morrow, 2001). Unfoldment Theory is applicable as a grounding theoretical framework for literacy center research studies because both emphasize the importance of a motivating environment, a child's natural curiosity, and engaging activities as routes to learning. Morrow (2002) has conducted extensive research related to the use of literacy centers in the classroom. In her work she describes the effects of literacy center activities on children's literacy development. Factors examined included the physical layout of the classroom literacy center, the use of teacher-modeled literacy center activities, and the types of collaborative activities that occur during children's independent reading and writing time. Morrow's research demonstrated that children's engagement in literacy center activities resulted in increased enjoyment of reading and writing, and improved skills in print recognition, phonemic awareness, phonics, reading comprehension, vocabulary development, oral reading fluency, and writing.

Researchers and graduate students interested in framing a contemporary research study with Structuralism would most likely be working in the areas of perceptual and neurological processes of reading. Although more current theories, known as cognitive processing theories, now exist to explain the perceptual and neurological facets of the reading process (see Chapters 7, 8, and 9), Structuralism may still be used for historical purposes to establish the root of cognitive processing research. Cognitive processing theories and models are the contemporary extension of the structuralist theoretical stance of years past because both share the central goal of explaining the biological aspects of the reading process.

As described earlier in this chapter, the first research studies related to reading were grounded in the Structuralism theoretical perspective. Research by Catell (1886, 1890), Quantz (1897), Dearborn (1906), and Huey (1908) form the foundational cornerstone of this theory. Shaywitz et al. (2000) exemplify research in the modern-day extension of Structuralism. Their cognitive processing investigations using state-of-the-art imaging technology have been designed to study the biological differences of the brains of normal versus dyslexic readers. Shaywitz et al.'s research has shown definite biological differences in brain function between these two groups of readers consistent with the *specific phonological deficit hypothesis*, the belief that the primary difference between normal and dyslexic readers lies in dyslexic readers' difficulty in processing speech sounds.

## SUMMARY

Before the 20th century, the educational theories that held implications for understanding reading stemmed from four theoretical roots: Mental Discipline Theory, Associationism, Unfoldment Theory, and Structuralism. Mental Discipline Theory suggests that the mind is akin to a muscle and needs to be exercised and strengthened for learning to occur. Associationism emphasizes the ways in which learning occurs in the mind through thought processes that make connections between things. Unfoldment Theory focuses on the natural emergence of the intellect through the fostering of a child's curiosity, the creation of a stimulating environment for the child, and the use of play. Structuralism seeks to explain learning through the study of perceptual processes. Mental Discipline Theory, Associationism, and Unfoldment Theory are nonexperimental philosophies applicable to all areas of general education. Research related specifically to the field of reading began with experimental, perceptual studies of cognitive processing that fall under the theoretical umbrella of Structuralism. The theories presented in this chapter are primarily linked to each other by their emergence in chronological history. Although they are all rooted in antiquity, examples of their application can still be found in modern-day classrooms. Furthermore, each of the theories can still be used as a theoretical framework for current research.

# CHAPTER 3

# Behaviorism

## The Dominant Educational Theory for 50 Years (1900–1950s)

Despite advances made by the early cognitive theorists studying perception during the late 1800s and the early 1900s (see Chapter 2), research studies related to reading turned from a cognitive processing theoretical orientation to a focus on instructional approaches beginning in 1910 (Venezky, 1984). During this period few additional research studies related to perceptual processes were conducted (Venezky, 1984). Instead, the emphasis on teaching and testing coincided with the rise in popularity of the theoretical perspective of *Behaviorism*. Behaviorism was the predominant educational and psychological theory for 50 years thereafter, persisting well into the 1960s (Woolfolk, 1998; Thomas, 1996). Behaviorism changed the depiction of reading from one of perceptual processing to one of reading as a behavior composed of isolated skills, each of which could be reinforced to increase student achievement. It continues to be significant today as the theoretical underpinning associated with direct instruction.

According to Thomas (1996), Behaviorism arose as a theoretical response to theories of Mentalism, such as the Psychoanalytic Theory advocated by Freud (1933). In Mentalism, actions and behaviors are seen as being driven by unobservable, and in some cases even unconscious, feelings, drives, impulses, and wishes. According to Thomas, behavioral theorists such as Watson (1913) doubted the existence of many of the mental elements proposed by Freud, and suggested instead that human behaviors needed to be studied and explained through observable actions. According to Thomas, Watson considered Mentalism to be unscientific. Watson and other early behaviorists believed that the documentation of observable actions related to learning would be the key to making the field of psychology a true science. Watson asserted this view in his 1913 publication "Psychology as a Behaviorist Views It," and with it launched the behaviorist movement (Thomas, 1996).

## WHAT IS BEHAVIORISM?

Behaviorism is a theoretical perspective on learning that focuses on observable changes in behavior. From a behavioral perspective, the outcome of learning is an observable change in behavior.

Two underlying assumptions are present in all theoretical versions of Behaviorism. The first is the belief that behavior is the result of an organism's, or person's, response to stimuli. The second is the belief that external stimuli can be manipulated to strengthen or reduce an organism's or an individual's behavior (Greeno, Collins, & Resnick, 1996). There are three major behavioral theories: Classical Conditioning Theory, created by Ivan Pavlov; Connectionism, put forth by Edward Thorndike; and Operant Conditioning Theory, established by B. F. Skinner. All three theories are built on the early foundation of Associationism, as discussed in Chapter 2. While Classical Conditioning Theory has few direct implications for reading instruction and reading research, it is briefly presented here because it is the primary precursor to Operant Conditioning Theory, which remains a powerful and prominent theory in educational thought and practice.

## CLASSICAL CONDITIONING THEORY

Pavlov created *Classical Conditioning Theory* as a result of his research studying dogs' digestion in the 1920s. During his research Pavlov noted that his dogs began to salivate at the sight of their food bowls, even when the bowls were empty. Pavlov postulated that the dogs were salivating because they associated the presence of their dishes with the arrival of their dinners. In other words, the dogs had *learned through association* to connect their food bowls with their dinners. Intrigued with the concept, Pavlov continued to experiment with other forms of associational learning. Eventually, Pavlov was able to produce salivation in his dogs by simply ringing a bell. This *conditioning* was achieved by the repeated pairing of bell ringing with the delivery of food to the dogs. Thus, the ringing of the bell, even in the absence of the food dishes, was enough of a stimulus to produce the salivation response in the dogs. This form of associational learning became known as classical conditioning. Slavin (1997) writes, "Pavlov's emphasis on observation and careful measurement and his systematic exploration of a number of aspects of learning helped to advance the scientific study of learning" (p. 153). Pavlov's research focused primarily on the exploration of Behaviorism in the biological sciences. John Watson (1878–1958), an American, was the first behaviorist to apply the concepts inherent in Classical Conditioning Theory to the realm of human behavior (Pierce & Epling, 1999). As a result, according to Sternberg (1996), Watson is acknowledged as the father of Behaviorism.

Classical Conditioning Theory exemplifies Behaviorism because it focuses on observable changes in behavior and responses to stimuli as demonstrative of learning. An example of classical conditioning is when children come to school hesitant and nervous about learning to read, and, through numerous experiences that are positive, become happy and successful learners. In contrast, when children come to school as curious and engaged learners and then are exposed to experiences that are negative, their responses to learning to read change for the worse. Both are examples of classical conditioning because the initial response of the child is changed over time as a result of associations made in school.

## CONNECTIONISM

While Pavlov and Watson were primarily interested in events that preceded actions, Edward L. Thorndike extended the study of Behaviorism by showing that "stimuli that occurred after a behavior [also] had an influence on future behaviors" (Slavin, 1997, p. 154). Thorndike created the theory of *Connectionism* and proposed its four laws: the Law of Effect, the Law of Readiness, the Law of Identical Elements, and the Law of Exercise. Slavin (1997) explains the Law of Effect:

Thorndike's Law of Effect states that if an act is followed by a satisfying change in the environment, the likelihood that the act will be repeated in similar situations increases. However, if a behavior is followed by an unsatisfying change in the environment, the chances that the behavior will be repeated decreases. Thus the consequences of one's present behavior were shown to play a crucial role in determining one's future behavior. (p. 154)

Thorndike's Law of Effect is also known as the "Principle of Reinforcement."

Thorndike also postulated the Laws of Readiness, Identical Elements, and Exercise.

- The *Law of Readiness* states that learning is facilitated when easier tasks precede those that are related but more difficult.
- The *Law of Identical Elements* states that the more elements (i.e., content and procedure) of one situation are identical to the elements of a second situation, the greater the transfer, and thus the easier the learning in the second situation.
- The *Law of Exercise* states that the more stimulus–response connections are practiced, the stronger the bonds become. The less the connections are used, the weaker the bonds.

Hiebert and Raphael (1996) comment on the implications that Thorndike's laws had on classroom instruction in the early 1900s:

The same laws of learning—effect, exercise, readiness, and identical elements (Thorndike, 1903)—were applied across subject areas but, because of the place of reading and writing in the 3 Rs, considerable attention was paid to the pedagogy of reading and writing. The law of readiness meant that the critical behaviors of reading, which were viewed as recognizing the most frequently used words, needed to be sequenced. The laws of identical elements and exercise dictated that students practice repeatedly on specific sets of target words (or, prior to that, letters) to ensure a connection between stimulus and response. The law of effect meant that correct responses such as the reading of a story made up of the target words or filling in a target word within a workbook exercise should be praised. (p. 554)

Thorndike's Connectionism is considered a behavioral theory because, like Pavlov and Watson, Thorndike equated learning with observable changes in behavior. In contrast to Pavlov and Watson, however, Thorndike concentrated on the effects of varying stimuli that occurred after a behavior rather than the consequences of varying stimuli that occurred simultaneously to, or before, a behavior.

---

### TEACHER'S ANECDOTE: CONNECTIONISM

All of Thorndike's laws from Connectionism are observable in my classroom. The Law of Effect, also known as the Principle of Reinforcement, is clear because my students respond very well to positive reinforcement. I try to "catch my students doing something well" and praise them for it. I'll say something like "Look at how well Samantha is focused on her work," and most of the other students will look up at her and then go back to their work with increased attention. The Law of Readiness is apparent in the way that I structure my lessons throughout the week. On Mondays I try to start with an introductory lesson on a concept. As the week progresses, my subsequent lessons on the concept get harder. Not all of my students get through all of the harder lessons on every topic, but that is how I individualize in my classroom. I am reminded of the Law of Identical Elements when I think about my students' abilities in the areas of reading and writing. I find that my better readers are also my better writers. Since reading and writing share the elements of both being language processes, the better my students are at one, the better they will likely be at the other. The Law of Exercise makes me think of my students who do, and do not, read at home. The students who do read at home tend to be much better readers than those who don't.

—STACI KLEIN, fourth-grade teacher

---

## OPERANT CONDITIONING THEORY

Skinner continued Pavlov and Watson's work on the importance of association in learning. He also continued Thorndike's work regarding the relationships between behavior and its consequences. However, in contrast to his predecessors, Skinner believed that Classical Conditioning Theory and Connectionism only accounted for a small percentage of learned behaviors (Woolfolk, 1998). Skinner believed that not all human learning is so automatic and unintentional. Most behaviors are not elicited by stimuli, they are emitted or voluntarily enacted. People actively "operate" on their environment to produce different kinds of consequences. These deliberate actions are called *operants*. The learning process involved in operant behavior is called operant conditioning because we learn to behave in certain ways as we operate on the environment. (Woolfolk, 1998, p. 208)

Thomas (1996) explains the ways in which Skinner's work, called *Operant Conditioning Theory*, built on the behavioral theories that preceded it. He writes:

> One problem that early behaviorists met was that they often could not identify accurately what stimulus was bringing about the responses they observed. Hence they were forced to assume the operation of stimuli they actually could not locate. In the 1930's Skinner suggested a solution to this common problem. He proposed that there was not one kind of conditioning but two. One was the classical S–R [stimulus–response] relationship demonstrated by Pavlov. The other, and by far the more frequent in human behavior, Skinner labeled *operant* or *instrumental conditioning*. Instead of the behavior being drawn out or elicited by a stimulus, the behavior (response) was simply *emitted* or expressed without any observable stimulus evoking it.
>
> For example, a pigeon in a cage just naturally does pigeon-like things—walking about and pecking. A baby in a cradle just makes natural baby movements—wiggling its arms and legs in a random way. In Skinner's opinion, it is not important to identify the stimulus that started the pecking and the arm and leg movements. Rather, if we are to understand why behavior occurs, it is far more important to inspect the consequences of these movements, for the consequences are what come to control actions. (p. 172)

Skinner's research focused on the use of reinforcement and punishment in changing behavior. He also explored the effects of variations in using reinforcements and punishers such as schedules of consequences. Rewards for desired behaviors increased their frequency, and appropriate responding could be shaped through the reinforcement of behaviors that successively approximated the desired behaviors. An assumption underlying his work was that the behavior of both animals and people could be changed using similar techniques (Brumbaugh & Lawrence, 1985).

## CLASSROOM APPLICATIONS

Skinner called his classroom application of Operant Conditioning Theory "programmed learning," also known as "programmed instruction." In programmed learning, instruction is carefully broken down into small, successive steps that are carefully designed to maximize the likelihood of students' success, and to minimize the likelihood of students' frustration and failure. As students successfully accomplish each step they are rewarded (Brumbaugh & Lawrence, 1985). Teaching from a strict behavioral position, therefore, requires the arrangement of the instructional situation, inasmuch as it is possible, to produce errorless learning.

Programmed instruction is usually implemented through the use of behavioral objectives. A *behavioral objective* is a statement that is created to identify a target behavior in need of change, as well as to identify what behavioral change will constitute success. For example, a teacher might create the following classroom management behavioral objective: *Students will independently rotate through the classroom centers. Success will be achieved when students are able to complete their center rotations for 1 month with three or less teacher assists per day.* After identifying a behavioral objective, teachers will then employ Operant Conditioning Theory methods to achieve their objective. As stated earlier, these methods include the use of positive and negative consequences and schedules of reinforcement to shape behavior. With regard to the example above, on the first day of addressing her behavioral objective, a teacher might positively reinforce her students after just 3 minutes of independent center work. On the second day, reinforcement would occur after 5 minutes, and so on, until longer and longer periods of independent work were attained. In this case, the *schedule of reinforcement*, that is, how often the reinforcement is delivered, is being manipulated to achieve the behavioral objective.

Another common technique used in behavior management to achieve behavioral objectives is called "shaping." In the process of *shaping*, gross approximations of a behavior are initially reinforced with the use of positive reinforcement. Subsequently, however, only more and more refined approximations of the desired behavior are reinforced. For example, when children are very young we may reinforce them for looking at a book and telling the story in their own words. As children mature, however, our expectations of their ability to read begins to increase and gradually we reinforce them only as their reading becomes more and more conventional.

Chaining is an additional behavioral management technique. *Chaining* "enables a person to hook together a sequence of small, individual conditioned acts to compose a complex skill" (Thomas, 1996, p. 176). Chaining is a central element of Skinner's application of operant theory to the classroom.

Behaviorism has also had a significant impact on the construction of educational software products (Thomas, 1996). Many educational software products are built on the behavioral principles of breaking complex tasks down into simpler tasks that can then be mastered, and sequencing tasks in order of difficulty in order to ensure learners' success. Another element of Behaviorism seen in educational software programs is the delivery of immediate feedback to students regarding the accuracy of their responses to a learning task.

Regarding the overall importance of Skinner's contributions to our understanding of learning, Woolfolk (1998) stated that Skinner's work totally changed the way educators think about teaching and education.

Behaviorism has affected the specific field of reading in multiple ways including the way the task of reading is understood, perceptions of how reading instruction should proceed, the creation of reading materials, and the assessment of reading progress.

Behaviorism created a new perception of the task of reading as a complex act consisting of component parts. The component parts of reading were viewed as visual discrimination (the ability to discriminate shapes and letters), auditory discrimination (the ability to discriminate the sounds of the alphabet), left-to-right progression during reading, vocabulary (word knowledge), and comprehension (understanding what you have read). This understanding of reading led to a subskills approach to reading. In the *subskills approach* the complex task of reading is broken down into its many component elements, and the emphasis of reading instruction becomes mastery of these components. Hiebert and Raphael (1996) comment on the way in which reading and reading instruction were viewed after the advent of Behaviorism:

> Skinner's (1954, 1965) view of operant conditioning gave behaviorism new life in the middle of the 20th century, especially as it pertained to school reading instruction. With this view of learning, a content area such as reading could be broken into steps, each of which could be the basis for exercises in text or on a machine. Each element of an exercise required an overt response, which was followed by immediate feedback. When a student's response was correct, the feedback was reinforcing. When the student responded incorrectly, the student was told

to give another response until he or she got it right. Learning to read became the center of activity, as researchers devised hierarchies of seemingly endless skills that were made up of subskills that themselves had subskills, and so forth. . . . (p. 554)

*Direct instruction* is one form of reading instruction that is clearly linked to a behavioral theoretical perspective. In direct instruction teachers explicitly focus children's attention on specific reading concepts such as phonics, vocabulary, and comprehension skills, and provide information to students about those skills. Often direct instruction emphasizes discrete skills and subskills perceived as necessary for students' reading success. Kame'enui, Simmons, Chard, and Dickson (1997) acknowledge that "direct instruction is made distinctive, pedagogically and philosophically, by its originator, Siegfried Engelmann, and the 40 or so curriculum programs that he and his colleagues have authored over the past 25 years" (p. 61). In direct instruction reading teachers have a clear understanding of those skills that are necessary for successful reading and know how to assess their students' abilities in these areas. Teachers then proceed to teach those skills directly.

Kame'enui et al. (1997) report on the foundational principles of direct instruction: (1) the teacher is responsible for children's learning; (2) the key to successful instruction is to find out what the student has not been able to learn; (3) teachers need to find ways to respond to children's individual differences; (4) "the more carefully that the skills are taught, the greater the possibility that the child will learn them" (p. 62); and (5) "teach children in a way that provides maximum feedback on what they are learning and where they are having difficulty" (p. 62). According to Kame'enui et al. (1997), in direct instruction "children's failure to learn is unacceptable and unnecessary if we understand what we want to teach and design the teaching carefully, strategically, and with full consideration of the learner" (p. 62).

Direct instruction is currently a prominent approach to teaching reading. According to Carnine, Silbert, Kame'enui and Tarver (2004), direct instruction is the most effective and efficient approach to reading instruction. It is based on the teaching of six steps: (1) specifying objectives, (2) devising instructional strategies, (3) developing teaching procedures, (4) selecting examples, (5) sequencing skills, and (6) providing practice and review. As stated above, objectives must be very specific and based on observable behaviors. The use of strategies in direct instruction means that students need to be taught methods and approaches that they can independently apply during reading, rather than just taught to memorize information. The teaching procedures used in direct instruction are very explicit. Carnine et al. (2004) explain the steps involved in the direct instruction teaching procedure:

> Formats often contain two stages: introduction and guided practice. In the introduction stage of a format, the teacher demonstrates the steps in a strategy and then provides structured practice in using the strategy. In the guided-practice stage, the teacher gradually reduces help and prompting, and eventually the students apply the steps in the strategy independently. Including teacher guidance from prompted application to independent application of a strategy is referred to as scaffolded instruction. A final step in the guided practice stage, called discrimination, includes the teacher presenting a set of examples that provide practice on items applicable to the new strategy and items from similar previously taught strategies. (p. 26)

Selecting examples and sequencing skills are also critical components of effective direct instruction (Carnine et al., 2004). Examples that are used by the teacher in the early phases of the direct instruction lesson should be ones that are easy for students to apply what they have learned. Examples that are used later in the lesson can be more complex and require students to use discriminatory skills. Similarly, careful sequencing of skills is another critical element of a well-designed direct instruction lesson. Carnine et al. (2004, p. 27) describe the five steps to be taken in teaching a skill:

1. Preskills of a strategy are taught before the strategy itself is presented.
2. Instances that are consistent with a strategy are introduced before exceptions.
3. High utility skills are introduced before less useful ones.
4. Easy skills are taught before more difficult ones
5. Strategies and information likely to be confused are not introduced at the same time.

Finally, the direct instruction lesson is concluded with independent practice, repeated practice, and review.

Like direct instruction, *reading readiness* is another form of reading instruction that is reflective of a behavioral theoretical orientation. In reading readiness instruction educators focus on facilitating reading development through instruction in skills and subskills identified as prerequisites for reading. Traditionally, in the reading readiness approach these skills have been taught through direct instruction. Skills associated with reading readiness include auditory discrimination (the ability to identify and differentiate familiar sounds, similar sounds, rhyming words, and the sounds of letters); visual discrimination (including color recognition, shape identification, and letter identification); left-to-right progression; visual–motor skills (such as cutting on a line with scissors and coloring within the lines of a picture); and large-motor abilities such as skipping, hopping, and walking on a line. Typically, instruction of the desired subskills takes place through the use of worksheets.

Early childhood literacy instruction based on the reading readiness model implies that one prepares for literacy by acquiring a set of prescribed skills. These skills are taught directly and systematically, consistent with a behavioral approach to learning and teaching. In today's literacy classrooms for young learners, many readiness activities are still relevant, but additional experiences are also used to teach children about the comprehensive act of reading. This perspective, Emergent Literacy Theory, is explained in Chapter 5.

Shannon (1990) writes that in addition to Behaviorism changing educators' perceptions and instruction of the reading task, it affected the ways in which students' progress in reading was tracked and the creation of reading materials. Shannon refers to educators committed to a behavioral orientation as "scientific managers." Shannon argues that during the rise of scientifically managed educational practices (Behaviorism), three groups became very powerful in the field of reading: reading experts, basal publishers, and state departments of education. In Shannon's opinion, all three of these entities acted in ways that promoted behavioral practices in reading. These practices included dividing literacy into discrete skills, focusing on the attainment of objectives, and relying heavily on the use of testing to monitor reading achievement.

With regard to present-day effects of Behaviorism on reading, Shannon (1990) writes that

> social, economic, and political circumstances, and the public's fascination with business, science, and behavioral psychology, have enabled advocates of the scientific management position to dominate American reading lessons since the 1920's through the nearly universal use of commercially prepared basal reading materials. (p. 14)

## RESEARCH APPLICATIONS

Researchers and students whose studies focus on observable changes in behavior may be interested in using Classical Conditioning Theory as a theoretical framework for their research. In the field of reading, studies linked to classroom behavior, time on task, and frequency of independent reading can be conducive to a Classical Conditioning Theory context.

Montare (1988) published the first research article demonstrating that Classical Conditioning Theory could be applied to the subject area of reading. In his study, 4-year-old nonreaders were shown 22 pictures of known objects (e.g., a dog, a cat, a chair), followed by the printed word for that object (*dog, cat, chair*). The pictures and words were shown to the children via a tachistoscope. No reinforcement of any kind was provided. Following 10 conditioning trials for each word–picture pair, retention was measured by presenting each child with the printed word prompt. Results revealed a 95% retention rate, indicating that in 95% of the cases children were able to correctly read the printed word in the absence of the paired picture. In Montare's words, "The printed word was classically conditioned to become a signal of the picture which itself had been a previously learned signal" (p. 619). In his writing, Montare noted that while classical conditioning could be demonstrated in single-word identification, it was unlikely to be applicable to the reading of connected text that requires higher levels of cognition.

Researchers and graduate students conducting studies in any of the areas related to Thorndike's laws may choose to situate their studies in Connectionism. Studies related to the effectiveness of sequencing instruction according to difficulty, as well as studies of transfer and practice effects, could be appropriately placed in this theoretical framework as long as the effects being assessed were observable behaviors.

As stated earlier, Thorndike's Law of Identical Elements states that the more elements (content and procedure) of one situation are identical to the elements in a second situation, the greater the transfer, and thus the easier the learning in the second situation. This theoretical belief can be seen as underlying research in the realm of the reading–writing connection. Research in the area of the reading–writing connection emphasizes the similarities between the two cognitive processes including the viewpoint that both reading and writing are acts of composing. Implicit in this research line is the belief that since reading and writing both rely on similar cognitive processes, strengthening writing skills will have a beneficial effect on reading ability, and vice versa.

In one study that investigated the reading–writing connection, Koskinen (1993) compared the effects of integrated language arts instruction with the effects of traditional instruction. The integrated, literature-based program was designed to increase motivation for independent reading and writing and contained three primary components: (1) careful design of the physical elements of the classroom including the establishment of a literacy center; (2) the use of teacher-guided literature activities to provide models for students' independent activities; and (3) implementation of an independent reading–writing period. Results of the study indicated that the students who participated in the program in which reading and writing were taught in an integrated manner significantly outperformed the control group on measures of language development, comprehension, and writing. Koskinen's research findings are consistent with Thorndike's Law of Identical Elements.

Research studies that can be situated within an Operant Conditioning Theory context are those that focus on the effects of consequences, including reinforcers and punishers, shaping, extinction, schedules of reinforcement, maintenance, and the role of antecedents on students' learning. As in all behavioral research, the use of this theoretical framework is limited to studies examining observable behavior and behavioral changes. A recent study by Burns and Kondrick (1998) directly examined the applicability and effectiveness of Operant Conditioning Theory to reading instruction. In their work 10 parents were taught to implement a behaviorally based reading intervention with their fourth-grade children with reading disabilities. During the intervention program children received tokens for correctly reading target words, paragraphs, and stories, and for correctly answering comprehension questions. The children could exchange these tokens for money. Pretest and posttest comparisons demonstrated that children showed significant improvement on several subtests of the Woodcock Reading Mastery Tests—Revised (Woodcock, 1987), and on the Gray Oral Reading Tests—Revised (Wiederholt & Bryant, 1986), and that parents expressed a high level of satisfaction with the project. A major weakness of the study, however, was the absence of a control group.

Research studies related to the effectiveness of direct instruction can also be viewed as situated in a behavioral theoretical orientation. Kame'enui et al. (1997) conducted the largest evaluation of direct instruction in the 1960s and 1970s as a component of Project Follow Through. This project sought to evaluate the relative effectiveness of a variety of programs designed to increase at-risk students' academic achievement. Included in the variety of the nine tested programs were (1) five that were based on individualized, child-centered, constructivist-oriented learning built on the work of Piaget, Freud, and Dewey; (2) one program based heavily on parent involvement; (3) one program based heavily on bilingual and language education; and (4) two programs that emphasized isolated skill development, consistent with direct instruction and a behavioral theoretical orientation. According to Kame'enui et al. (1997), "The results of Project Follow Through revealed that the Direct-Instruction approach produced greater gains in basic skills (i.e., word identification, mathematics computation, spelling), cognitive problem solving (e.g., reading comprehension, mathematical reasoning), and affective learning (e.g., self-esteem, locus of control) than other educational models" (p. 65).

Finally, research related to reading readiness can also be viewed from a behavioral theoretical orientation. Walton and Walton (2002) studied the effects of several early literacy instructional approaches on 99 prereading kindergarten children. The children were exposed to instruction that included one or more of the following treatments: (1) isolated skill development instruction consistent with reading readiness, (rhyming, initial phoneme identity, and letter–sound relationships); (2) rime analogy reading instruction in which children were taught word identification primarily through the study and manipulation of word families; and (3) listening to stories (this was the control condition). Children who received a combination of reading readiness and rime analogy instructional treatments outperformed children who received either of those treatments in isolation. Additionally, children in the control group performed less successfully on tasks of early reading skill than did children in the other treatment groups. Despite this finding, the authors underscored that having young children listen to stories is still a vital part of early literacy programs because it builds capabilities such as familiarity with story structure, children's vocabulary, and pleasure associated with storybook reading. The study demonstrates that the reading readiness approach to early reading instruction is still one that is valued and applied in current investigations of children's literacy development.

## SUMMARY

Behaviorism is a theoretical perspective of learning that focuses on observable changes in behavior. Two underlying beliefs of Behaviorism are that behavior is the result of an organism's, or person's, response to stimuli, and that external stimuli can be manipulated to strengthen or reduce an individual's behavior. Behaviorism was the predominant psychological and educational theory in the United States from approximately 1910 to the end of the 1950s.

This chapter examined three prominent behavioral theories: Pavlov's Classical Conditioning Theory, Thorndike's theory of Connectionism, and Skinner's Operant Conditioning Theory. Built on the foundation of Associationism (discussed in Chapter 2), Pavlov's Classical Conditioning Theory articulates the concept of conditioning in which learning is observed through the repeated pairings of conditioned stimuli. While Pavlov and his disciple Watson were primarily interested in events that preceded actions, Thorndike extended the study of Behaviorism in his theory of Connectionism by demonstrating that stimuli that follow behavior also have an effect on learning. Thorndike is most famous for his Laws of Effect, Readiness, Identical Elements, and Exercise. Skinner further expanded the findings of the earlier behavioral theorists with his explanations of operant behaviors—the ways in which people learn to operate on their environments based on the antecedents and consequences of their behaviors. All three behavioral theories presented in this chapter hold implications for classroom practice and are viable theoretical contexts for researchers studying observable behaviors related to reading. The current popularity of direct instruction for teaching reading underscores the applicability of Behaviorism in today's classrooms.

# CHAPTER 4

# Constructivism
## (1920s–Present)

## CONSTRUCTIVISM: THE GENERAL CONCEPT

In approximately the same time period that Behaviorism was developing and impacting the American educational system, Constructivism was also influencing American educators. *Constructivism* is a theory of learning that emphasizes the *active construction of knowledge* by individuals (Woolfolk, 1999). From a constructivist viewpoint, learning occurs when individuals integrate new knowledge with existing knowledge. In this theoretical perspective, the integration of new knowledge with existing knowledge can only occur when the learner is actively engaged in the learning process.

In addition to presenting learning as a by-product of active mental engagement, constructivism views learning as a natural and ongoing state of mind. Christie, Enz, and Vukelich (1997) share the words of Frank Smith (1971), a famous proponent of the constructivist model, to explain this aspect of Constructivism: "Learning is not an occasional event, to be stimulated, provoked, or reinforced. Learning is what the brain does naturally, continually" (p. 7).

In addition to its description of the learner as an active, natural builder of knowledge, Constructivism has three other major components. First, in contrast to the behaviorist view that learning is observable, Constructivism holds that learning takes place through internal mechanisms that are often unobservable to the external viewer. Thus, in Constructivism, learning can often take place without any external, noticeable indicators. Second, in the constructivist perspective, learning often results from a hypothesis-testing experience by the individual. For example, a child might not know what a word is when she is reading. According to the constructivist view, she may make a guess (a hypothesis) as to what the word is. She will try the word. If the sentence makes sense with that word—that is, if her hypothesis proves to be correct— she will keep reading. If the sentence does not make sense—that is, if her hypothesis is incorrect—she will revise her hypothesis and try another word. Thus hypothesis testing is a central component of constructivist theory. Third, according to Constructism, learning results from a process known as "inferencing." *Inferencing* is the process of "filling in the meaning gaps" (Ruddell & Ruddell, 1995, p. 54). It is also known as "reading between the lines." Anytime a reader figures out something that is not explicitly stated in the text, he or she is making an inference. Constructivism has been applied directly to the study of reading as an explanation of the way in which readers construct messages, or comprehend, during the reading process (Anderson & Pearson, 1984).

Constructivism, and its application to the field of reading, has developed as a result of the efforts of a wide variety of educators and psychologists. In this chapter we note the contributions of several of the most prominent of them, including Anderson and Pearson (1984), Bartlett (1932), Brown (1978), Dewey (1916), Flavell (1976), Goodman (1967), Guthrie (2004), Pressley (2000), Rosenblatt (1978), and Smith (1971). However, before proceeding, it is important to note that there is a branch of Constructivism known as Social Constructivism (see Chapter 6) that emphasizes the social aspects of learning. Due to the large scope of both of these topics, and because each of these theories emerged during different points in history, the two are treated in separate chapters in this text.

## INQUIRY LEARNING

John Dewey (1859–1952) was one of the first American constructivists. His work has had a profound influence on American education since the early 1900s, and especially from the 1920s to the 1950s (Morrow, 2001). When Behaviorism was at its peak during the 1950s, Dewey's influence was less apparent. However, beginning in the 1960s Dewey's work was reevaluated and had a growing impact. The key elements of his writings are still affecting education in the 21st century (Gutek, 1972). Gutek, a historian of educational theory, writes that Dewey's work contributed to defining the characteristics of education in the 20th century.

Dewey's notion of learning was based on the Unfoldment theory as developed by Rousseau, Pestalozzi, and Froebel, previously described in Chapter 2. Incorporating the work of these classic philosophers and educators, Dewey emphasized the growth of the individual, the importance of the environment, and the role of the teacher in students' learning. Dewey's philosophy of education became known as *inquiry learning*. Inquiry learning was designed, first and foremost, to produce involved citizens capable of successfully participating in and contributing to a democratic society. With that goal in mind, the curriculum emphasizes the development of students' cognitive abilities, such as reasoning and decision making (Seefeldt & Barbour, 1994).

Consistent with a constructivist perspective, Dewey's work also emphasized a problem-based learning approach to education, central to which was motivating learner's interest (Woolfolk, 1998). Inquiry learning suggests that to optimize learning students need to formulate hypotheses, collect data to test hypotheses, draw conclusions, and reflect on the original problem and the thinking processes needed to solve it. Dewey criticized competition in education, and instead promoted collaboration, cooperation, and use of a democratic style in education (Woolfolk, 1998).

Dewey opened an experimental school based on inquiry learning at the University of Chicago. Here he created the "Activity Curriculum" based on his beliefs. According to historian Nila Banton Smith (1986), the curriculum was designed to provide students with interesting experiences that were likely to promote their curiosity. Once their curiosities were stimulated, students were encouraged to identify, investigate, and solve problems. The problem-based learning experiences were conducted in small, social groups. The curriculum encouraged the ongoing process of problem-based learning. Thus, after the students solved one problem, they were encouraged to identify another one. Dewey believed that this process of education would best prepare students for the real-world, adult activities needed to support a democratic society.

Many components of high-quality education have been drawn from Dewey's work. These include emphases on the role of the environment in education, problem-based learning, and social collaboration. The centrality of motivation in learning was also emphasized in Dewey's teachings. Dewey was a constructivist because he saw that, although it is the teacher's job to create an enticing curriculum and a supportive, motivating environment in the classroom, in the end it is the student who must actively create his or her own learning. Furthermore, inquiry learning is constructivist in nature because it emphasizes the active construction of knowledge by individuals and views learning as an internal, not necessarily observable, phenomenon. Dewey's Activity Curriculum emphasized hypothesis testing and inferencing, two additional characteristics of a constructivist approach to learning.

---

### TEACHER'S ANECDOTE: INQUIRY LEARNING

Dewey's preference for collaboration over competition directly relates to the cooperative learning that I use in my classroom. I employ cooperative learning and encourage my students to work collaboratively on a daily basis and in every subject area. Based on my own experiences, collaboration is more effective than competition. Rather than competing for my approval or attention, my students work with each other to solve problems and they help each other to produce a final project. Collaboration provides my students with the opportunity to converse, which motivates them since they are naturally social. Working together and learning from each other also provides them with the opportunity to construct their own meaning rather than looking to me as the sole source of information.

In my experience, literature circles have been the most effective collaboration and active learning tools in reading. In my classroom we are currently reading, *The War with Grandpa* and *The Chalkbox Kid* in literature circles. All of my students, even the weakest readers, have been successful in the literature circles. By choosing their own vocabulary, asking their own thought-provoking questions, and highlighting the passages that are most meaningful to them, my students construct their own knowledge and play an active role in what they extrapolate from the texts. They have been motivated to read and to perform their jobs well so that their groups are successful.

Dewey believed that solving problems that arise in groups helps students to become more effective problem solvers in other areas. At the end of our literature circles each day students evaluate their groups on their work habits and skills. They discuss the changes that they must make in order for their group to be more successful next time.

Dewey's theories of collaboration and problem-based learning also relate to conflict resolution. In my classroom we have a social problem-solving meeting once a week. At these meetings we all sit in a circle for half an hour and collaborate to solve issues or problems that arise on the playground or in the classroom. These meetings evoke a sense of community and eliminate competition between classmates. Each child shares his or her feelings about a single problem and we collaborate to reach the most effective way to solve it.

—MICHELLE HILKE, third-grade teacher

## SCHEMA THEORY

Schema Theory is another constructivist theory. In general, the theory strives to explain how knowledge is created and used by learners. According to *Schema Theory*, people organize everything they know into schemas, or knowledge structures. People have schemas for everything in their lives including people, places, things, language, processes, and skills. For example, people have schemas for their grandmothers (everything they know about their grandmothers) and going to restaurants (everything they know about all the restaurants they have ever visited and learned about) and dogs (everything they know about dogs). Their schemas for language includes everything they know about their language(s), and their schemas for cooking includes everything they know about cooking.

An important characteristic of Schema Theory is that everyone's schemas are individualized. A person who cooks a great deal will have a much more elaborated schema for cooking than someone who rarely cooks. A sailor will have a much different schema for boats than someone who has never sailed. According to Schema Theory, these differences in existing schemas greatly influence learning. Schema Theory suggests that the more elaborated an individual's schema for any topic (e.g., cooking, boating, or dogs) is, the more easily he or she will be able to learn new information in that topic area. The theory also suggests that without existing schemas it is very hard to learn new information on a topic.

Another important characteristic of Schema Theory is that knowledge structures are pliant and expandable. For example, even if a child has only eaten at "fast-food" restaurants, just one fine dining experience will quickly cause his or her schema for restaurants to be elaborated. So too for a child who has only been exposed to small dogs; if she or he meets a Great Dane, her or his dog schema will rapidly change to accommodate this new knowledge. Thus Schema Theory suggests that existing knowledge structures are constantly changing.

Schema Theory articulates three processes through which knowledge structures change: accretation, tuning, and restructuring (Widmayer, 2004). In *accretation*, learners take in new information but have no need to change existing schemas (e.g., a gardener who is familiar with many types of flowers learns of a new variety). In *tuning*, an existing schema is modified to incorporate new information (e.g., a child who has only seen small pleasure boats sees an oil tanker). In *restructuring*, a new schema must be created by the learner because the old one is no longer sufficient (e.g., a person who has held a stereotype abandons it as a result of a new experience).

Bartlett (1932) has been credited with the creation of the term "schema" as we use it today in education, and the initial, general application of that term to the field of reading. In tracing the history of Schema Theory, Anderson and Pearson (1984), explain that Bartlett viewed a schema as "an active organization of past reactions, or past experience" (p. 257). Bartlett studied the concept of schema by having research subjects read texts and then recall what they had read after varying periods of time. To Bartlett, one's schema was what was recalled after reading was concluded (Hiebert & Raphael, 1996).

Anderson and Pearson (1984) wrote a seminal chapter about the application of Schema Theory to the reading process and its implications for reading instruction. In their writing, Anderson and Pearson asserted that, in addition to having schemas for content (e.g., people, places, and things), readers have schemas for reading processes (e.g., decoding, skimming, inferencing, and summarizing) and for different types of text structures (e.g., narrative texts, expository texts). They argued that differences in readers' schemas in these realms are related to differences in comprehension. For example, a reader who has an elaborate schema for hiking will comprehend a text on that topic much differently than someone who has a very limited schema on hiking. Similarly, how well developed readers' schemas are in the areas of skills and text structures will also influence their reading comprehension. Relatedly, without adequate existing schemas regarding the topic of the text, the skills needed to read the text, and the structure of the text, reading comprehension will not occur.

Schema Theory has most influenced reading instruction by highlighting the central role of existing knowledge (i.e., schemas) in processing new knowledge. Now that educators understand how important existing knowledge is to the acquisition of new knowledge, many classroom teachers have become adept at building and activating students' background knowledge (schemas) prior to reading texts with students. Instructional practices such as webbing, vocabulary activities, anticipation guides, and previewing all build and activate students' schema prior to reading. Instruction related to reading process and text structures are also valuable in developing students' schema.

Schema Theory is consistent with a constructivist perspective because of its emphasis on the central role of activity in the learning and reading processes. In Schema Theory, students actively construct and revise their schemas as they read and learn. Furthermore, as they read and learn, students use their existing schemas for language and content to assist with new reading and learning experiences.

## TEACHERS' ANECDOTES: SCHEMA THEORY

A recent experience comes to mind when discussing Constructivism and Schema Theory. When introducing stories to my students I always ask about any experiences that they may have that are related to the story. I feel this helps them relate to the story and it also allows me to see what they know about the story topic. In this way I can tell which concepts need to be further developed before we start reading.

In this case we were going to read a story called "Let's Go Fishing." I started by telling my students that the story was about a little girl who lived on a farm and liked to go fishing in the creek there. My students are inner-city children, most of whom are from low socioeconomic backgrounds. None of them knew exactly what a "creek" was and they called out words such as *pond*, *lake*, *ocean*, and *sea*. Also, most of them had not had any personal experiences of going to a farm or going fishing. Some of them thought that putting a stick in the water was equivalent to fishing. On the other hand, the few students who had actually fished before could tell the class about the experience and even used words such as *bait*, *hook*, and *reeling in a fish*. As we progressed in the lesson and I tried to build the students' schemas in these areas, I found that those students who had really been to farms and those who had really been fishing seemed more interested in the story and were better able to engage in the conversations about it. They seemed to better understand it. The only exception to this was that in some cases the children seemed to confuse their real experiences with the story experience. I see now that they were trying to integrate the new information from the story with their already existing schemas on the topics.

—JOHANNAH ROGERS, first-grade teacher

I based my introduction of the book *Anne Frank: The Diary of a Young Girl* on Schema Theory. My students had learned about World War II in history class. When I introduced the book, the class and I created a web depicting their background knowledge. One area of the web was World War II. We discussed what took place in Europe. We discussed what happened to the Jewish people living in countries that were overtaken by the Germans. Another area of the web was for friends and families. We discussed the importance of both and the types of interactions we have with them. Allowance and budget were also discussed and added to the web.

Each of these topics helped the students create an idea of what Anne Frank was going to go through in the book. The students predicted what they thought the book was going to be about based on what they knew about the time period. The students would look back at the web whenever we read something in the book that was connected to a topic from the web. This lesson was an example of Schema Theory because the students activated their prior knowledge prior to reading. The students then connected what they learned from the book to what they had previously known.

—JENNIFER WITT, sixth-grade teacher

## TRANSACTIONAL/READER RESPONSE THEORY

Louise Rosenblatt (1978) further extended the application of Schema Theory to the field of reading. Based on the idea that every individual is unique with regard to what constitutes his or her schema in any particular area, Rosenblatt argued that every reading experience is therefore unique to each individual as well. The notion that all read-ers have individualized reading experiences because each reader has unique background schemas forms the cornerstone of Rosenblatt's *Transactional/Reader Response Theory*. As an example of the main idea of this theory, imagine that two children are reading the same story about migrant farmworkers. Johnny has never known anyone who works on a farm, not has he ever known any migrant workers. In contrast, Billy is quite familiar with the lives of migrant farm-workers: both his parents are migrant workers. Rosenblatt's Transac-tional/Reader Response Theory states that Johnny and Billy will have different reading responses to the migrant farmworker story as a result of the differences in the amount and kinds of background schemas each possesses.

Additionally, Rosenblatt's work adds the distinction of two kinds of responses that all readers have to texts. These are known as "effer-ent responses" and "aesthetic responses." *Efferent responses* are fact-oriented. *Aesthetic responses* are personally and emotionally based. Hennings (2000) elaborates on the differences between the two:

> Efferent meaning-making requires readers to personally disengage when reading, to obtain facts. Important in efferent reading response is what remains *after* the reading—the understanding acquired, the inferences made, the conclusions developed, the opinions generated. In contrast, aesthetic meaning-making is subjective and personal. . . . What readers are "living through"—what they see, hear, and feel—as they interact with the text is important. Rosenblatt calls this pro-cess of selecting ideas, sensations, feelings, and images and making something unique and personal with them "the literary evocation." Readers who assume an aesthetic stance connect emotionally with the story or poem they are reading to become as one with it. They are—in the words of Judith Langer (1995)—envisioning "text worlds in the mind." (p. 131)

With regard to the classroom implications of Transactional/Reader Response, when designing lessons for our students we must remember that the purposes of reading informational texts and reading literature are very different. When designing lessons around expository text, we should focus on obtaining efferent responses from our students. In con-trast, when designing lessons using literature, we should target our in-struction on promoting children's aesthetic responses to the texts. One method of evoking aesthetic responses in children is to elicit connections between the text and their own lives.

Transactional/Reading Response Theory is constructivist in nature because it emphasizes the active role of the reader in meaning making. Furthermore, Transactional/Reader Response Theory recognizes the centrality of internal, nonobservable events to learning and knowledge construction. McGee (1996) summarizes:

> According to Rosenblatt (1978), readers construct literary meaning using the text merely as a blueprint. Literary works are filled with gaps or places in which readers must supply critical information left out by the authors (Iser, 1978). When reading for aesthetic purposes, readers fill in gaps by focusing on the unique images, impressions, feelings, and reactions they bring to mind while reading. These brief and fleeting images, feelings, impressions, and thoughts work along with their respective responses to form the reader's unique and personal understanding of the literary work. (p. 195)

## TEACHER'S ANECDOTE: TRANSACTIONAL/READER RESPONSE THEORY

Rosenblatt's Transactional/Reader Response Theory of reading and writing relates to a variety of practices that I incorporate in my reading class. The idea of reading as an individualized process relates to the reading response log questions that I give to my students when we are not using literature circles. Questions like "What do you think of . . . ?" or "How would you have handled the situation if you were the main character?" allow my students to have an individual aesthetic experience with the text. Each student's personal experiences will produce a different response, allowing for more colorful discussions. During independent readings of the texts I often ask my students to list any observations, connections, and wonderings that they have. The text-based observations that they make become efferent experiences because the same events happened for each student. The connections that my students make to the text, and the questions that they are left wondering about, become aesthetic experiences because they differ for each reader. Connections and wonderings are dependent upon each student's emotional response to the text and his or her own unique background experiences.

One group of students is currently reading *The Chalkbox Kid*. They recently experienced a very aesthetic response to this text. The particular children in this group came from loving families who are involved in their children's lives. Therefore, these six students became very angry with the mother in the story for not wanting to see her son's artwork or his special place. They could not comprehend her indifferent attitude because they had never experienced such neglect. Other children in my class may have considered the mother's negative attitude to be normal. They would not have had the same aesthetic experience because of their different backgrounds.

Similarly, as a personal journal question, I asked the students who are reading *The War with Grandpa* if they sided with Peter or with Grandpa in the room argument. Depending on their background experience, students had different answers. The children who have always had their own room claimed that Grandpa was right and that Peter was being immature. But my students who are forced by their parents to share a room with a sibling argued for Peter. The children had a hard time comprehending the other's point of view because it was so different from their own experiences. What an incredible lesson in reading as an individualized experience!

—MICHELLE HILKE, third-grade teacher

## PSYCHOLINGUISTIC THEORY AND WHOLE LANGUAGE THEORY

Psycholinguistic Theory is another theory that can easily be classified as contructivist in nature. *Psycholinguistics* is the study of the links between psychology and language. As Shannon (1990) writes, "Psycholinguistics is the intersection at which the study of the language system meets the study of how humans acquire, interpret, organize, store, retrieve, and employ knowledge" (p. 133).

At the core of the psycholinguistic perspective on reading (Goodman, 1970, 1967, 1976; Smith, 1971) is the assumption that reading is primarily a language process. A central component of the Psycholinguistic Theory of reading is that readers rely on language cueing systems to help them rapidly read text. Although there are multiple cueing systems that readers use, those most often cited in conjunction with Psycholinguistic Theory are the systems of syntactic, semantic, and graphophonic information. *Syntactic cues* are those related to the gram-

matical structure or syntax of the language that enable readers to predict
the next words in the text. *Semantic cues* are those related to the meaning of the words and sentences that allow readers to predict the next
words in the text. *Graphophonic* cues are those that are derived from
the visual patterns of letters and words and their corresponding sounds
that, again, allow readers to predict the next words in the text. According to Psycholinguistic Theory, after young children successfully, albeit
unconsciously, internalize these cueing systems in their oral language
they are able to use these cueing systems to guide their reading

In addition to its emphasis on using language cueing systems to
guide reading, Psycholinguistic Theory argues that readers use their
knowledge about language, and the world in general, to drive their
thinking as they engage in the reading process. The theory suggests that
as they read, readers make predictions about what the text will say
based on their knowledge in these areas. If the text is consistent with a
reader's expectations, then reading proceeds easily and fluidly. If, however, the text is inconsistent with the reader's expectations, then the reading process will become slower and more laborious and the reader will
need to decode the text word by word, and sometimes letter by letter. As
Heilman, Blair, and Rupley (1986) state, according to Psycholinguistic
Theory "the more familiar a reader is with a given topic, the less she
needs to rely solely on the printed text. The readers' knowledge of the
topic and her language competence allow her to predict information and
rely less on print" (p. 38).

Psycholinguistic Theory regards prediction as a key part of the reading process in which the reader makes and tests hypotheses as he or she
reads. In this context, a *hypothesis* is what the reader thinks/predicts
that the text will say. Psycholinguistic Theory suggests that readers test
their hypotheses by attending to the first letters in words as they read. If
the text matches their hypotheses, then reading proceeds quickly. If the
text differs from the reader's hypotheses, then the reader slows down
and reads from more of a text-driven, or "bottom-up," stance. According to the psycholinguistic perspective, the use of prediction and hypothesis testing during reading occurs very rapidly and unconsciously. Furthermore, these processes are viewed as a means of allowing the reader
to progress quickly through texts by sampling words and comparing
them to his or her predictions or hypotheses, rather than reading every
word that is printed on the page. Proponents of Psycholinguistic Theory
argue that such sampling aids rapid reading and stands in contrast to
reading every word printed on the page, which would be cumbersome
and slow for readers. Based on the perception of reading as a process of

confirming and rejecting hypotheses founded on linguistic knowledge, Goodman (1967) described reading as a "psycholinguistic guessing game" in which the child attempts to reconstruct, in light of his or her own knowledge of language and of the world, what the author has to say.

Adherents of Psycholinguistic Theory gain insights into the cueing systems that readers use by analyzing their miscues. *Miscues*, a term coined by Goodman (1967), are a reader's responses to the text that differ from what the text actually says. Miscues are not just another name for what has traditionally been called "reading errors." The term "miscue" was deliberately used by Goodman in an attempt to put a more positive light on the deviations that readers make from the actual text during the act of reading. According to Goodman, reading miscues can be examined to illuminate the reader's thinking process during reading. As such, he referred to the examination of miscues as "windows" into a reader's mind.

Psycholinguistic Theory emphasizes the idea that readers are active participants in the reading process who try to construct a coherent, meaningful interpretation of the text as they read. In this regard, Psycholinguistic Theory can be viewed as a constructivist theory.

In 1971, Smith applied concepts from Psycholinguistic Theory to the teaching of reading in his highly influential book *Understanding Reading*. This work laid the foundation for *Whole Language Theory*, a theory of literacy learning and instruction that has had a powerful impact on literacy education since the 1980s. From a content analysis of 64 professional articles related to Whole Language Theory, Bergeron (1990) composed this definition of Whole Language:

> Whole language is a concept that embodies both a philosophy of language development as well as the instructional approaches embedded within, and supportive of, that philosophy. This concept includes the use of real literature and writing in the context of meaningful, functional, and cooperative experiences in order to develop in students' motivation and interest in the process of learning. (p. 319)

Whole Language Theory is a philosophy about how children learn from which educators derive strategies for teaching. The philosophy encompasses and extends Psycholinguistics Theory. Whole Language Theory suggests that reading, like oral language, is a natural process that children will acquire if immersed in high-quality literacy environments and exposed to meaningful, authentic literacy experiences and high-quality literature. It is also based on the beliefs that listening, speaking, reading, and writing are all interconnected, and that advances in any one area will promote advances in the other areas. Whole Language Theory is a child-centered philosophy that borrows from and builds on the motivational aspects of Unfoldment Theory.

Whole Language Theory is consistent with a wide range of instructional strategies. Importantly, Whole Language Theory literacy instruction uses authentic pieces of high-quality children's literature rather than commercially prepared basal reading series as the primary materials for the language arts program. The literature is also used as a springboard for activities in other content areas. A wide variety of genres of reading materials are housed in a literacy center. The classroom itself is designed as a rich literacy environment. Center-based activities comprise a large part of the school day. There are large blocks of time for reading and writing workshop. Most activities are designed to promote active, social interactions. A major objective of classrooms based on Whole Language Theory is the development of a child's desire to read and write. Assessment is varied, ongoing, and growth-oriented, often using portfolio assessment and conferencing as major components of the process.

Instruction based on Whole Language Theory can be implemented in many different ways, depending on the needs and interests of those involved. There is no one right way to create a Whole Language Theory program because one program cannot satisfy everyone's needs. Whole Language Theory is a theory of how children learn language arts that holds strong implications for classroom practices. Additional instructional strategies associated with Whole Language Theory are presented in the "Classroom Applications" section of this chapter.

TEACHER'S ANECDOTE:
PSYCHOLINGUISTIC THEORY
AND WHOLE LANGUAGE THEORY

In one of my guided reading books we were reading about the Special Olympics. We had already made predictions about what the Special Olympics are based on the cover of the leveled book. The students began to read their guided books individually. Part of my assessment in guided reading instruction is to go around the table and tap the kids on the shoulder to hear them read. While they are reading I do a brief running record on them. During the reading I came upon a child who always has a great deal of difficulty reading. When it was his turn to read, he correctly read words such as *handicapped*, *wheelchair* and *exceptional*, but could not read the words *jumped* or *hurdled*. Now I know what happened. In my book talk before the students started reading I used the terms "handicapped," "wheelchair," and "exceptionally challenged" and we discussed the meaning of these terms. It is now evident to me that the child used that information to read these words in the story. I am assuming he also made a connection between the word *wheelchair* and the picture of the Asian child in a wheelchair. I now understand why the child read the difficult words correctly but had trouble with the easier ones. Goodman's theory helped me realize that this child had a prior sense of what was meaningful in the text, based on what we had discussed earlier in the group discussion.

—DAWN SPRINITIS, reading specialist

## METACOGNITION

Metacognition is the process of thinking about one's own thinking. The concept of metacognition, when applied to the field of reading, contributes to a constructivist understanding of how reading comprehension occurs, as well as to a body of knowledge regarding instructional strategies that can be used to facilitate reading comprehension.

Research on the general concept of metacognition was introduced in the mid-1970s by Flavell (1976) and Brown (1978), who studied the development of children's ability to be aware of and control their own cognitive processes (Baker, 2002). Interest in developing students' metacognitive abilities with regard to the reading process arose in response to Durkin's (1978–1979) research, in which she argued that the technique teachers used most often to develop reading comprehension, the directed reading lesson, was not effective in promoting students' ability to *independently* comprehend texts (Duffy, 2002). In traditional directed reading lessons, teachers introduce a reading selection to students, guide their reading of the selection, and then discuss the reading with them. This approach to reading instruction, although still popular and advocated in many basal reading series, leaves many students in a teacher-dependent state, offering them little in the way of tools that they can independently apply to facilitate their own reading comprehension.

In response to Durkin's (1978–1979) findings, educational researchers began to search for alternatives to the directed reading lesson that they hoped would offer greater opportunities for building students' independent reading comprehension abilities (Duffy, 2002). The study of metacognition as a way of understanding the reading comprehension process, and as an approach to reading comprehension instruction, was one outcome of this search (Duffy, 2002). Studying the topic of metacognition, researchers determined that proficient readers employ a number of metacognitive strategies during reading that assist them in understanding the text (Pressley, 2000). For example, proficient readers are aware of whether or not they comprehend what they are reading, and employ "fix-up" strategies such as rereading, slowing down, or looking up word meanings when comprehension failures occur. Proficient readers also engage in goal setting, self-questioning, summarizing, and visualizing during the reading experience (Brown, 2002; El-Dinary, 2002). Additional metacognitive processes that proficient readers intuitively use include "being aware of their purpose in reading . . . overviewing the text . . . reading selectively . . . making associations to ideas presented . . . and revising prior knowledge that is inconsistent with ideas in the text" (Pressley, 2000, p. 550).

Not only has research demonstrated the effective use of metacognitive strategies by good readers, it has also consistently shown that poor readers have far less metacognitive awareness than their higher achieving peers and that young readers have less than older readers (Baker, 2002). These findings have encouraged researchers to investigate the effectiveness of teaching all readers to master the metacognitive strategies used by excellent readers. This approach to comprehension instruction has become known by a number of terms including "metacognitive instruction," "strategy instruction," "direct explanation of strategies," and "transactional strategy instruction." For the purposes of our discussion, we will refer to this body of knowledge as metacognitive instruction.

The goal of metacognitive instruction is to help readers become more aware of their own thinking during the reading process. During metacognitive instruction, educators provide *explicit* instruction on the use of metacognitive techniques that students can apply during reading. *Explicit instruction* means that teachers attempt to be especially clear, organized, and detailed regarding the nature of the metacognitive strategy they are explaining, and when and how that strategy should be applied by the reader during the reading experience.

In addition to the central notion that metacognitive instruction must be explicit is the idea that metacognitive instruction must take place through a gradual transfer, or "release," of responsibility from the teacher to the student for the application of the metacognitive strategy

(Baker, 2002). In gradual transfer of responsibility, the instructional approach begins with the teacher's explicit description of the metacognitive strategy, and then the modeling of how, when, and why the strategy can be used. The modeling often takes place through think-aloud methods used by the teacher. The modeling phase is followed by a guided-use phase in which the teacher helps the students apply the strategy with teacher direction. Over a period of time, students gradually become able to independently initiate and use the target strategy. At this point it can be said that the responsibility for that specific metacognitive tool has been successfully transferred from the teacher to the student. Then the teacher can begin instruction of another metacognitive strategy.

Below, one teacher explains how she has used metacognitive instruction in her classroom teaching.

## TEACHER'S ANECDOTE: METACOGNITION

William Butler Yeats once said, "Education is not the filling of a pail but the lighting of a fire." I have always felt drawn to this quote as it inspires me to be the best teacher I can be. My goal is to motivate my students to take control of their learning and achievement. Initially, I decided to become a reading specialist because I felt helpless when it came to facilitating my students with their reading. Now that I have completed my thesis on metacognition and comprehension skills, I feel equipped with the strategies and statistics to achieve this goal and adequately guide my students toward success.

Often, students expect reading to come naturally. When it doesn't, they become less motivated to read, especially since they believe they can obtain all their information and entertainment needs through other, less challenging mediums. Struggling students need to "buy into" the fact that these reading practices are ongoing and overnight success will not be achieved. Through repetition, construction, development, and encouragement, slowly they will come around and begin to employ the strategies. With this concerted effort students will begin to achieve small successes and to develop ownership of their own learning.

Since implementing metacognitive instruction and practices in my classroom, my students appear more focused and self-aware. The students seem actively engaged beyond the literal level. The metacognitive comprehension skills notably build confidence and help dependent readers become more actively involved and self-aware. They make the switch from being disengaged to seeing themselves as learners who embrace the learning process.

After reviewing different metacognitive strategies, and providing modeling and practice, I present the students a laminated bookmark with reminders of these strategies. Even my most challenged readers embrace the strategies and frequently can be seen referring to the bookmark. As the year goes on the readers become cognizant of self-challenges and reading challenges and now know how to describe and discuss these challenges and how to ask for focused help.

—NICOLE MATTIVI, eighth-grade English teacher

Research on the effectiveness of metacognitive instruction as it applies to improving students' reading comprehension ability shows that this type of instruction does, in fact, lead to significantly strengthened reading comprehension abilities (Block & Pressley, 2002). Unfortunately, however, metacognitive instruction is time-consuming and challenging for teachers to learn and implement (El-Dinary, 2002). While many educators do believe that the time and effort required to use metacognitive instruction is worthwhile and therefore have chosen to pursue the approach in their work with students, this powerful instructional approach to comprehension instruction is still not widespread in American schools (Block & Pressley, 2002).

Metacognitive instruction reflects contructivist theory because of its depiction of the readers' active, internal cognitive engagement as central to the reading process. While metacognition has a social component in its initial phases of instruction, it is not classified as a form of Social Learning Theory because a focal goal of metacognition is to help readers to independently employ these strategies.

## ENGAGEMENT THEORY

Engagement Theory (Guthrie, 2004; Guthrie & Wigfield, 1997, 2000) seeks to articulate the differences between "engaged" and "disengaged" readers, and to provide direction to educators on how to help students become more engaged. According to the theory, *engaged readers* are those who are intrinsically motivated to read and who therefore read frequently. Engaged readers are also mentally active, using metacognitive strategies to build their understanding of the conceptual content of texts. Engaged readers are frequently social, often talking with others about what they are reading and learning. Thus Engagement Theory contains the central elements of Metacognitive Theory but also emphasizes motivational, conceptual, and social aspects of learning.

There are vast differences between the achievement gains of engaged and disengaged readers. For example, engaged readers spend 500% more time reading than do disengaged readers (Guthrie, 2004). Additionally,

> For 9-year-olds on the National Assessment of Education Progress (NAEP) in 1998, the correlation between the indicator of engaged reading and reading comprehension achievement was higher than any demographic characteristic such as gender, income, or ethnicity (Guthrie et al., 2001). Even more surprising and significant was the finding that 9-year-olds whose family background was characterized by low income and low education, but who were highly engaged readers, substantially outscored students who came from backgrounds with higher education and higher income, but who themselves were less engaged readers. Based on a massive sample, this finding suggests the stunning conclusion that engaged reading can overcome traditional barriers to reading achievement, including gender, parental education, and income. (Guthrie, 2004, p. 5)

Educators interested in the concept of engagement have begun to investigate ways to increase students' reading engagement. Guthrie (2004) created Concept-Oriented Reading Instruction (CORI). This approach to reading instruction has five major components: (1) the use of themes in reading instruction, (2) an emphasis on student choice for both reading texts and responses, (3) the use of hands-on activities, (4) the availability of a wide variety of text genres chosen to interest students, and (5) the integration of social collaboration into reading response activities. Research on the effects of CORI indicates that students involved with this program demonstrate increased motivation for reading, increased use of metacognitive skills, and increased gains in conceptual knowledge (Anderson & Guthrie, 1996).

## CLASSROOM APPLICATIONS

Constructivism, based on Dewey's foundational work, has had a powerful impact both on the ways in which the reading process is understood and on the ways in which reading instruction is implemented in class-rooms. As a result of Constructivism, educators can view the reading process as one in which the reader constructs his or her own messages while reading. The work of Bartlett (1932) and Pearson and Anderson (1984) helps us understand the ways in which already existing knowl-edge (organized as schemas) influences the construction of these mes-sages (comprehension). Similarly, the work of Rosenblatt (1978) helps us understand the ways in which everyone constructs individualized interpretations, based on the uniqueness of their personal schemas, dur-ing reading. Psycholinguistic Theory and Whole Language Theory strengthen our awareness of the role of language as children work to construct meaning during reading. Metacognitive Theory further ex-tends our understanding of the message construction process, or com-prehension, by elaborating on the ways in which proficient readers men-tally engage with a text during reading. Each of these constructivist theories has generated a number of classroom practices consistent with its interpretation of the importance of Constructivism in the learning experience.

Dewey's original conceptualization of Constructivism has probably influenced reading practices in the classroom most by laying the founda-tion for the understanding of learning as a constructivist experience. When teachers engage in practices that are consistent with the belief that their students' learning is dependent on their students' ability to construct knowledge within themselves, they are using instructional approaches grounded in Dewey's work. Dewey was also famous for advocating the importance of problem solving in learning, and for the use of small groups of students to stimulate social learning during problem-solving learning experiences. When classroom teachers engage their students in problems-based learning situations, and in problems-based learning small-group experiences, they are using instructional approaches based on Dewey's work.

The work of Anderson and Pearson (1984) on Schema Theory is most famous for generating the classroom practices of brainstorming and webbing. In *brainstorming*, teachers guide students through activi-ties in which they aim to get students, first, to activate any background information (schemas) they have on a topic, and second, to extend their already existing background knowledge on the topic. Brainstorming activities are based on the premise that reading comprehension will improve when students' schemas are activated and strengthened prior to reading. When engaging students in these activities teachers traditionally gather students into a group and then have them openly "brainstorm" on the topic, which means to suggest any related ideas to the topic. Teachers then write the students' ideas on a blackboard, whiteboard, or easel for the group to see and discuss.

*Webbing* is a more organized form of brainstorming. In contrast to brainstorming, in which student-generated ideas are written down randomly, in the order in which they are introduced, in webbing, student-generated ideas are organized into categories by the teacher as he or she records them. In a semantic web activity, for example, a teacher uses a large sheet of chart paper to draw a diagram with his or her students. In the center of the chart paper the teacher draws a circle and prints the key concept to be discussed, for example, "beach." The teacher then asks the students to generate ideas they associate with the beach, such as "shells," "waves," "sun," "suntan lotion," "surfing," "umbrellas," and so on. The teacher and students organize these ideas into categories as they are generated, such as "things that people bring to the beach," "things that people do at the beach," and "things that are part of nature at the beach."

One popular form of webbing is the *KWL approach*. In this activity, prior to reading, teachers ask students to generate what they already know (K) about a topic and what they would like to know about it (W). Following reading, students complete the chart by discussing what they learned (L) as a result of their reading. As stated above, all of these popular classroom instructional activities are based on the belief that children construct their own knowledge during the reading process and that this construction process can be facilitated through learning experiences that activate existing schemas and build new schemas prior to the reading of texts.

Rosenblatt's (1978) Transactional/Reader Response Theory also has significant implications for classroom practice. Rosenblatt's theory draws attention to the different types of responses (efferent and aesthetic) that readers can have during the reading experience, and to the ways in which readers' schemas ultimately provide each reader with an individualized interpretation of the text. Rosenblatt's work has also helped educators appreciate the importance of designing learning activities that elicit a variety of individual efferent and aesthetic responses to reading.

As a result of Rosenblatt's writings, it is now common for teachers to create follow-up activities to reading that encourage a wide range of creative and individualized responses. For example, Cox (1996) presents postreading activities that stimulate a broad spectrum of reading responses: writing in literature response journals, talking about books in literature response groups, readers' theater, storytelling, puppetry, video-taping, dioramas, bookmaking, story boxes, story maps, and story quilts. In each of these activities, children's individual responses to reading, both efferent and aesthetic, are reinforced.

One popular activity based on Rosenblatt's Transactional/Reader Response Theory is drawing students' attention to the use of three different types of connections during reading. The first type of connection is the "text to self" connection. Here readers are helped to attend to the ways in which the story or passage is related to the reader's personal life. The second type of connection is the "text to text" connection. In this area readers are helped to make connections between the text that they are currently reading and others that they have read in the past. The third type of connection is the "text to world" connection. As the name suggests, in this activity readers focus on the relationships between what they are reading and the world at large. When first using this activity, teachers often present it in a teacher-directed lesson. After practice, however, students can be helped to make and record these connections spontaneously during reading. Again, the foundational premise in this activity is that students' comprehension of text will be enhanced as the links between what they are reading and what they already know are underscored.

Like Schema Theory and Transactional/Reader Response Theory, Psycholinguistic Theory and Whole Language Theory have deeply influenced classroom practices regarding literacy learning. The application of Psycholinguistic Theory in the classroom is most apparent in the use of running records during guided reading lessons. In *guided reading lessons*, teachers meet with small groups of students with similar levels of reading skill and provide them with reading texts that are matched to their level of reading achievement. As the guided reading session progresses, and after all students are familiar with the text and have read it both silently and aloud as a part of the group, students are asked to read aloud individually. At this point, the teacher may conduct a "running record" of the child's oral reading during which the teacher records the types of errors, or "miscues," that the student makes. As Psycholinguistics Theory suggests, these miscues are viewed as "windows into the mind" of the student that help the teacher determine what types of cuing systems the student is relying on during the reading experience. Running records are also used during Reading Recovery lessons with at-risk students. Additionally, a Psycholinguistic Theory orientation is observable in the classroom when teachers use cues based on prompts such as "Does that make sense?" during students' oral reading.

As with Psycholinguistic Theory, aspects of Whole Language Theory are visible in many classrooms. Whole Language Theory is associated with all the following instructional strategies:

- Use of real, high-quality literature for literacy learning.
- Use of real, meaningful contexts for literacy activities.
- Child-centered instruction based on children's interests.
- Heavy emphasis on student choice.
- Use of thematic instruction.
- Use of active, social learning experiences.
- Use of "teachable moments."
- Use of a variety of grouping systems.
- Use of large blocks of time for integrated literacy activities.
- Use of alternative systems of assessment, such as portfolio assessment.
- Use of centers in the classroom.

As a result of the large number of instructional strategies with which Whole Language Theory is associated, it is impossible to adequately cover the application of this topic to the classroom in this text. Instead, one aspect of Whole Language Theory instruction, thematic instruction, has been chosen to provide some insight into the ways in which this theoretical orientation influences literacy instruction.

*Thematic instruction* is a form of instruction that is integrated through the use of a unifying concept or theme. As Morrow (2001) explains, "Literacy learning becomes meaningful when it is consciously embedded into the study of themes and content area subjects" (p. 16). Morrow writes that thematic units vary, but are unified by their goal of providing literacy instruction in interesting and authentic contexts. Morrow then presents three types of thematic units that are popular. The first type is organized around a literacy genre or a particular author. For example, the classroom teacher might prepare a thematic unit on fairy tales or on the author Tomie dePaola. In this type of unit the teacher shares many examples of literature from the chosen genre or author, and prepares lessons and activities that use reading and writing to further explore the genre or author.

The second type of popular thematic unit identifies a theme that has a science or social studies thrust. Reading materials related to that theme are then used as the basis of many lessons. Morrow writes, "For example, if the theme was the farm and one of the stories used in the unit was *The Little Red Hen,* some related activities might be to bake some bread, role-play the story, or write another version of the story in which the animals are all helpful in making the bread" (p. 16).

The third type of popular thematic unit uses a science or social studies topic and consciously integrates literacy into all content area lessons, including music, art, play, math, social studies, and science. Many selections of children's literature are used as a major part of the unit; however, the literature itself does not drive the unit—the topic of the unit is the main focus. In this type of unit, the classroom centers are filled with materials that relate to the topic, including literacy materials to encourage reading and writing. Reading and writing are purposefully incorporated into all science and social studies lessons. Skills are taught when they seem appropriate—for example, in the unit on the farm, when the class hatches baby chicks in an incubator, journals may be kept on the progress of the chicks, and the digraph "ch" could be emphasized. Unit topics are incorporated into the entire school day in all content areas. Topics may be predetermined by the teacher, selected by the children and teacher together, or decided on spontaneously based on something of interest that occurs in the school, in someone's home, or in the world.

We hope that these brief descriptions illustrate the significant impact that the use of thematic units can have in the classroom. Additionally, it is important to remember that the use of thematic units is just one of many aspects of Whole Language Theory instruction that can be implemented in the classroom.

Metacognition is another theory that can also be used to influence literacy instruction in powerful ways. The goal of metacognitive instruction is to help students become more aware of their own thinking during the reading experience. Metacognitive instruction is also designed to promote students' independent use of metacognitive strategies during the reading experience. The keys to effective metacognitive instruction are that the teacher is very explicit about when and how any particular metacognitive strategy is implemented, and that the teacher uses a gradual release of responsibility to transition the student from being dependent on the teacher regarding when and how to use the strategy to being independent in its use.

An example of metacognitive instruction is teaching students to monitor whether or not they are comprehending what they are reading. The teacher would probably begin the lesson by explaining to students that good readers monitor whether or not they are understanding what they are reading, and if they realize that they are not comprehending the text they employ "fix-up" strategies to try and correct the problem. The teacher would then explain why it is important to monitor whether or not you are understanding what you are reading, and why you should employ fix-up strategies if you are not understanding what you are reading. Following this, the teacher would explain that this strategy (i.e., comprehension monitoring) should be used whenever students read, no matter what they are reading. After the teacher has fully explained the target strategy and why and when it should be used, she or he will progress to modeling the use of the strategy her- or himself. This technique is based on the use of "think-alouds" in which the teacher reads each paragraph and then thinks aloud to illustrate to the students the way she or he is thinking about the text and whether or not she or he understands it. At this point the teacher can also model a comprehension breakdown and the use of a fix-up strategy.

After the teacher has completed the modeling and explanation phase of strategy instruction, she or he should help students to begin to practice with the target strategy in a supported way. This means that students should be given an easy passage or text on which to practice, and that practice should occur in a group setting with much teacher involvement. For example, students may be asked to read a single, easy paragraph and then discuss whether or not they comprehended it. Practice should continue on progressively longer and more difficult texts, with progressively less teacher involvement as students' success is demonstrated. Eventually, students will be able to independently use the metacognitive strategy that has been taught to them. Then the teacher can begin instruction on a new strategy.

## RESEARCH APPLICATIONS

Dewey (1916) supports the central role of the learner as the constructor of his or her own knowledge, and focuses especially on the areas of problem-based learning and social collaboration within a constructivist orientation to learning. Additionally, Dewey's theory emphasizes the role of the physical environment in learning. Researchers and graduate students initiating research projects within any of these domains may choose to situate their studies within Dewey's Inquiry Learning.

Morrow, Pressley, Smith, and Smith (1997) used Dewey's Inquiry Learning to frame their literacy research on the effects of a literature-based program integrated into literacy and science instruction. One hundred twenty-eight third-grade children from diverse backgrounds were assigned to either a literacy/science program in which both their literacy and science programs received a literature-based intervention, or to a literacy-only program in which only their literacy program received a literature-based intervention. Additionally, one group of children was assigned to a control program in which they received traditional reading instruction from a non-literature-based, basal reading text. The interventions ran for the course of a full academic year. Pre- and posttest comparisons revealed that students in the literacy/science group performed significantly better than did children in the literacy-only group on all measures used. Furthermore, children in the literacy-only group performed significantly better than the control children on all but one measure. The researchers framed their work in terms of Dewey's Inquiry Learning because of the theory's emphases on the importance of curiosity and interest in learning. Using this lens, the authors suggested that the differing levels of literacy achievement might have been attained because the varying levels of literature infusion stimulated corresponding levels of curiosity and interest in the students.

Researchers and graduate students working from a constructivist perspective may prefer to frame their research from a Schema Theory context if they are particularly interested in the ways in which students' organization of knowledge affects their reading abilities. Schema Theory is particularly useful for studies in the area of reading comprehension. Research regarding the effectiveness of activities designed to activate and build background knowledge are often framed from this viewpoint.

The role of background knowledge on reading comprehension in first and second language reading was investigated in a study by Droop and Verhoeven (1998). In this case, the particular schema investigated was that of cultural background knowledge. In the study, third-grade students read three text selections that were matched for reading difficulty. The context of the first text selection was consistent with their own cultural background (Dutch). The context of the second text selection was Near Eastern (Moroccan and Turkish), which was foreign to these students. The third text was designed to be neutral and did not identify a cultural context. Results of read-aloud protocols, retellings, and comprehension assessments demonstrated that student familiarity with the cultural context of a text was associated with increased comprehension for students reading in their first language. For students reading in their second language, this effect was limited when texts were linguistically complex, suggesting that "because of a limited proficiency in the target language, these children cannot profit from their background knowledge if texts are linguistically more complex" (p. 267). The results of the study were interpreted as consistent with a Schema Theory view of reading.

The Transactional/Reader Response Theory is appropriate for researchers and graduate students who are primarily interested in students' individual responses to literature and the qualitative nature of those responses. In one study employing a Transactional/Reader Response Theory lens, Bean and Rigoni (2001) investigated the reader response patterns of five pairs of students as they read a young-adult, multicultural novel. Analysis of weekly dialogue journals between the pairs of students, instructor reflections, and participant interviews showed that students used the text "as a means of helping them make sense of their own lives and the lives of those around them" (p. 233). In their conclusion, the authors emphasized the importance of their work in that it "offers an alternative to homogenized, fact-driven learning" and "can reduce the limitations of the teacher as the central, omniscient authority" (p. 246). Indeed, both of these statements are associated with literacy instruction that includes aspects of Transactional/Reader Response Theory.

Psycholinguistic Theory remains an important theory that influences classroom practices in literacy instruction. However, Stanovich (2000) argues that, from a research perspective, the value of Psycholinguistic Theory for explaining the reading process has diminished through the years. The devaluation of Psycholinguistic Theory as a comprehensive model to explain the reading process is due to the recent disproving of a central tenet of Psycholinguistic Theory. Stanovich (2000) writes, "The hypothesis that the superior word recognition skills of the better readers were due to their superior context-use skills—a hypothesis that once had great popularity in the reading literature—is now known to be false" (p. 406). Stanovich continues:

> A large amount of research has consistently indicated that the word recognition of better readers is not characterized by more reliance on contextual information. It is the poorer reader who is more reliant on contextual information at the word recognition level. The reason for this finding eventually became apparent— ... the word recognition processes of the skilled reader are so rapid and automatic that facilitation from less reliable contextual information is not needed. (p. 406)

With regard to research in the area of metacognition, a study by Dole, Brown, and Trathen (1996) has received much attention. In the first phase of their project, the metacognitive skills of 67 fifth- and sixth-grade students from an at-risk school were examined. The students were randomly assigned to one of three conditions: metacognitive strategy instruction, story content instruction, and basal control instruction. Following a 5-week intervention, the students in all three groups performed similarly on reading materials that had been used for instruction. However, the strategies instruction group significantly outperformed the other two groups when they were asked to read texts that were new to them. In the second phase of the research, two students' metacognitive skills were investigated more closely. Results from this investigation revealed that students possessing different reading achievement levels appear to respond to metacognitive strategy instruction differently.

## SUMMARY

Constructivism is a theory of learning that emphasizes the active construction of knowledge by individuals. The theory is characterized by the notions that learning can occur in the absence of observable indicators, that learning often results from a form of hypothesis testing, and that the process of making inferences is central to the learning process. Constructivism has been applied directly to the study of reading as an explanation for the way in which readers construct messages, or comprehend, during the reading process.

Six constructivist theories were presented in this chapter: Inquiry Learning, Schema Theory, Transactional/Reader Response Theory, Psycholinguistic Theory/Whole Language Theory, Metacognitive Theory, and Engagement Theory. Inquiry Learning, developed by Dewey (1916), emphasizes the importance of problem solving, social collaboration, and motivation, based on interest and curiosity in learning. Schema Theory, first suggested by Bartlett (1932) and later expanded by Anderson and Pearson (1984), conceptualizes the way in which knowledge is organized in the brain, and the implications of that organization for learning and reading. Transactional/Reader Response Theory, put forth by Rosenblatt (1978), further extends the application of Schema Theory by arguing that all readers have unique responses to reading texts due to the unique nature of their background schemas. Psycholinguistic Theory emphasizes the role of language in the reading process, and Whole Language Theory uses that information as the cornerstone of a theory of literacy learning and instruction for students. Metacognitive Theory stresses the importance of specific types of mental engagement during the reading process to ensure accurate comprehension and comprehension monitoring experiences. Finally, Engagement Theory incorporates the central features of Metacognitive Theory while also emphasizing the roles of motivation, conceptual knowledge, and social interactions during learning. All of the theories presented in this chapter are built on the premise that individuals are active in the construction of their own knowledge, and hold current value for both classroom instruction and research. Theories of Social Constructivism are treated separately in Chapter 6.

# CHAPTER 5

# Theories of
# Literacy Development
## *(1930s–Present)*

During the early 1900s, at about the same time that constructivist theorists such as Dewey (1916) were trying to explain the ways in which individuals create internal understanding, and behaviorists such as Watson (1913) and Thorndike (1903, 1931) were trying to explain how learning could be understood in terms of observable behavior, developmental theorists were trying to explain literacy growth from a longitudinal perspective. Theorists working from a developmental perspective attempt to explain the growth of specific behaviors and abilities across time.

Developmental theorists in reading aim to address such questions as:

- How does early reading ability develop?
- In what ways can early reading development be facilitated?
- What are some symptoms of developmental problems in early reading ability?

This chapter examines several different theories of development. These include Piaget's Theory of Cognitive Development (Piaget &

Inhelder, 1969), Maturation Theory (Morphett & Washburne, 1931), Holdaway's Theory of Literacy Development (1979), Stage Models of Reading (Frith, 1985; Chall, 1983), Emergent Literacy Theory (Clay, 1985), and Family Literacy Theory (Taylor, 1983). As in the preceding chapters, the theories are accompanied by reflections written by classroom teachers on the relationship between their own teaching experiences and the theories, and examples of classroom and research application.

## THEORY OF COGNITIVE DEVELOPMENT

Slavin (1997) describes Piaget as the best-known psychologist in history. A Swiss, born in 1896, Piaget received his PhD in biology and wrote his dissertation on mollusks. His work with children originally started as a way of understanding issues related to epistemology (i.e., the study of the nature of knowledge) from a biological perspective (Brumbaugh & Lawrence, 1963). Study of his own children inspired many of the ideas in Piaget's writings. In particular, he sought to explain the different ways in which his children processed information throughout their development.

Piaget can be classified as both a constructivist and a developmental theorist. Consistent with a constructivist viewpoint, Piaget stressed the importance of the child as an active organism as he or she progressed in cognitive development (Slavin, 1997). As Seefledt and Barbour (1994) write, "Piaget made it clear that children learn through direct experiences and social interaction with peers. Play and activity, according to Piaget, were equated with intellectual growth" (p. 11).

However, in addition to being a constructivist, Piaget was also a developmental theorist. As a result of many years of studying children's cognitive development, Piaget created the *Theory of Cognitive Development,* which describes the ways in which the quality of children's thinking changes over time. According to Woolfolk (1998), Piaget identified four factors that affect the quality of an individual's thinking as she or he grows: biological (i.e., physical) maturation, activity, social experiences, and equilibration. *Biological maturation* refers to the individual's genetic heredity that is present at birth and that will ultimately affect his or her growth. *Activity* refers to the physical experiences that the child has, through which he or she will construct much of his or her knowledge base. *Social experiences* refer to the child's interactions with others as she or he grows, and which will also affect her or his growth. Equlibration is the child's search for cognitive balance when cognitive imbalance, or dissonance, occurs.

In addition to identifying these four factors as central to children's cognitive development, Piaget identified four stages of qualitatively different types of thinking through which children progress in their journey toward adult thinking. These have become known as *Piaget's Stages of Cognitive Development*. The first stage is the *sensorimotor* period (birth–2 years) in which the child's thinking is based on his or her sensory exploration of the world. In this stage the child's cognition is a function of what he or she sees, hears, feels, and tastes. During this period of development the child does not yet have sufficient language to document his or her experiences with words. The second stage is the *preoperational* period (2–7 years) in which rapid language development occurs. Here the child begins to categorize and organize his or her world with words. The child's thinking is very concrete at this point in development. The third stage is the *concrete operational* period (7–11 years). In this period the child is able to use concrete objects as a vehicle for beginning to think about abstract concepts. In the fourth and final stage, the *formal operational* period (11–adult), the child is able to move beyond the concrete to use language in an abstract way (Hennings, 2000; Slavin, 1997; Woolfolk, 1998). These cognitive stages have been widely studied in research, although the most recent work in developmental psychology emphasizes the flexibility of these periods.

Piaget's writings are foundational for explaining the ways in which children cognitively develop. Teachers need to understand the ways in which children think at different stages of development in order to create developmentally appropriate lessons and activities for them. Piagetian development has been examined in relation to the development of reading skill, with research indicating that improvements in reading comprehension, word attack, and vocabulary are positively associated with children's cognitive development (Cartwright, 2002). In summarizing the impact of Piaget's Theory of Cognitive Development on classroom practices, Hennings (2000) concludes that it "provides teachers with a framework for understanding the way children at different age levels are likely to think about objects and events" (p. 88). For a good summary of Piaget's contributions, see "Piaget and Education," by H. P. Ginsburgh (1985).

## MATURATION THEORY

Judging from the professional literature of the early 1900s, little attention was paid to a child's literacy development before he or she entered school. It was generally assumed that literacy began with formal instruction in first grade. A strong influence on reading instruction during this time came from developmental psychologists who advocated maturation as the most important factor in learning to read. Preschool and kindergarten teachers during the early 1900s generally ignored or avoided reading instruction, but did follow the Unfoldment Theory-based teachings of Pestalozzi and Froebel, as presented in Chapter 2.

Influenced by the climate of the times, Morphett and Washburne (1931) supported the postponement of reading instruction until a child was developmentally old enough to be successful with the tasks of early reading. Morphett and Washburne conducted research to determine the optimal age at which this would occur. Their research concluded that children with a mental age of 6 years and 6 months did better on a test of reading achievement than did younger children. Their study became the cornerstone of what is now known as *Maturation Theory*. This theory stated that reading instruction should not be implemented until students reached the age of 6 years and 6 months. Recommendations related to this theory suggested that parents not attempt to teach reading to their children at home either. The prevailing belief associated with this theory was that parents as well as educators would cause damage to children's reading ability if they attempted to teach reading to children who were too young.

Maturation Theory was the dominant theory in reading education from the 1930s until the 1950s, affecting the literacy instruction of millions of American children. As a result of this theory, formal reading instruction was withheld from children both at home and at school until children reached the mental age of 6 years and 6 months. In the 1950s, however, the position taken by Maturation Theory was challenged by both Behaviorism (see Chapter 3) and Constructivism (see Chapter 4). The behaviorists were most successful in challenging Maturation Theory (Shannon, 1990). The result of the behaviorists' success was the popular depiction of reading as a complex behavior that could be broken down into component skills. This subskills approach to reading, which also yielded the reading readiness approach to early literacy development, was the dominant approach to reading instruction for 50 years thereafter. It is fully described in Chapter 3.

## TEACHER'S ANECDOTE: MATURATION THEORY

Most theories of literacy learning have advanced beyond the con-
straints of the Maturation Theory. There are some recent examples,
however, of this kind of thinking impacting the teaching and learning of young readers. Recently, many educators adopted a system of
"invented spelling" as an acceptable spelling strategy for elementary
school children. Invented spelling varied in its application in
schools, but from my personal observations, many schools used it
to allow children to invent the spelling of new words according to
what they heard in the word or what they believed looked right.
The theory was based on a belief that interfering with young children's spelling as they wrote would only frustrate them and was not
developmentally appropriate. Children were permitted and even
encouraged, to experiment with spelling and were not formally
instructed or corrected until later grades. Teachers defended the process by insisting that children would learn to spell the words correctly "when they were ready." Teachers who used invented spelling
as the dominant spelling curriculum in the classroom were basing
their practices on the Maturation Theory because they did not
believe in teaching children a system of spelling until they were
developmentally ready. In fact, these teachers believed it could be
detrimental to students' confidence and writing skills if taught too
early.

—ELIZABETH SORIERO, third-grade teacher

## THEORY OF LITERACY DEVELOPMENT

Following Maturation Theory, Holdaway's (1979) Theory of Literacy
Development was the next major developmental theory to arise. Close to
50 years elapsed between the emergence of the two. The *Theory of Literacy Development* can be described as having three dimensions: explanation of the developmental nature of literacy learning, explanation of the
four processes he viewed as central to literacy learning, and explanation
of a method of teaching designed to promote developmental literacy
learning.

In Holdaway's theory, learning to read is viewed as a natural developmental occurrence. Holdaway (1979) writes that learning to read

begins in the home when children first see their parents read and have stories read to them. In this theory, parents are the models for children, and children strive to emulate what their parents do. This emulation results in children's first attempts, or approximations, at reading, which are usually quite inaccurate, or in Holdaway's words, "gross approximations." Nonetheless, Holdaway believes that these first attempts at reading are, and should be, reinforced by parents. Gradually, according to this theory of literacy development, as the child's attempts at reading are reinforced and the child's skill grows, the child begins to read for real. Thus, in Holdaway's theory, the development of reading is natural and very much mimics children's natural development of oral language skills.

Morrow (2001) summarizes the processes that, according to Holdaway (1979), are components of this natural process:

> The first is observation of literacy behaviors—being read to, for example, or seeing adults reading and writing themselves. The second is collaboration with an individual who interacts with the child, providing encouragement, motivation, and help when necessary. The third process is practice. The learner tries out alone what has been learned, such as reading and writing activities—and experiments without direction or adult observation. Practice gives children opportunities to evaluate their performances, make corrections, and increase skills. In the fourth process, performance, the child shares what he or she has learned and seeks approval from adults who are supportive, interested, and encouraging. All of the processes that Holdaway views as central to early literacy learning are grounded in the notion of meaning-based instruction. (p. 134)

Holdaway advocates certain characteristics of literacy instruction that he believes facilitate natural literacy development. These characteristics are consistent with a rich home literacy environment and with the parent–child interactions of modeling and reinforcement described above. He recommends creating a rich literacy classroom environment, labeling key items around the room, using a classroom management style that fosters children's independence and self-regulation, and immersing children in meaningful language experiences with high-quality children's literature (Burns, Roe, & Ross, 1999). Holdaway is also a strong advocate of promoting peer interaction among students. Among his most famous recommended instructional strategies is the use of big books and shared reading techniques in classroom instruction. These instructional approaches are discussed in the "Classroom Application" section of this chapter. While Holdaway's theory is primarily a theory of literacy development, it is also consistent with Whole Language Theory (see Chapter 4).

---

In terms of my own literacy experiences, I would agree with Holdaway's theory. For instance, as a child, my earliest memory of reading was with my mom. Although I did not have a lot of books, the ones I had were very special. My first book was Dr. Seuss's *One Fish, Two Fish, Red Fish, Blue Fish*. I can remember my mom reading that book to me over and over. Eventually, however, I wanted to be able to read the words by myself. I would make gross approximations of the words and my mom would help me practice until I finally learned several simple words. The first day I read a whole page by myself to my mother was the happiest day of my life because I really wanted to please her and show her that I could do it.

—LISA HAMILTON, middle school special education teacher

---

## STAGE MODELS OF READING

Beginning in the 1980s, educators interested in the development of reading ability began to propose different models regarding the stages through which readers pass as they move toward reading proficiency. Since reading development is ongoing, continuous, and gradual, it is somewhat artificial to separate its growth in terms of stages (Gunning, 2003). As Gunning writes, "This is done, however, to provide greater understanding of the reading process. By having a sense of what readers have accomplished, what stage they are in now, and what stage they are headed for [educators] should be able to be better able to understand and plan for their needs" (p. 11).

Another central point unifying Stage Models is the common belief that the ways in which children approach the task of reading qualitatively change as they mature (Goswami, 1998). Stage Model theorists believe that as children's reading skills develop they increase both the number and type of strategies that they can use during reading experiences. Furthermore, Stage Model theorists believe that the strategies associated with the earlier stages of development remain available to readers even as more refined reading skills associated with later stages of development are attained. Stages of reading development have been proposed by a number of reading theorists including Ehri (1991); Chall (1983); Gough, Juel, and Griffith (1992); and Frith (1985). According to Stahl and Murray (1998), however, "In all of these models, the development of word recognition goes through roughly three stages, what Ehri (1991) called visual cue reading, phonetic cue reading, and phonological recoding" (p. 75).

Stahl and Murray (1998) summarize the characteristics of the three stages common to the Stage Model theorists. They label the first stage that readers attain *visual cue reading*. At this stage, called the "logographic stage" by Ehri (1991), children use visual cues as their primary method of word recognition. In this stage children memorize words by their shape. Word identification at this stage of development is not yet related to letter–sound knowledge. Contextual information, such as the familiar colors, fonts, and logos in the word *McDonald's* are the types of cues that children use when they are in the visual cue reading stage of development.

According to Stage Models, reading logographically in a language that is alphabetic, such as English, is very inefficient. As children mature, they gradually transition to the second stage of development, the *alphabetic stage* of word identification ability. This stage is also called "phonetic cue reading." When children are in the beginning of the alphabetic or phonetic cue reading stage, they use some letter–sound cues to help them identify words. As Stahl and Murry (1998) write, "In phonetic cue reading, the beginner uses some letters in words (typically the initial or boundary letters) to generate one or more sounds in the spoken equivalent of the word, thereby narrowing the ranges of choices for contextual guessing" (p. 76). Phonetic cue readers are capable of finger-point reading of highly predictable or memorized texts, and of pairing spoken and printed words in these simple passages (Stahl & Murray, 1998). As children mature, they rely more and more heavily on their letter–sound knowledge to aide them in accurate word identification.

The third stage of word identification in Stage Models is the *phonological recoding stage*, also called the "orthographic stage" and "cipher reading" (Gough et al., 1992). At this point in development readers use their automatic knowledge of sound–letter relationships to help them read using letter patterns within words. These letter patterns, also known as "word families" or "phonograms," help readers process text more quickly. Reading through the use of word patterns within words has been identified as a primary route by which mature readers process text (Adams, 1990).

---

## TEACHER'S ANECDOTE:
## STAGE MODELS OF READING

In the beginning of the school year, I observe my students reading in small-group instruction and I notice that most of them read at the alphabetic stage. They are taught to sound out unknown words by identifying the letter sounds and look for meaning within the sentence. I begin to model to the students how they should point to the words as they read them. By the middle of the year, I start to see some of my higher readers move toward the phonological stage. At this point in time, they already have an understanding of the letters and sounds and I begin to see them sound words out using different chunks. I recently gave a reading test where I could give very little assistance. One of my little girls got stuck on the word *sand*. She asked me what the word was and I told her I couldn't tell her but we could sound it out together. First she gave me the sound that was represented by the letter *s*. As I covered up the letter *s*, she then told me the letters *a-n-d* and said, "And." The little girl showed me that she was able to sound out the word by knowing and recognizing the chunk *and*. This is an example of the Stage Models of Reading because in the classroom you begin to see the different stages or levels your students go through as they read.

—REBECCA YEDLOCK, first-grade teacher

---

## EMERGENT LITERACY THEORY

The Stage Models and their theorists have been invaluable in helping educators understand children's early reading development. Their work, however, has primarily focused on the word recognition dimension of the reading experience. Other theorists and researchers, interested in studying early literacy development from a perspective broader than word recognition, began to investigate complementary aspects of literacy development in approximately the same time period that the stage theorists worked. These theorists and researchers created what is now known as *Emergent Literacy Theory*. Emergent Literacy Theory both explains early literacy development and provides instructional guidance to promote early literacy growth. The term "emergent literacy" refers to a period in a child's life between birth and when the child can read and write at a conventional (approximately third-grade) level. Marie Clay (1966) was first to employ the term. It is important to remember that the term "emergent literacy" refers to a functional level of performance rather than to a chronological age. Precocious children may become conventional readers (i.e., able to read at the third-grade level) long before they are actually in third grade. Similarly, students with serious disabilities may stay in the emergent phase of development long after their third-grade year of schooling has ended, and even remain in that stage for the rest of their lives.

Emergent Literacy Theory is built on a set of beliefs regarding the ways in which children's early literacy development occurs. One of the central tenets of Emergent Literacy Theory is that children's development in the areas of listening, speaking, reading, and writing are all interrelated (Morrow, 2005). This means that children who are already proficient with listening and speaking tend to excel at early reading and writing tasks. Conversely, children who have difficulty or are delayed in the areas of listening and speaking tend to be more at risk for reading difficulty (Snow, Burns, & Griffin, 1998). The interrelatedness of these skills also suggests that positive growth in one area of literacy development will have a beneficial effect on the other areas of development. According to Teale and Sulzby (1986), all children go through a period of emergent literacy in which they become increasingly aware of the relationships between spoken and written language. Emergent literacy theorists believe that children's gradually increasing awareness of these relationships is what aids youngsters in their early attempts with reading and writing. Many of the beliefs on which Emergent Literacy Theory are based are consistent with Whole Language Theory.

A second central belief of Emergent Literacy Theory is that literacy development starts at birth and is continuous and ongoing (Morrow, 2005). This belief is in sharp contrast to Maturation Theory, described above, which suggested that literacy learning should not be addressed until a child is 6.5 years old. This belief also contrasts with those Stage Theories that ignore literacy growth until the child is beginning to focus on word identification. Emergent Literacy Theory stresses the idea that children's earliest experiences of being talked to and read to are all part of their early literacy development.

Not surprisingly, since Emergent Literacy Theory argues that children's listening, speaking, reading, and writing skills begin at birth, it also emphasizes the critical role that children's home environments have on the development of these abilities. Research has indicated that children who come from literacy-rich home environments tend to have stronger, more accelerated, literacy skills. *Literacy-rich home environments* are ones in which a large number of books are available for both children's and adults' reading; parents frequently read to children and frequently read themselves; parents read a wide variety of material including books, newspapers, and magazines; reading is associated with pleasure; parents frequently take children to the library and to bookstores; children have access to writing materials; and the social, emotional, and intellectual climate of the homes are conducive to literacy growth (Morrow, 2005). Emergent Literacy Theory underscores the finding that although many factors are important to children's reading success, including parents' education, occupation, and socioeconomic level, the quality of the literacy environment correlates most closely with children's early literacy ability (Morrow, 2005).

Gunning (1996, pp. 26–27) lists the essential understandings that children need to master in the emergent literacy phase of development. These concepts, which can be mastered in children's homes, in their classrooms, or both, include:

- What we say and what others say can be written down and read.
- Words, not pictures, are read.
- Words are made up of letters, and sentences are made up of words.
- Reading goes from left to right and from top to bottom.
- A book is read from front to back.
- What we say is divided into words (e.g., some students may believe that "How are you?" is a single word).
- Space separates written words. Students must be able to match words being read orally with their written counterparts.
- Sentences begin with capital letters.
- Sentences end with periods, question marks, or exclamation marks.
- A book has a title, an author, and sometimes an illustrator.

These understandings are often referred to as "concepts about print" and "concepts about books" that children must learn to be successful with reading. Coupled with the word recognition information articulated by proponents of Stage Theory, Emergent Literacy Theory outlines much of what children need to learn in their early years to be successful with later reading.

---

## TEACHER'S ANECDOTE: EMERGENT LITERACY THEORY

Clay's Emergent Literacy Theory seeks to explain how literacy develops and what instruction is needed during the emergent literacy period. Unlike Maturation Theory or Stage Model theories, Clay believes that literacy development begins at birth and that the home environment plays a major role in a child's literacy ability. In my own experiences as a child I cannot recall a time without books. My mother is an avid reader and has worked in our township library since I was 2 years old. My siblings and I received official library cards as soon as we were old enough to write our own names. Then we were allowed to check books out of the library on a weekly basis. My parents read to us often and they regularly read themselves. We were always writing in notebooks and I loved going to work with my mother so that I could type at her desk. According to my mother, during our elementary school years reading, writing, and speaking came naturally for us. There is no doubt in my mind that those early experiences helped my brother, sister, and I become successful readers. Our experiences are examples of Emergent Literacy Theory because our home environment helped facilitate our literacy development.

—DEIRDRE M. TAYLOR, K–3 literacy support teacher

---

## FAMILY LITERACY THEORY

The concept of "family literacy" was initially proposed by Taylor (1983) in her seminal work on the topic. *Family literacy* has been defined as the study of the relationships between families and the development of literacy (Tracey, 1995). The term "Family Literacy Theory," rather than referring to a unified theory put forth by a single researcher, refers to a series of ideas proposed by many researchers who share viewpoints on

(1) the design, implementation, and evaluation of programs to facilitate the literacy development of family members (Morrow, 1995;

Neuman, 1995; Paratore, 1993; Shanahan, Mulhern, & Rodriguez-Brown, 1995); (2) the relationships between literacy use in families and students' academic achievement (Leseman & DeJong, 1998; McCarthy, 1997; Purcell-Gates, 1996; Senechal, LeFerve, Thomas, & Daley, 1998; Snow, Barnes, Chandler, Goodman, & Hemphill, 1991; Taylor, 1995); and (3) the ways in which literacy is naturally used within the context of the home (DelGado-Gaitan, 1992; Purcell-Gates, 1995; Taylor, 1983). (Tracey & Young, 2002, p. 729)

Jordan, Snow, and Porche (2000) summarize a few of the key points regarding Family Literacy Theory. Drawing on the work of Bus, van IJzendoorn, and Pellegrini (1995), Hart and Risley (1999), and Scarborough and Dobrich (1994), they write that research has now demonstrated that literacy-rich home environments contribute more powerfully to children's early successful literacy development than do excellent preschool and kindergarten classrooms. Furthermore, referring to the work of Edwards (1995) and Edwards, Pleasants, and Franklin (1999), they write that "although excellent formal reading instruction can ensure success in literacy even for high-risk readers, substantial efforts to recruit the partnership of families greatly increase the chances of success" (p. 524).

Studies central to the development of Family Literacy Theory have investigated homes in which children learned to read without direct instruction before coming to school (Durkin 1966; Holdaway, 1979; Taylor, 1983). Such homes provide rich reading environments that include books and other reading materials. Family members serve as models of involvement in literacy activities. For example, they answer children's questions about books and print, read to children frequently, and reward them for participating in literacy activities. In addition, parents of successful readers most often are involved at school and seek information about their children's literacy development. These homes are rich in the supportive and interactive behaviors conducive to learning to read. Specific studies of home storybook readings have provided information on the kinds of interaction that encourages literacy development. Analyses of the recorded questions and comments of parents and children during shared book experiences at home demonstrate that the following variables are associated with children's increased literacy abilities: the total number of words spoken by the child during the storybook reading; the number of questions asked by parents before and after reading; the number of high-level, critical thinking questions asked by parents; and the amount of positive feedback given to the child (Flood, 1977; Tracey & Morrow, 2002).

Family Literacy Theory overlaps with Emergent Literacy Theory regarding the ways in which at-home experiences contribute to children's literacy success. Family Literacy Theory also extends previous conceptualizations of literacy learning by emphasizing the critical role that parents and parent involvement have on children's literacy development.

---

## TEACHER'S ANECDOTE:
## FAMILY LITERACY THEORY

I entered school with a strong literacy foundation and was already reading due to the fact that I grew up in a rich literacy environment. I still have the book, worn and torn, that my mother would read to me each night. The book had 365 stories, all dated, and the story of the day would be read as she tucked me into bed. Year after year it was read and, even though the stories didn't change from year to year, I was still eager to have it read to me. Eventually, I started reading along. Just a few years ago my mother was cleaning out the basement and getting rid of "old junk." That book was one of the few pieces I took out of the pile of garbage and insisted on saving.

Growing up, I lived about eight blocks from the library. The kids up the block and I would walk there weekly, almost daily in the summertime. First, we'd stop at Angelo's for a slice of pizza and soda with the $2.00 our parents gave us. Then, we'd go to the library and cool off in the air conditioning, look at books, and check out as many as we could carry home. Those trips, which I thought of as a treat and adventure each time we went, never lost their novelty, and are some of my fondest childhood memories. I remember doing this from the time I was about 7, when it was still OK for parents to let a group of 7-year-olds walk to the library on their own.

All my reading experiences as a child were positive. I grew up loving to read. Even now, when I need a break, I curl up with a book. When I tell my students this, they think I'm just saying it because I'm a teacher and that's what teachers say.

—RENEE BEN-DAVID, seventh-grade special education teacher

## CLASSROOM APPLICATIONS

Piaget's theory provides literacy educators with a framework for under-standing how students at different developmental points are likely to think (Hennings, 2000). Children's literacy development in the pre-operational period (ages 2–7), in which rapid language development occurs, is likely to be greatly affected by their experiences with at-home and in-class storybook reading. Children's literacy development in the concrete operational period (ages 7–11), in which children use concrete objects as vehicles for beginning to think about abstract concepts, will likely benefit from the use of semantic organizers such as charts and webs to help them organize their thoughts related to reading comprehension and writing. Students in the formal operational period (ages 11–adult), during which language can be used in abstract ways, will be able to take advantage of complex strategies related to reading instruction. It is likely that older students' success with metacognitive instruction is related to their having reached this level of cognitive development.

Morphett and Washburne's (1931) Maturation Theory is no longer used to explain children's literacy development. This theory has been included in the present chapter because of the central role it held in the history of instructional approaches to children's literacy development. As stated previously, from 1931 until the advent of the reading readiness approach in the 1950s, literacy instruction was withheld from students who were younger than 6.5 years old in the belief that providing instruction before children were "ready" would be detrimental to their development (Morrow, 2005). Although this fundamental premise of Maturation Theory has been proven false, the concept of maturation remains an important one in literacy education today. The other theories discussed in this chapter (Theory of Literacy Development, Stage Models of Reading, Emergent Literacy Theory, and Family Literacy Theory) all incorporate the concept of maturation, but in a more contemporary fashion.

Holdaway's (1979) Theory of Literacy Development presents literacy growth as a natural process that begins in a young child's home. Holdaway recommends practices that teachers can use in classrooms based on processes that foster literacy growth in children's homes. Among his most famous techniques are the use of big books as a teaching tool and the procedure of shared reading.

Holdaway (1979) recommends the use of big books as a technique to foster natural literacy development. A *big book* is a high-quality children's book that is printed by the publisher in a greatly enlarged size. Big books are typically sized to be 2–3 feet high and 2–3 feet wide. The teacher reads a big book to a group of young children, who usually sit at her or his feet on an area rug. The purpose of using big books is to create a feeling in every child that he or she is sitting on his or her parent's lap for a story. In Holdaway's view, big books can be used in the classroom to create the same kinds of positive feelings about story time that children have when they sit in their parents' laps and are read to at home. Furthermore, Holdaway argues that these natural storytelling situations are ideal for fostering literacy skills such as strengthening children's oral language, helping children track print from left to right, and building children's concepts of letters, words, and story grammar.

Holdaway (1979) is famous for advocating a particular technique used for storybook reading known as "shared reading." Shared reading can be implemented with big books and also with regular-sized books. The shared reading technique begins with the teacher's selection of high-quality books appropriate for the listening audience (Reutzel & Cooter, 1996). Reutzel and Cooter (1996) describes several criteria that should be considered when selecting books for a shared reading activity:

> Books and stories chosen for sharing need to be those that have been proven to be loved by children. Any book or story (including those selections in basal readers) to be shared should have literary merit and engaging content. The pictures should match the text and tell or support the telling of the story in proper sequence. The text should be characterized by repetition, cumulative sequence, rhyme, and rhythm to entice the children and "hook" them on the language patterns. . . . Finally, and perhaps most importantly, the books chosen for shared book experiences need to have a visual impact on 30 children similar to the impact that a standard-sized book would have on the knee of a child or in the lap of a parent. (p. 365)

Following the selection of a high-quality text, the shared reading lesson is divided into three segments: before reading, during reading, and after reading (Reutzel & Cooter, 1996). In the *prereading phase* the teacher introduces the reading selection. He or she reads the book title to the students, shows them the book's cover, predicts what the story may be about from a "picture walk," and activates and builds the students' background knowledge related to the story's content. After the book is introduced, the teacher begins the *reading phase*. His or her reading should be done with enthusiasm and expression. If the text contains predictable sections, such as the use of repeated phases, the teacher should encourage the students to join in the reading. Another way of involving students during the reading is to ask them questions and have them make predictions regarding the story. When the teacher finishes reading the story, he or she starts the *postreading phase* of discussion and follow-up activities. During this phase the teacher should ask questions that are on a variety of levels, from those designed to enhance simple factual recall, to those designed to encourage high level, open ended, critical thinking. Ideally, follow-up activities will provide students with choices regarding the ways in which they can respond to the story's content. Popular choices include writing, drawing, story retelling, and dramatization. Activities that integrate art, music, movement, and social collaboration are usually especially motivating to students. The shared reading activity almost always includes the rereading of stories on subsequent days. Rereading can build reading fluency and story comprehension. Note, that stories should not be reread to the point of boredom. The technique of shared reading has been shown to be effective in promoting students' literacy development in the areas of word recognition, vocabulary, comprehension, and fluency (Reutzel, Hollingsworth, & Eldredge, 1994).

Stage Models of Reading also generate much direction for children's literacy activities in the classroom. A wonderful activity for children in the logographic stage of development (the stage in which words are memorized by shape and context) is to collect samples of familiar environmental print and place them in a photograph album. For example, items such as paper bags, napkins, and labels bearing the logos and names of brands such as McDonald's, Burger King, Wendy's, Dunkin Donuts, Cheerios, and Gatorade can be cut up and placed in a photo album in the literacy center. Similarly, coupons for easily recognizable products such as cat food, dog food, groceries, and cleaning products can be placed either in a photograph album or in a coupon box. Because children see these logos frequently in their environments, they will be among the easiest print for young children to "read." Successful experiences "reading" these logographs will help young readers develop the confidence and motivation that they need to move into the next stage of literacy development.

Children in the alphabetic stage of development (when they are beginning to use letter–sound cues to read words) will benefit from activities that help them master automatic letter recognition, and activities such as puzzles, word card games, and sorting games that help them focus on the initial, ending, and medial sounds within words. Morrow (2001) describes many of these activities. She notes that children learn letters that are meaningful to them (e.g., their initials, the letters in their first name) most easily, and that this approach is more successful than teaching one letter per week. In order for children to become proficient with letter–sound relationships, they must first master the alphabet. Children should be encouraged to explore a wide variety of manipulative letter exercises such as letter puzzles, felt letters, magnetic letters, wooden letters, and letter stamps. They should also have access to alphabet letter books and tapes, as well as to software that teaches letters through animation.

Key letters can be taught to accompany thematic instruction, such as b for boat, t for train, and c for car to accompany a unit on transportation. Children can search through magazines to locate the letters they are learning, and also search for target letters in the logographic materials described above. Games such as finding objects in the classroom that begin with a target letter, identifying objects by touch in a bag that begin with a certain letter, and old-fashioned letter bingo are also popular activities for building early letter–sound familiarity. Students who have a collection of "Very Own Words" may have specific letters that they will want to learn, if asked, and children are almost always interested in learning the letters of their names and those necessary to write key words in their life such as mom, dad, and love. Students can independently work on learning an initial letter such as p and sort picture cards of items that do and do not begin with the letter. These materials can be created to be self-correcting if the teacher chooses by preparing the cards in a puzzle-like formation (e.g., only the picture cards of those items that begin with letter p will fit together). Another idea is to create an alphabet journal for each child with one page of the journal devoted to each letter of the alphabet. Children can then print words that they learn and paste words that they cut from magazines on these pages. Many additional ideas for building letter–sound knowledge are available in professional resources.

Finally, children in the phonological recoding stage (characterized by automatic letter recognition and the use of letter patterns when reading) will benefit from activities that strengthen their awareness of word families in single and multisyllable words. The Reading Teacher's Book of Lists (Fry, Kress, & Fountoukidis, 2000) is a valuable resource that lists most of the word family patterns in the English language and words associated with each family. An ideal way to help children learn letter patterns within words is to provide them with one card of a word family, such as an, and many cards with individual letters on them such as b, c, d, and so forth. The students' job is to write a list of all the an words that they can make. Activities such as this can be done in small mixed-ability groups that will allow more able students to help their less able peers. Variations on this activity can be made using word wheels and slide rule designs. Games that focus on rhyming, the use of literature that emphasizes rhyme, and poetry are also activities that can often be modified to help students master letter patterns within words. After students have mastered letter patterns within one-syllable words, they can be taught how to use letter patterns within words as an approach to reading multisyllable words.

All of the activities described above, from big books and shared reading to lessons that promote logographic, alphabetic, and ortho-graphic skill development, comprise instructional experiences that are used in the emergent literacy classroom. Teachers interested in building a classroom that is additionally reflective of Emergent Literacy Theory can begin by thinking about designing instruction that is consistent with its central tenets: (1) listening, speaking, reading, and writing are interrelated; (2) literacy development is continuous and ongoing; and (3) parents have a powerful influence on children's literacy development.

Teachers with an emergent literacy orientation often begin by creating rich literacy environments in their classrooms. Educators striving to enhance the richness of their classrooms' literacy environments create environments similar to those found in literacy-rich homes. These classrooms are marked by the extensive presence of books, environmental print, writing materials, and numerous opportunities for children to interact with these items in meaningful ways. Emergent literacy classrooms are also designed to be appealing and to encourage children's curiosity to engage with books, audiotapes, and related storytelling props. Emergent literacy classrooms should all have well-supplied literacy centers. Detailed information on the creation of classroom literacy centers is presented in Chapter 2.

A wide array of instructional practices are associated with Emergent Literacy Theory. These include the use of multiple assessment tools to track literacy growth; the use of thematic instruction in the classroom (also known as "learning across the curriculum"); the use of high quality, authentic children's literature as a teaching tool; an instructional approach that promotes social interaction between students; and the use of a literacy center in the classroom as an essential component of literacy instruction (Morrow, 2001, 2005). Of course, daily storybook readings and related activities are a cornerstone of literacy-rich classrooms that promote emergent literacy development. Many resources are available for educators interested in infusing practices consistent with Emergent Literacy Theory into their classrooms (Morrow, 2005).

Educators interested in classroom practices that incorporate Family Literacy Theory will strive to create partnerships with parents that are built on mutual respect and two-way communication (Paratore, 2001). In such relationships, teachers devote equal attention to *gathering information from parents* about their family's literacy practices at home, and *distributing information to parents* about how to promote their children's literacy growth.

In egalitarian teacher–parent relationships parents, grandparents, and guardians are encouraged to spend time in their children's schools and classrooms. In this capacity visitors can be invited to share special skills or hobbies that they have (e.g., sewing, cooking, carpentry, weaving, and music) with students. These skills and hobbies can be shared with the whole class or as a center activity. Many parents are able to serve as guest readers, as reading and writing tutors, and/or as assistants at learning centers. Adult visitors can also be sources for information related to areas of classroom study. For example, one child's grandfather visited his granddaughter's third-grade classroom to share his recollections of the past as a German Jewish refugee during World War II.

Teachers interested in integrating Family Literacy Theory in the classroom will be committed to gathering information about each student regarding his or her home life. One approach to doing this is the development of family stories (Buchoff, 1995). Buchoff uses a thematic unit on the topic of families as a springboard for having students create stories about their families. Students create stories to share family experiences through a variety of media including oral retellings, audio- and videotaped recordings, and written family accounts. Other options include creating family photograph albums, either in a traditional form or electronically, and keeping family journals. Students are encouraged to ask their family members for input when creating their stories. Teachers can provide family members with prompts to promote such input, such as "Tell your child about the neighborhood where you lived when you were young" or "Tell your child about your favorite relative when you were young." Through assignments such as these teachers learn about children's home lives while at the same time enhancing family literacy interaction for their students.

## RESEARCH APPLICATIONS

Researchers and graduate students conducting research that focuses on the cognitive processes used by students during reading and learning may want to choose Piaget's Theory of Cognitive Development as the theoretical framework for their work. Similarly, those interested in the qualitative changes in students' thinking across developmental stages may also want to consider this theoretical context. Bryant (2002) used elements of Piaget's Theory of Cognitive Development to explain his research findings from a number of studies regarding the ways in which children learn spelling (also called orthographic) rules. In his work, Bryant determined that children first learn to use a single spelling pattern. Then, when children find that the single pattern is inadequate for spelling all words, they learn an alternative spelling pattern, but overgeneralize it. Finally, children learn the full range of orthographic rules. Bryant described the pattern of development through which children progress as reflective of Piaget and Inhelder's (1969) conceptualization of the ways in which children construct knowledge of rules about the world.

Although the central principle of Maturation Theory—that children can't really learn to read until they are 6 years and 6 months of age—has been debunked, the general concept of studying maturation as a variable in literacy research is still very much applicable. In one such project (Viise, 1996), the spelling development of children in kindergarten through the fifth grade was studied and then compared to the spelling development of adult literacy learners. The primary finding of the study was that adult literacy learners proceed through many of the same stages of spelling development as do young children. These stages consist of the *prephonetic stage*, in which spellers correctly produce the first consonant of the word: the *phonetic or letter name stage*, in which the spellers make attempts to represent each sound in the word with a letter; the *within-word pattern stage*, in which spellers progress to a more sophisticated understanding of letter–sound rules in single-syllable words; and the *syllable-juncture stage*, in which spellers negotiate multisyllable words. A final stage is the *spelling–meaning connection*. This study is reflective of the general concepts in Maturation Theory because it emphasizes the natural stages of development through which spellers progress as they mature.

Korkeamaki and Dreher (1996) investigated the application of a meaning-based early literacy program with first-grade students in Finland using Holdaway's Theory of Literacy Development (1979, 1989), emphasizing meaning-based literacy instruction as a theoretical frame. As the authors describe, a meaning-based instructional approach contrasts sharply with the typical Finnish literacy instruction that emphasizes visual and auditory readiness, as well as synthetic phonics instruction. In the study, the literacy development of nine first graders were tracked during the literacy intervention, which included the use of predictable books, the use of a literacy-enriched classroom environment including a voluminous library center, and minilessons that featured specific skills related to story reading experiences. These minilessons included direct instruction on letter names, letter sounds, and letter–sound relationships, all of which were embedded and related to a child's literature selection, but were not drill-like in form. The findings of the study indicated that "the students progressed rapidly and started to use phonic strategies to figure out words despite the lack of emphasis on drills" (p. 29). The authors continued: "The children made good progress during the 6-month period, despite the fact that they were not taught with the phonics drills typically used with Finnish first graders" (p. 30). The results of the investigation supported Holdaway's Theory of Literacy Development that emphasizes the importance of meaning-based literacy instruction.

Cardoso-Martins (2001) examined the basic assumptions of the Stage Models of Reading in her study of the early reading development of Brazilian Portuguese children. In this research project children at very low levels of early reading ability were instructed with one of two types of early reading instruction. The first group was provided with whole-word reading instruction for 3 months, followed by a phonics-based program that emphasized syllable identification for another 3 months. The second group received traditional phonics-based instruction for all 6 months of the project. The children's literacy abilities were assessed and tracked at multiple points during the intervention using a variety of measures. The results of the study indicated that children in the whole-word treatment group did not spontaneously begin to engage in traditional decoding (phonological recoding) during the whole-word phase of their literacy instruction, as the Stage Models of Reading would suggest. Instead, the results of the study suggested that the ways in which the young children approached the task of early reading was greatly influenced by the instructional approach used to teach them. The results of the study, therefore, while using Stage Models as a lens of analysis, did not lend support to the Stage Models of Reading.

Emergent Literacy Theory has prompted a wide variety and an extensive number of research studies (Yaden, Rowe, & McGillivray, 2000). These include studies of storybook reading, sociodramatic play, emergent writing, the home literacy environment, and metalinguistic awareness (Yaden et al., 2000). Emergent Literacy Theory was used to frame an investigation of the literacy development of two first-grade

Hispanic children (Fitzgerald & Noblit, 1999). The central research question investigated was whether these two, young, English as a Second Language (ESL) learners would show patterns of emergent literacy development similar to their non-ESL peers. The researchers tracked the children's growth using a variety of assessment measures including anecdotal observations, writing samples, formal and informal tests, running records of the children's oral reading, videotape and audiotape analyses, teachers' journal transcriptions, and general field notes. The data were analyzed through an inductive approach, consistent with qualitative research methods, as the researchers searched for "an overarching sense of the two children's patterns of growth" (p. 178). The results of the study revealed that "Roberto's fuller and Carlos's incomplete pathways paralleled the routes typically taken by native-English-speaking emergent readers as described in other literature" (p. 166). This study, therefore, was one of the first in the professional literature to demonstrate the similarities between the emergent literacy development of ESL and non-ESL young learners.

Jordan et al. (2000) conducted a research study on the effects of a family literacy program on the development of kindergarten children's early literacy skills. In their research, parent education sessions, at-school parent–child activities, and at-home book-mediated activities were provided for 177 children and their families in the experimental intervention, Project EASE (Early Access to Success in Education). According to the authors, the primary goals of the project were to "increase the frequency and quality of language interactions through book-centered activities, and to give parents information about the opportunities for engagement in their children's developing literacy abilities" (p. 525). The results of the study demonstrated that the children whose families participated in the project demonstrated significantly greater early literacy achievement than did control children. Furthermore, the greatest observed gains were in the children whose literacy skills were weakest at the beginning of the program, but whose parents demonstrated strong program involvement.

## SUMMARY

This chapter summarizes key theories that have been used to explain children's literacy development. The theories presented in this chapter include Piaget's Theory of Cognitive Development (Piaget & Inhelder, 1969), Maturation Theory (Morphett & Washburne, 1931), Holdaway's (1979) Theory of Literacy Development, Stage Models of Reading (Ehri, 1991; Frith, 1985; Chall, 1983), Emergent Literacy Theory (Clay, 1985; Morrow, 2001, 2005), and Family Literacy Theory (Taylor, 1983). Piaget's Theory of Cognitive Development, one the most famous theories used to explain children's overall cognitive development, can be used to help literacy educators understand the learning stages through which students progress as they mature and their relationship to literacy achievement. Maturation Theory (Morphett & Washburne, 1931) promoted the idea that literacy instruction should be delayed until children are 6.5 years old, supposedly the age at which children would be most successful at learning to read. Countering Maturation Theory, Holdaway's (1979) Theory of Literacy Development suggested that literacy development begins much earlier, in children's homes, and is based on meaningful learning experiences. Holdaway created activities such as the use of big books and shared reading to help educators re-create the kinds of early literacy experiences that were found in the homes of precocious readers. Stage Models of Reading (Ehri, 1991; Frith, 1985; Chall, 1983) describe the stages through which children progress in the development of their word identification abilities. Emergent Literacy Theory (Clay, 1985; Morrow, 2005) describes a broader set of abilities than do the Stage Models, and explains how these abilities develop from birth onward. Finally, Family Literacy Theory focuses on the unique role of the home and parents in children's literacy development.

# CHAPTER 6

# Social Learning Perspectives

## *(1960s–Present)*

The social learning perspective incorporates several different theories, all of which emphasize the central role of social interaction in the development of knowledge and learning. When applied to the field of reading, the social learning perspective emphasizes the importance of social influences and social interaction on literacy learning. The social learning perspective includes Sociolinguistic Theory (Bernstein, 1972a, 1972b; Bloom & Green, 1984; Heath, 1982), Socio-Cultural Theory (Au, 1997; Bronfenbrenner, 1979; Moll, 1992, 1994), Social Constructivism/Socio-Historical Theory (Vygotsky, 1978, 1986), and Social Learning Theory/ Social Cognitive Theory (Bandura, 1986). While these terms are often used as if they are interchangeable, this chapter will aim to clarify their distinctions. An additional area of special interest within the social learning perspective is Critical Literacy Theory (Siegel & Fernandez, 2000; Freire, 1970; Gee, 1990; Shannon, 1990). All these theories are examined in this chapter. Before reading about them, however, you may want to ask yourself the following questions that are related to a social learning perspective:

- How does the social community in which students live affect their literacy learning?
- How does the social community within the classroom affect students' literacy learning?

- How do parent–child language interactions affect student literacy learning?
- How do students' interactions with each other affect their literacy learning?
- How do teachers' interactions with students affect their literacy learning?

## SOCIOLINGUISTIC THEORY

As stated above, the social learning perspective incorporates several different theories, all of which emphasize the central role of social interaction in the development of knowledge and learning. The first application of the social perspective to the field of reading emerged in the 1970s with Sociolinguistic Theory. As the name suggests, from the sociolinguistic perspective, reading is viewed as both a social and a linguistic process. Bloom and Green (1984) write, "As a social process, reading is used to establish, structure, and maintain social relationships between and among people. As a linguistic process, reading is used to communicate intentions and meanings, not only between an author and a reader, but also between people involved in a reading event" (p. 395).

Sociolinguistsic Theory is rooted in the fields of anthropology, linguistics, and literary analysis. According to Bloom and Green (1984), anthropology provided the perspective that reading and writing could be viewed as cultural events. Anthropology also provided the perspective that cultures affect social practices such as reading and writing. The field of linguistics contributed the notion that language differences between social classes are related to differences in all language practices, including reading and writing (Bernstein, 1972a, 1972b). Linguistics also added the perspective that the ability to read is related to social functioning, that is, that individuals learn to read as a means to accomplish personal goals related to basic life functioning (Halliday, 1975). The third root of Sociolinguistic Theory, literary analysis, added the understanding that during the reading process meaning is constructed by, and located in, the reader (Rosenblatt, 1978, 1994).

Sociolinguistic theorists believe that oral language is the foundation upon which children's reading and writing achievement is built (Apel & Masterson, 2001; Snow, Burns, & Griffin, 1998). As such, oral language knowledge provides children with an intuitive understanding of the structure of language (i.e., its syntax) that helps them predict text and read fluently at a later age. From this perspective, oral language is also

the foundation for vocabulary learning that later helps children comprehend the words and messages that they read (Carnine et al., 2004; Hart
& Risley, 2003). Often preschool children from at-risk communities do
not acquire the high-quality oral language foundations that children
from more affluent communities acquire. For example, children from at-
risk communities often do not gain a familiarity with conventional English syntax because the primary language spoken in their homes is not
English, or, if it is English, it is a dialect rather than Standard English.
Furthermore, it has been demonstrated that children from at-risk communities are exposed to significantly less vocabulary than their more
affluent peers. Hart and Risley (1995, 1999) estimate that within a
year's time period, children from professional homes are exposed to 11.2
million words, children from working-class homes are exposed to 6.5
million words, and children from welfare homes are exposed to 3.2 million words. Since vocabulary knowledge is essential for reading success,
this discrepancy places preschool children from at-risk communities at a
grave disadvantage and necessitates prolonged, multifaceted interventions.

Many research studies now viewed as classic reflections of the social
learning perspective were originally presented as studies of Sociolinguistic Theory by Bloom and Green (1984). For example, Shirley
Brice Heath's (1982) work is a seminal study in the field of reading that
was framed from this perspective. Heath studied the daily oral and written literacy practices of three different communities in the southeastern
United States in the early 1970s. She gave the three communities pseud-
onyms: Maintown, Roadville, and Trackton. Maintown had a "mainstream, middle-class, school-oriented culture" (Heath, 1982, p. 49),
Roadville was a "white working-class community of families steeped for
four generations in the life of the textile mill" (p. 59), and Trackton was
a "black mill community of recent rural origin" (p. 49). Heath's work
revealed that the "three communities differ[ed] strikingly in their patterns of language use and in the paths of language socialization of their
children" (p. 49). Maintown parents interacted with their children in
patterns of language and socialization labeled as "mainstream" (p. 54).
Children in Maintown were socialized to books at ages as young as 6
months. Through patterns of interaction repeated hundreds of times a
year for all of their early development, these children learned to listen to
stories, look at illustrations, and answer questions of many types about
story content. Health determined that these patterns of interaction
closely paralleled the book-oriented interactions to which children
would be exposed once they entered school. In contrast to Maintown,

early literacy socialization in Roadville focused on more isolated elements of storybook reading such as letter and number identification and item labeling. In this community adults were likely to simplify complex story texts by paraphrasing stories in easier language for their children. Furthermore, in Roadville parent–child conversations rarely included high-level questions by parents that demanded critical thinking or extensive language use by their children. Health concluded that as a result of this pattern of socialization, Roadville children did well in literacy learning in the lower grades at school but had greater and greater difficulty in the upper grades when their schoolwork demanded higher levels of critical thinking that they had not developed in their early years at home. Trackton children's primary form of socialization to literacy was oral rather than print. Trackton children were more likely to hear their parents tell them oral stories than they were to listen to stories in books read to them by their parents. Similarly, Trackton children were encouraged to develop their own oral, storytelling skills rather than to learn to read text-based materials. Bedtime stories were not a cornerstone of Trackton children's early literacy development as they were in the Maintown and Roadville communities. Heath argued that as a result of this socialization pattern, Trackton children were less familiar with, and therefore less prepared for, the demands of school-based literacy learning than were their peers from Maintown and Roadville. This difference led to greater school-based literacy learning difficulties for the Trackton children.

In short, Sociolinguistic Theory is a theory from the social learning perspective that particularly emphasizes the role of individuals' language in reading acquisition and reading ability. Furthermore, Sociolinguistic Theory asserts that language is learned as a result of people's social interactions with each other. Varying patterns of social and language interactions subsequently lead to differences in individual reading skill.

## TEACHER'S ANECDOTE: SOCIOLINGUISTIC THEORY

I can directly relate to Heath's findings. I tutor a student from a white, middle-class community who succeeds in the classroom because the child's home environment mimics the school environment. The parents have always provided a nurturing, language-rich environment for the child to thrive in, and he has. He has brought this rich background to school with him and this has given him an advantage from the beginning of his school career.

I teach another child who comes from a white, low-SES family. I find that this child has some deficits with language. However, what she lacks at home she gains in school and she uses those experiences to her advantage. She lives with her mother, who works full time but gets out in time to pick up her children at school. The mother is very nice but she is always rushing. Her child gets many wonderful experiences outside of school, but I don't think that the mother takes the time to make them language-rich experiences, with her child being a participant rather then a listener.

The child that I teach that falls into Heath's third group comes from a low-SES family. The child came to school with severe language delays and has made little progress throughout the year. The child comes from a foster family situation where children in the home pick him up from school and often take care of him until bedtime. The child does not get help with homework and watches a lot of television. He doesn't interact with children his own age outside of school. He also doesn't interact with many people, in general, outside of school. I find that he knows a lot less than other children his age. In the classroom when we have discussions he has a hard time participating because he does not have background knowledge in the things we discuss. For example, we recently looked at different types of vegetables because we discussed the letter *v* and the other children got into a discussion about the supermarket. He had a hard time participating because he has rarely been to the supermarket. He could not identify even the most common vegetables. He even has a hard time expressing what interests him. The only thing he talks about is television.

Heath's work really put these situations into perspective for me. It is so much easier to deal with these issues when you know what you are up against. The work these researchers have done really exemplifies what a crucial role social interactions play in learning. This knowledge definitely helps teachers to fully understand what shapes their students' learning.

—MARIANNE PANARESE, first-grade teacher

## SOCIO-CULTURAL THEORY

*Socio-Cultural Theory* emphasizes the roles of social, cultural, and historical factors in the human experience. Woolfolk (1999) states that in this theoretical perspective, "Knowledge is constructed based on social interactions and experience" (p. 279). Socio-Cultural Theory is similar to Sociolinguistic Theory because both emphasize the social aspect of learning, but Sociolinguistic Theory focuses more on the language aspects of these interactions, while Socio-Cultural Theory focuses more on the broader concept of culture, which includes, but is not limited to, language.

The socio-cultural perspective has its roots in the work of Bronfenbrenner (1979). Bronfenbrenner posits that concentric levels of influence affect children's development. Bronfenbrenner (1979) suggests that these layers of influence can be imagined as "a set of nested structures, each inside the next, like a set of Russian dolls" (p. 3). According to Bronfenbrenner, three spheres of influence affect human development: the microsystem, the mesosystem, and the exosystem. *The microsystem*, the first and innermost level of influence, is the child's immediate environment, his home and/or classroom. *The mesosystem*, the second level of influence, is the layer of interaction that exists between the child's home and school life. *The exosystem*, the third level of influence, is the child's parents' work situations. Bronfenbrenner calls his perspective an "ecological view of development," or an Ecological Model of human development, because it illustrates the power of "wide-ranging" developmental influences (p. 4).

Au (1997) appears to have built on Bronfenbrenner's (1979) Ecological Model, adapting the general concept of an exosystem to that of culture at large. According to Au (1997), Socio-Cultural Theory emphasizes the idea that "the human experience is mediated by culture" (p. 183). Au writes that culture can be viewed both as a factor that is stable and persists over a long period of time, and as a factor that is unstable and constantly evolving and changing. For example, we can consider all of the 20th century as a single cultural experience, defined by such inventions as the automobile, the television, the computer, and space travel. However, if we viewed the 20th century as a factor that was ever evolving and changing, the culture of the 1920s would be regarded as drastically different from that of the 1940s, 1950s, or 1960s. As Au (1997) explains, "In one view, culture is seen as a relatively stable, integrated whole encompassing a people's knowledge, beliefs, and ways of life. In the other view, culture is seen as an active process of change, growth, and development" (p. 182). In the socio-cultural perspective, culture is viewed as tremendously important in affecting children's literacy development.

In addition to emphasizing the cultural influences of learning, Socio-Cultural Theory emphasizes the social nature of learning. Au

(1997) writes, "Socio-cultural research on school literacy learning attempts to explore the links among historical conditions, current social and institutional contexts, inter-psychological functioning [that which takes place between people], and intra-psychological functioning [that which takes place within the individual]" (p. 182). She continues:

> In short, a socio-cultural perspective begins with the assumption that reading, like other higher mental functions, is essentially social in nature. Even reading a book alone can be considered a social activity, because the reader is engaged with the author, the book is written in a language developed through long periods of use by other people, and the reader's concepts and schemata for responding to the book borrow from the thinking of others and result from previous social interactions. (Au, 1997, p. 184)

Au concludes by stating:

> School literacy learning is seen as a social process, affected not only by present but historical circumstances. Learning to read cannot logically be separated from the particular milieu in which it takes place. When children learn to read, or fail to learn to read, they do so in a particular social, cultural, and historical environment. Their success or failure in reading cannot be understood apart from that environment. (p. 184)

This statement illustrates the emphasis on both culture and the social nature of learning that Socio-Cultural Theory underscores.

Moll (1992, 1994) writes about the application of Socio-Cultural Theory to the literacy learning of marginalized students, especially those from Hispanic backgrounds. Moll asserts that mainstream classrooms are not typically designed in ways that allow Hispanic children to showcase their "funds of knowledge," that is, the sources of knowledge that are central to their homes and communities. As a result, all too often Hispanic children are perceived as coming from homes with limited intellectual capital and possessing limited intellectual capability. This perspective has been called a "deficit" perspective. Instead, Moll argues that teachers must begin to value children's funds of knowledge, bringing them into the classroom and using them as vehicles for literacy learning. For example, one student that Moll (1994) studied was the child of a farmer whose family had a long history of farming. Although the farmer was not formally educated, he possessed a tremendous amount of knowledge related to farming: knowledge of planting, watering, fertilizing, rotating crops, harvesting, marketing, and farm equipment. The father and the student also possessed a shared, rich family history of farming. Moll reports that the student's teacher invited the father into the classroom to talk about his work and lifestyle. After he left, the children wrote about what they had learned and completed other extension activities related to his visit. The experience was so successful in generating positive self-esteem and meaningful literacy learning that the teacher subsequently had six other parents representing a variety of occupations and avocations to the classroom. Moll's work is socio-cultural because it emphasizes the central role of social influence on literacy learning.

## TEACHERS' ANECDOTES: SOCIO-CULTURAL THEORY

Christine is usually a very quiet little girl. She infrequently participates in class discussions. She is a Vietnamese student who has good command of the English language. One of the story selections read this year was called "We Don't Look Like Our Mom and Dad." This story told of two adopted Korean children and how they were assimilated into an American family. It spoke of the Korean culture, foods, and customs that the children brought with them. Christine responded well to this story. She offered to bring to school a traditional Vietnamese costume that she wears for special occasions. Through this story she was able to relate her background knowledge to the school curriculum.

—LU ANNE TOYE, fourth-grade teacher

The majority of the population in my school district is upper-class, white-collar, European American families. The minority is mostly lower socioeconomic, blue-collar, Hispanic families. Each year when we review our standardized test scores we find that the white children perform significantly better than the Hispanic children in language arts and reading. Part of the reason for this is that many of the European American families have the opportunity, finances, and education to offer their children extra support at home. I think, though, that another reason for the discrepancy is that the literature in our basal readers and in the chapter books that we read focuses on European American culture. The majority of the stories that we read have European American characters. Some have African American characters, but there are very few with Hispanic heroes and heroines. Even in social studies, when we teach immigration, we focus on the European immigrants, failing to mention immigrants from South America or Africa. Mathematical word problems still tend to use names such as "John" and "Elizabeth." We very infrequently encounter ethnic names in our textbooks. Perhaps if our curriculum and teaching materials related more to the Hispanic population's background, these students would be more successful in school and on standardized tests.

—MICHELLE HILKE, third-grade teacher

## SOCIAL CONSTRUCTIVISM

Lev Semionovich Vygotsky, a Russian scholar, was one of the earliest and most famous theorists from the social learning perspective. Although Vygotsky's theory is literally entitled the "Socio-Historical Theory of Cognitive Development" (Dixon-Krauss, 1996), it is commonly referred to as "Social Constructivism." Vygotsky's professional life spanned only 10 years, but during that time he wrote more than 180 works (Dixon-Krauss, 1996). Vygotsky died from tuberculosis in 1934 at the age of 38. After his death, his work was banned in the Stalinist Soviet Union for 20 years. Even in the United States his work was not widely read until the 1970s (Slavin, 1997). Now, however, Vygotsky's work is extremely prominent and influential in the fields of psychology and education.

Most prominent in Vygotsky's work is the belief that children learn as a result of social interactions with others. Woolfolk (1997) writes:

> Whereas Piaget described the child as a little scientist, constructing an understanding of the world largely alone, Vygotsky (1978, 1986, 1987, 1993) suggested that cognitive development depends much more on interactions with the people in the child's world and the tools that the culture provides to support thinking. Children's knowledge, ideas, attitudes, and values develop through interaction with others. (p. 44)

A second key idea in Vygotsky's Social Constructivism is that development depends on the sign systems with which individuals grow up. *Sign systems* include a culture's language, writing, and counting systems.

Vygotsky argued that children's learning is most affected by their mastery of language, as evidenced by their mastery of sign systems such as the alphabet, words, listening, speaking, and writing. Vygotsky postulated that it is through the use and manipulation of these signs that children have the tools to think about and respond to the world. He called the process of using these signs systems "semiotic mediation." He further argued that children learn the most about language and corresponding sign systems from the people around them with whom they interact.

An extremely influential concept within Vygotsky's Social Constructivism is the zone of proximal development. *The zone of proximal development* refers to the ideal level of task difficulty to facilitate learning which, according to Vygotsky, is the level at which a child can be successful with appropriate support. Tasks that children can independently complete do not fall within the zone of proximal development and therefore, according to this theory, are not ideal for promoting children's development.

Another key idea in Vygotsky's Social Constructivism is scaffolding. *Scaffolding* refers to the assistance that adults and more competent peers provide during learning episodes. This support can take the form of "clues, reminders, encouragement, breaking down the problem into steps, providing an example, or anything else that allows the student to grow in independence as a learner"(Slavin, 1997, p. 48). Children learn during experiences within the zone of proximal development as a result of others' scaffolding.

Vygotsky's theory suggests guidelines for the ways in which cognitive development occurs. A child must experience the use of higher mental functioning in social situations before he or she can internalize such functioning and independently use it. Similarly, children must learn about cultural communication systems in social situations prior to independently using the systems. Au (1997) labels these transitions as ones that move from interpsychological (between people) to intrapsychological (within an individual). She suggests that the process of learning to read follows this pattern as well.

Slavin (1997) compared and contrasted the ways in which Piaget and Vygotsky conceptualized development. Both theorists agreed that development occurred in a series of stages that is the same for all learners. Piaget, however, proposed that development precedes learning. In Slavin's words, Piaget suggested that "specific cognitive structures need to develop before certain types of learning can take place" (p. 46). Vygotsky, however, believed that learning results as a function of interacting with others.

## TEACHER'S ANECDOTE: SOCIAL CONSTRUCTIVISM

Vygotsky's idea of the zone of proximal development relates closely to a practice in my district called "differentiated instruction." The idea of the zone of proximal development is that children should be provided with the opportunity to learn at their own individual level. The same theory guides differentiated instruction. If children are presented with tasks that are not challenging enough, or that are too complicated, they will not learn.

At the K–5 level in my district we do not use any type of grouping or leveling in any subject. Knowing, however, that in a given math, reading, or language arts class there will be a minimum of three different ability levels, the administration encourages teachers to employ differentiated instruction. I often practice differentiation, particularly in reading and math. It is quite advantageous to students because each of them is able to learn and succeed at his or her individual ability level.

For example, when the class is initially introduced to a basal story, they read it in one of three ways. My more advanced students read the story independently. Children at the middle level read the story with a partner, a practice we call "buddy reading." My three lowest readers listen to the story on tape and follow along in their texts. While each child experiences the story in his or her own way, I am free to walk around the room and interact with the students. I ask children individual questions and scaffold, or clarify parts of the story for them, if they do not understand.

I incorporate the idea of the zone of proximal development, or differentiated instruction, in other areas of my reading program as well. When we use our basal readers I pretest my students to determine if they are already familiar with certain skills to be presented in a given theme. I have repeatedly discovered through pretesting that the skills presented by the basal are often too easy for two-thirds of my class. If I were to continue to teach them basic skills from the basal they would grow bored and little learning would occur. Therefore, I challenge these students by teaching them higher level thinking skills through reading supplemental literature. The children who do not understand certain concepts, as demonstrated by the pretest, are able to practice these skills on their level using the basal.

Based on my experiences, Vygotsky's zone of proximal development makes sense. In the classroom, children who are above a certain level do not waste their time relearning information that they already know. Similarly, children who require reinforcement in some areas have the advantage of receiving scaffolding from the teacher, of learning with other children at their level of development, and of having tasks broken down into smaller steps for them.

—MICHELLE HILKE, third-grade teacher

## SOCIAL LEARNING THEORY

Albert Bandura (1969, 1977, 1986, 1997), a Canadian psychologist, developed another theory within the social learning perspective. Originally called "Social Learning Theory," but recently renamed "Social Cognitive Theory," this general theory of human behavior combines features of Behaviorism with those of social learning. Bandura's primary premise in creating Social Learning Theory was that a behavioral explanation of learning (see Chapter 2) did not take into account the phenomenon of *vicarious learning*, the notion that people learn from observing others. In fact, Bandura argued that people learn more from observing others than they do from the consequences of experiencing things themselves. Bandura suggested that it is fortunate that humans are capable of observational learning; without it we would all have to experience everything ourselves in order to learn. Instead, we learn by observing others— their successes, failures, efforts, and styles. In Social Cognitive Theory the people from whom we learn are called "models." Similarly, "modeling," is the action performed by the model.

Bandura writes that there are four stages to observational learning (Slavin, 1997). The first is the attentional phase during which the observer watches the model. The second stage is the retention phase in which the observer thinks about and processes what he or she has observed. The third stage of observational learning is the *reproduction phase*. In this phase the observer repeats the behavior that has been modeled. The fourth stage is the *reinforcement phase*. Bandura suggests that observers are often reinforced as they repeat modeled behaviors. For example, as children begin to learn to say "please" and "thank you" as a result of adults around them modeling these conversational courtesies, adults often reinforce them for the acquisition of these manners.

Social Learning Theory was largely developed as a result of Bandura's research investigating the effects of media, such as television, on children's learning. In these studies, children were exposed to cartoons in which the characters displayed varying amounts of aggression, and were then either rewarded or punished for their hostile behaviors. After watching the cartoons, the children were observed during play sessions, most famously, playing with a large, plastic, Bobo doll that could be knocked down repeatedly. Bandura's research showed that the children who were exposed to the most aggression in the cartoons were the most likely to display aggression during their play sessions following the viewings. Furthermore, the research indicated that whether or not the characters in the cartoons were rewarded or punished for their hostile actions also predictably affected the likelihood that the children would repeat the aggressive behavior during play.

As stated above, Bandura recently changed the name of the Social Learning Theory to the Social Cognitive Theory. With this change Bandura wanted to emphasize that much cognition is used during observational learning. During learning humans interpret the behaviors of others: they don't just thoughtlessly imitate the behaviors of those around them. Bandura's newest research and writings also emphasize the role of self-efficacy in learning. *Self-efficacy* refers to one's belief that he or she possesses the abilities to attain specific goals. According to Bandura, people with high perceived self-efficacy try more, accomplish more, and persist longer at a task than do people with low perceived self-efficacy. Furthermore, individuals can have perceived self-efficacy that is equivalent to, exceeds, or falls short of their actual abilities.

Bandura's writings have had a tremendous impact on the fields of psychology and education. Teachers frequently use the concept of observational learning as a basis for classroom management. For example, many teachers will compliment (reinforce) the behavior of one student in the classroom with the expectation that other students in the classroom will imitate that desired behavior. Here, the teachers are counting on observational learning to be effective. Such use of observational learning is a widely recommended classroom management practice.

The concepts of modeling and observational learning have been particularly prominent in the field of literacy learning. Modeling and observational learning are cornerstones of the field of emergent literacy (see Chapter 5). These terms are often used to explain the ways in which young children learn about reading and books at home from their parents. The techniques themselves are also central to practices that teachers use during literacy instruction. When teachers read from big books, use a morning message, or invite guest speakers into the classroom, they are often hoping that their students will engage in observational learning. Similarly, the widespread use of D.E.A.R. time (Drop Everything and Read time) throughout the country, during which everyone in the school stops what they are doing and reads for a set amount of time, is a popular literacy instructional approach grounded in observational learning. Although Bandura's Social Learning/Social Cognitive Theory is not one that is frequently seen in framing reading research, the theory has had a large and lasting impact on children's literacy learning both at home and in school.

---

### TEACHER'S ANECDOTE: SOCIAL LEARNING THEORY

I found that I really identified with the work of Bandura when I think about my own children. Ryan and Leanna will do whatever I model for them, whether it is positive or negative. They see my wife and I do a lot of reading and we have a loving and caring home and this transfers to them. They love to read or be read to and are very affectionate toward other people. Also, when we eliminated television from their daily lives the violent behaviors that would occasionally pop up seemed to disappear. They now really have nowhere to observe these types of behavior. I also observe my students' behavior at school during recess. In talking to the students and observing their behavior there is a definite connection between their actions and what they watch on television.

—JOSEPH TUCKER, special education teacher

---

## CRITICAL LITERACY THEORY

In addition to spawning Sociolinguistic Theory, Socio-Cultural Theory, Social Constructivism, and Social Learning Theory, the social learning perspective has also provided the foundation for writings and investigations related to the political aspects of literacy education. Work that uses a political lens to examine literacy education falls under the umbrella of "Critical Literacy Theory." *Critical Literacy Theory* considers the political aspects of literacy education such as the ways in which schooling reinforces persistent inequalities in contemporary society, and the opportunities that exist within education to empower individuals to overcome such social oppression.

Critical Literacy Theory challenges the traditional belief that education is a politically neutral process designed to promote the individual development of all children. According to Siegel and Fernandez (2000), "The image of schooling as an opportunity for social mobility based on merit is replaced, in critical thought, by one that shows how schools reproduce the unequal distribution of wealth and power that is the hallmark of capitalist societies, and in so doing contribute to the maintenance of the status quo" (p. 141).

Freire (1970), author of *Pedagogy of the Oppressed*, is a key figure in the development of Critical Literacy Theory. Working in Brazil in the 1960's, Freire sought to find ways to understand, and then educate, the poor and uneducated masses. In his writings Freire argued that a "pedagogy of oppression" existed in Brazilian society. This pedagogy of oppression provided less than adequate educational services to the lowest classes of the Brazilian population, enabling society to continue to supply itself with a perpetual stream of poorly educated workers. These people were necessary for maintenance of Brazil's status quo. Freire's work presented illiteracy not as a personal failing, but "as a historically constructed product of a society structured to produce inequality" (Siegel & Fernandez, 2000, p. 146). Freire sought to create a "pedagogy of liberation" and was successful in educating many poor Brazilians until the government forced him into exile in response to his radical political beliefs and practices.

According to Bloome and Talwalker (1997), studies move into the realm of Critical Literacy Theory when they begin to examine the concept of power in relation to literacy learning. From this perspective, "The teaching of reading is viewed as a social process that can either foster or inhibit the empowerment of students" (Bloome & Talwalker, 1997, p. 109). Bloome and Talwalker note that Critical Literacy Theory seeks to examine "how reading and writing instruction might help students acquire a critical perspective on how written language is used to promote a particular cultural ideology and how it may inhibit the growth and maintenance of minority languages and cultures" (p. 109). Gee (1990), for example, writes that educators must investigate the ways in which literacy education has been used to "solidify the social hierarchy, empower elites and ensure that people lower on the hierarchy accept the values, norms, and beliefs of the elites, even when it is not in their interest to do so" (cited in Siegel & Fernandez, 2000, p. 142). Likewise, Shannon (1990) writes:

Current social relations are human artifacts developed over time through unequal negotiations between those with power and those without power. The goal of critical theory, then, is to reestablish the meaning of freedom based on human values, just social relations, and equality by illuminating the past and current social relations, documenting their consequences, and analyzing dialectically the society's contradictions as opportunities for change toward more just relations. (p. 148)

Critical Literacy Theory, which emerged in the 1960s, is the most recent theoretical development within the social learning perspective. Those who do work in the area believe that the field is still in its infancy.

## CLASSROOM APPLICATIONS

The social learning perspective is extremely popular among reading educators. Many current classroom practices in literacy instruction are built upon the premises of this theoretical perspective. Classroom practices consistent with the social learning perspective include, but are not limited to, the use of literacy centers in the classroom, shared readings, paired reading, cross-age reading/tutoring, guided reading, process writing, shared writing, guided writing, literature circles, morning meetings, and e-mail pals. All of these practices emphasize the social nature of learning, that is, the notion that students learn a great deal from the other people in their world, both adults and children. Several of these classroom practices are described in depth below.

### Sociolinguistic Theory Teaching Idea:
### Language Experience Charts and Morning Messages
### (Grades K–3)

The use of a language experience chart in the classroom is an instructional practice that reflects the social learning perspective, particularly Sociolinguistic Theory. A *language experience chart* is a story based on a shared experience that is written collaboratively by the teacher and young students on very large paper (chart paper). The processes of writing, reading, and rereading the story are used as teaching experiences. To begin a language experience chart, teachers call students to the rug in the classroom literacy center where a large pad of chart paper is propped on an easel. The teacher and/or students then decide on a topic for the language experience story. A language experience story is often based on a previous, shared experience, such as a class trip or a special event that has recently occurred. The teacher then asks students to think of a good sentence to start the story. When a student supplies the sentence, the teacher can either immediately accept what the student has said or ask the student or the class for additional ideas to strengthen the sentence. It is important that the teacher only uses sentences that are grammatically correct in this exercise. After everyone is satisfied with the starting sentence, the teacher begins to write the sentence with the class's assistance. The teacher may ask the students how to begin the sentence (with a capital) and how to spell many of the words. The teacher will also ask for punctuation marks as he or she is writing. After the first sentence is printed on the chart paper, the teacher asks the class to reread it, and then prompts the class to supply a second sentence. Construction of the language experience chart proceeds in this manner until the story is completed. At the conclusion of the lesson, students reread the entire story that they have helped to write. The teacher may also use the story as a teaching text at this point in the lesson, asking students to come up to the chart and find target words (e.g., words that begin with capitals, or those that have the -*ing* ending). Frequently, teachers laminate these stories and keep them on a stand or in the literacy center where students can reread them during literacy center time. Many educators believe that having children reread stories that they have helped to create, and that are based on experiences in which they have engaged, strongly benefits young readers' literacy development.

The teaching technique of using a morning message is a variation of the language experience approach described above. In the *morning message technique*, students and the teacher collaborate to write a message about what the day's activities will be. The teacher may prompt students with the content of the morning message (e.g., "Who can give me a sentence about going to music class?"), but the basic process of constructing and rereading the created text remain the same. The teacher can refer to the morning message throughout the day to remind students of that day's schedule. This practice reinforces the authenticity of reading for meaning.

The language experience approach and use of a morning message are practices consistent with the social learning perspective, particularly Sociolinguistic Theory, because they reflect the belief that learning is enhanced through social language interactions.

## Socio-Cultural Teaching Idea: Literature Circles (Grades 3 and Up)

The use of literature circles in the classroom is an instructional practice that is deeply grounded in the social learning perspective, and one that can be viewed as reflective of Socio-Cultural Theory. The concept of literature circles was developed by educators who believed that students would benefit from talking to each other about books, but who also believed that students' conversations needed to be structured in a way that would help them stay on task. The use of literature circles is consistent with a Socio-Cultural Theory perspective because it is built on the premise that students will learn from each other during literature circles (the social component). Additionally, the concept of literature circles emphasizes the importance of students bringing knowledge and artifacts from their own lives (their culture) into these discussions.

There are several different approaches for the design and use of literature circles in the classroom. In this chapter we present the work of Daniels (1994), one of the pioneers in the area, whose recommendations for literature circles are widespread and highly popular among teachers. Daniels suggests that students' conversations in literature circles should be organized according to jobs, or roles, that students perform in response to their reading, and then share during circle time. A selected number of these roles, and the job that the student does when he or she has that role, are highlighted below:

• *Discussion Director.* This student's job is to develop a list of three thought-provoking questions that the student's group might want to discuss about the reading assignment. The questions should help students talk over the main ideas in the reading and share reactions to the reading, not focus on details. Usually, the best questions come from the student's own thoughts, feelings, and concerns as he or she reads. During the literature circle the Discussion Director presents his or her questions and records the other students' answers to them.

• *Passage Master.* This student's job is to locate three special sections of the assigned reading to bring to the group's attention during literature circles. The idea is to help students in the group reexamine the sections of the text that are especially important or interesting. The Passage Master should identify the sections of the text that he or she found most important or interesting, and explain to the group the reasons for his or her choices. Then the Passage Master should record a summary of the group's responses to the selected passages.

• *Vocabulary Enricher.* This student's job is to locate and define five words that are unfamiliar or especially important to understanding the meaning of the assigned reading. During literature circles the Vocabulary Enricher helps the group locate the words in the text and better understand them.

• *Artist.* This student's job is to make some kind of creative, graphic response related to the assigned reading. The artistic response can be a sketch, cartoon, diagram, flow chart, collage, mobile, and the like. The idea or ideas represented in the artwork should reflect one or more of the important concepts in the reading and be accompanied by a short explanatory paragraph. During literature circles the Artist presents and explains his or her creative response to the group.

• *Connector.* The Connector's job is to identify meaningful connections between the assigned reading and real-world experiences. The connections may be related to the student's personal life, or events in the classroom, school, community, or larger world. The main focus here is to apply the reading to the real world. The student presents his or her connections during literature circles.

• *Investigator.* The Investigator's job is to locate additional, new information related to the assigned reading. Examples include magazine and newspaper articles, books, or information from the Internet related to the text. Interviews or visits to related locations are also appropriate. The Investigator may locate information about one or more concepts from the assigned reading, or find information about the text's author. The Investigator's job is to enhance the literature circle discussion with the extra information that he or she has found.

• *Summarizer.* This student's job is to prepare a summary of the assigned reading and share it with the group during literature circle.

## Implementing Literature Circles in the Classroom

The implementation of literature circles in the classroom should be flexible and in keeping with the maturity level of students in the classroom and the organizational style of the classroom teacher. There is no single, correct way to implement literature circles in the classroom. Practitioners are encouraged to try a variety of modifications when implementing this instructional approach, and to select the approach that works best for them. Some general guidelines that may be helpful are outlined below.

1. Literature circles are most easily implemented at third-grade level and above. While some teachers have successfully used literature circles at the second-grade level, many students are not yet ready for this degree of independence.

2. Students can either complete their assigned reading and role work as class work or as homework. Each has its benefits and drawbacks. If students do not complete their assigned work, they should not be allowed the "privilege" of participating in a literature circle.

3. Students can be placed in either heterogeneously or homogeneously based groups for literature circles. Each grouping arrangement has its benefits and drawbacks. Teachers should experiment to discover what works best for them and their students.

4. Students in every literature circle can read the same text, or different circles can work on different texts. Some researchers believe that self-selection of text/circle is an essential component of this instructional approach. Sometimes teachers will have access to many choices in this realm and other times they will not. Literature circles can be used with any text, including basal readers.

5. Teachers vary with regard to how often they use literature circles. Some teachers use them daily, others only once or twice a week. Still others set aside several months during the academic year for their use.

6. A combination of students' role work and informal observations of the literature circles can be used as sources of information for assessing students' performance. Traditional assessments such as tests and writing assignments can also be used as complements to nontraditional evaluations.

7. The highlights of literature circles have been presented here. Additional information can be found in books, professional journal articles, and on the Internet.

## Social Constructivism Teaching Idea: Cross-Age and Buddy Reading (Grades 3 and Up)

Like the instructional technique of literature circles, the instructional techniques of partner, buddy, and cross-age reading are also deeply embedded in the social learning theoretical perspective. Partner and buddy reading are consistent with the Social Constructivism theoretical perspective because the practices are built on the premise that children will scaffold each other's learning during the shared reading experiences. Although the terms are often used interchangeably, most often "partner reading" refers to pairing students from within the same class to read together, while "buddy reading" refers to pairing students from different grade classrooms to read together. The research on both forms of paired reading is positive. When Dixon-Krauss (1995) investigated the effects of partner reading on first and second graders, she found that the experience improved students' word recognition abilities and their attitudes regarding reading aloud. Small improvements in oral reading fluency were also reported. Below we present ideas for implementing partner reading followed by ideas for implementing buddy reading.

Many variations exist regarding ways to implement partner reading. As a general guideline teachers can assume that if their students are happily engaged in the paired reading process and staying on task, then the experience will be educationally valuable for their students. When planning to begin partner reading, teachers need to consider when and how to structure this component of their literacy program. Some teachers allow their students to choose partner reading as an optional activity within the literacy center portion of their day. Other teachers prefer that all of their students engage in partner reading at the same time. The pairing of students is a decision that can be made by the teacher, or one that can be made by the students themselves. Some teachers deliberately pair students possessing stronger reading skills with those possessing weaker reading skills, with the assumption that the better reader will be able to assist the struggling reader. Others pair students of equal reading skill with the idea that students will be best able to read material on their correct instructional level in this situation. Still other teachers allow students to decide with whom they want to work. The rationale for this approach is that students' motivation to read and attitudes toward reading will improve if they are given the opportunity to read with their friends.

With regard to reading materials during partner reading, many teachers allow student pairs to choose their own materials from the literacy center, thus making partner reading a variation of self-selected reading. Other educators assign specific materials from the classroom library, the guided reading texts, or the basal reading program. Teachers also differ in deciding how much direction and structure they provide to their students for this time. Some teachers give students specific rules stipulating how the students should organize their time during partner reading. Other teachers have students complete activity sheets or answer questions. Still other teachers just allow students to read together. Classroom practitioners beginning to experiment with this instructional technique are urged to try a variety of materials and methods. One approach may work better than others in specific classrooms, or, conversely, teachers may decide that it is beneficial to use an array of activities within the partner reading format.

Buddy reading is an alternative form of partner reading. In buddy reading teachers from two different grade levels work together to pair their students for partner reading. A central component of buddy reading is that the students within each pair are on different reading levels from each other. Most often, stronger readers from the upper grade are paired with stronger readers from the lower grade, and weaker readers from the upper grade are paired with weaker readers from the lower grades. In buddy reading students from the upper grade act as teachers or tutors during the paired reading experience. Sometimes classroom teachers instruct older students in techniques for helping the younger students with their reading (Morrow, 2002).

## RESEARCH APPLICATIONS

A large number of scholars in the field of literacy use a social learning perspective to present and interpret their research. In fact, in a recent prominent research synthesis, Gaffney and Anderson (2000) concluded that the major theoretical trends in the reading field today significantly reflect the social learning perspective. The areas of literacy research that have been investigated from a social learning perspective are numerous. In addition to those mentioned earlier in this chapter, examples include the classroom as a literacy learning community (Santa Barbara Discourse Group, 1994), the development of students' "funds of knowledge" (Moll & Greenberg, 1990), parent–child book reading experiences (Bus et al., 1995), home literacy experiences (Leseman & DeJong, 1998), and the nature of classroom discussions (Gambrell & Almasi, 1996).

Many literacy research studies currently use a Sociolinguistic Theory perspective. This perspective is most often seen in studies that examine language interaction in relation to children's reading development. Very often the focus of these studies is on parents', teachers', or peers' language use and its impact on children's literacy skills. A seminal example of this type of work is Snow's (1983) study of the relationship between children's literacy development and the language patterns that their mothers use with them. Snow revealed that mothers' language patterns associated with children's language growth included (1) the mothers' use of semantic contingency (e.g., the topical relatedness of adults' responses to their children's prior utterances), (2) scaffolding (e.g., the ways in which parents simplify their language in order to help children better comprehend it), and (3) accountability (e.g. mothers' demands that children speak in the most sophisticated language of which they capable—i.e., mothers don't encourage or tolerate "baby talk"). Snow's (1983) findings were later used to design a family literacy intervention in which parents were taught to increase the frequency of use of these types of language patterns during storybook reading time. The results of the intervention revealed that the language growth of children who participated in the program was significantly better than those who did not participate (Jordan et al., 2000). Researchers who are primarily interested in the effects of language on literacy development would be encouraged to choose a Sociolinguistic Theory perspective to frame their research.

As with Sociolinguistic Theory, many literacy scholars use a Socio-Cultural Theory perspective to frame their research. Researchers who use this perspective are most interested in understanding the effects of the broad concept of culture on literacy learning. As described above, Au (1994) has been a leader in this field. Other notable researchers from this perspective have been the Santa Barbara Discourse Group (1994), which investigated the classroom as a literacy learning community, and Moll and Greenberg (1990), who studied students' background knowledge, the ways in which their background knowledge ("funds of knowledge") matched or mismatched school demands, and the implications of these correspondences for students' literacy learning.

An example of recent research that uses a Socio-Cultural Theory perspective is a study of family literacy practices in immigrant households (Orellana, Reynolds, Dorner, & Meza, 2003). In this ethnographic work, the literacy experiences of 18 bilingual, young adolescents (fifth and sixth graders) engaged in translation and paraphrasing activities for their families were chronicled. The researchers examined 86 transcripts and 95 journal entries regarding these events, and contrasted the qualities of these interactions with traditional school-based literacy learning activities. The results of the study indicated that these bilingual immigrant youths played a "pivotal role" (p. 28) in the literacy events of their families. Children assisted their parents and other family members with tasks such as reading mail (letters, forms, ads, bills), responding to a jury summons, and interpreting memos from school. These interpretative and paraphrasing events occurred with great frequency in the studied families. When contrasting these experiences with traditional classroom-based literacy learning activities, the authors reported both similarities and differences. The authors urged educators to consider and build on the real-life literacy experiences of immigrant bilingual students when designing literacy tasks.

A current example of research employing a Critical Literacy Theory perspective is a study of the language and literacy practices of two Mexican schools (Jimenez, Smith, & Martinez-León, 2003). In this project, the literacy practices (reading, writing, speaking, and exposure to text) of students in four classrooms (two beginning primary classrooms, and two grade-four classrooms) were examined over a period of 6 months. Data sources included classroom observations, interviews with teachers and administrators, student-produced artifacts, and publicly displayed texts. The results of the study revealed that students in these classrooms had considerable freedom in their oral expression but that written expression was suppressed, or at best constrained, by teachers' emphasis on form rather than content. The researchers provided suggestions that Mexican educators could use to further develop their students' ability to reflect on the literacy practices that contributed to social injustices in their society. These included helping students respond more fully to publicly displayed texts and working on developing their students as "legitimate writers" as they had done in developing them as "legitimate speakers." This study is an example of one that uses the Critical Literacy Theory as a theoretical framework because the authors' intention is to examine classroom practices from the perspective of how they do, and do not, contribute to issues of social justice and inequality in the Mexican society.

## SUMMARY

This chapter summarizes the social learning perspective. The social learning perspective incorporates several different theories, all of which emphasize the central role of social interaction in the development of knowledge and learning. When applied to the field of reading, the social learning perspective emphasizes the importance of social influences and social interaction on literacy learning. The social learning perspective of Sociolinguistics Theory (Bernstein, 1972a, 197b; Halliday, 1975; Heath, 1982; Rosenblatt, 1978, 1994) emphasizes the importance of oral language in literacy learning and the central role of social interaction in all literacy acquisition. Socio-Cultural Theory (Au, 1997; Bronfenbrenner, 1979) emphasizes the broader effects of communities and cultures on styles of interaction and subsequently on students' learning. Social

Constructivism/Socio-Historical Theory (Vygotsky, 1962, 1978, 1986) describes the ways in which knowledge is constructed within individuals as a result of social interaction, and Social Learning Theory/Social Cognitive Theory (Bandura, 1986) describes the central role of modeling in human learning. Critical Literacy Theory (Freire, 1970; Gee, 1990; Shannon, 1990) examines the ways in which literacy and literacy instruction can be understood as vehicles of power to ameliorate social inequalities. While all of these theories share the common view that literacy learning is social in nature, each emphasizes different facets of that belief. Although the names of various social learning theories are often used as if they are interchangeable by writers, we have tried to clarify their distinctions and similarities, as well as articulate their implications for instruction and research.

# CHAPTER 7

# Information/Cognitive Processing Perspectives
## (1950s–1970s)

This chapter explores theories and models from the 1950s to the 1970s that contributed to the cognitive processing perspective of reading. Although research was conducted on basic physiological aspects of reading in the late 1800s and very early 1900s, as described in Chapter 2, a resurgence of interest in cognitive processing related to reading did not appear until the 1950s. This resurgence resulted from experimental psychologists' renewed interest in cognitive processes and the government's willingness to fund research investigations of this nature (Venezky, 1984). Hiebert and Raphael (1996) write: "The cognitive science revolution shifted the focus from the study of observable behaviors to attempts to describe unobservable mental processes. Because reading is an unobservable mental process, educational psychologists in the late 1960s and 1970s began to focus extensively on describing the underlying cognitive processes involved in reading" (p. 554). We first review the general characteristics of the cognitive processing perspective. Then we discuss some early cognitive processing theories and models specifically related to reading. Due to the very large scope of cognitive processing theories related to reading, discussion of this topic is spread over three chapters.

## GENERAL CHARACTERISTICS
## OF THE COGNITIVE PROCESSING VIEW

In describing the general characteristics of the cognitive processing perspective, Woolfolk (1998) writes: "The cognitive view of learning can
best be described as a generally agreed-upon philosophical orientation.
This means that cognitive theorists share basic notions about learning
and memory. Cognitive theorists believe, for example, that learning is
the result of our attempts to make sense of the world. To do this, we use
all the mental tools at our disposal" (p. 247). She continues, "The cognitive view sees people as active learners who initiate experiences, seek out
information to solve problems, and reorganize what they already know
to achieve new insights" (p. 247). Schwartz and Reisberg (1991) explain
that "cognitive psychologists, who focus on changes in knowledge,
believe learning is an internal mental activity that cannot be observed
directly. . . .Cognitive psychologists studying learning are interested in
unobservable mental activities such as thinking, remembering, and solving problems" (quoted in Woolfolk, 1998, p. 205). Sternberg (1996)
notes that "cognitive psychology did not become identified as a distinct
branch of psychology until the latter half of the twentieth century"
(p. 6).

## INFORMATION PROCESSING THEORIES

Information processing theories and models represent one perspective
within the cognitive theories and models orientation. According to
Slavin (1997), "Information processing theory is the cognitive theory of
learning that describes the processing, storage, and retrieval of knowledge from the mind" (p. 185). It has been the dominant theory of learning and memory for the past 20 years. Furthermore, these theories and
models are marked by a discrete, stage-by-stage, conceptual orientation
(Stanovich, 2000).

Information processing theories have been most notably represented
by Atkinson and Shiffrin's (1968) Information Processing Model (Figure
7.1). This widely accepted model, which dominated the field of psychological research in the 1970s–1980s, suggests that information moves
through different stages, or storage systems, as it is processed, reflected
upon, learned, saved, and retrieved.

Woolfolk (1998) and Slavin (1997) outline the components of
Atkinson and Shiffrin's (1968) Information Processing Model. In this

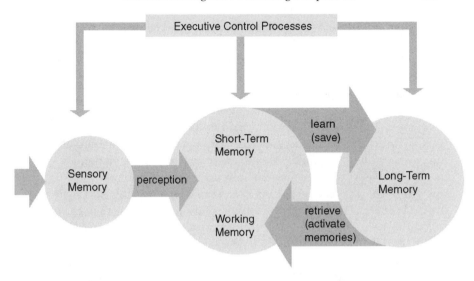

FIGURE 7.1. Atkinson and Shiffrin's Information Processing Model. From Woolfolk (1998). Published by Allyn & Bacon, Boston, MA. Copyright 1998 by Pearson Education. Reprinted by permission of the publisher.

model, the information processing system is organized by *executive control processes*. The executive control processes coordinate all the component systems of the model and guide information through the various stages of learning. According to this model, information is first perceived in the *sensory register*, also called *sensory memory*. Here, *perception* takes place, which is, according to Slavin (1997), "a person's interpretation of stimuli" (p. 186). Information can only be held for a few seconds in sensory memory, and perception takes place almost instantaneously. According to this model, after the information is processed in the sensory register, it is then processed in *working memory*, which is a temporary storage area. Working memory is also known as *short-term memory*. Woolfolk (1998) writes:

> Working memory is the "workbench" of the memory system, the component of memory where new information is held temporarily and combined with knowledge from long-term memory. Working memory is like the workspace or screen of a computer—its content is activated information—what you are thinking about at the moment. For this reason, some psychologists consider working memory to be synonymous with "consciousness." (p. 253)

Using an *articulatory loop* (the rehearsal mechanism of the mind), working memory saves information into, and retrieves information from, *long-term memory*. Slavin (1997) defines *long-term memory* as "the components of memory in which large amounts of information can be stored for long periods of time" (p. 191). Slavin also describes the various types of long-term memory: "Episodic memory . . . stores images of our personal experiences . . . Semantic memory . . . stores facts and general knowledge . . . Procedural memory . . . stores information about how to do things . . ., and Flashbulb memory [stores information about] important events that are fixed mainly in visual and auditory memory" (p. 191). The concept of *attention* is central to encoding information from short-term to long-term memory. Only information that receives sufficient attention when it is in short-term memory will be successfully encoded into long-term memory.

Once encoded, information is held in long-term memory in the form of *schemas*. Woolfolk (1998) defines *schemas* as "abstract knowledge structures that organize vast amounts of information" (p. 258). Slavin (1997) describes them as "mental networks of related concepts that influence understanding of new information" (p. 193). Schemas provide the structure through which information is stored, held, elaborated upon when new information is added, and retrieved from long-term memory. The information held in schemas is vulnerable to loss over time, known in information processing theory as *decay*. For additional information on schemas, see Chapter 4.

The Information Processing Model is illustrative of a cognitive processing perspective because it attempts to articulate the unobservable, underlying cognitive processes involved with the processing, storage, and retrieval of information. The highlights of the Information Processing Model have been presented here. For a complete understanding of this complex model additional resources should be consulted.

---

TEACHER'S ANECDOTE:
INFORMATION PROCESSING MODEL

The Information Processing Model is evident in the classroom in many ways. Students exercise short-term memory processes when they study for a quiz or a test and then forget most of the information after the test is completed. They may have repeated the information over and over in their heads when they were studying, but once they stopped rehearsing the information was lost. Long-term memory is executed when children read. Once a child is a good reader that skill is not forgotten. The letters of the alphabet and their sounds are not forgotten.

—KRISTEN CARRERO, fifth-grade teacher

## SUBSTRATA-FACTOR THEORY OF READING

One of the first applications of the cognitive processing perspective in the field of reading was made by Jack Holmes. In 1953, Holmes created substrata-factor analysis, a statistical application designed to identify the distribution of factors underlying reading ability (Singer, 1983). Holmes's work identified variables and subvariables that were correlated with reading ability. In his work he used subvariables in the variable categories of cognitive ability, verbal ability, fine motor skills, eye movements, and personality factors to predict the speed and power of an individual's reading ability (Singer, 1983).

Holmes used the substrata-factor statistical analysis procedure to create the *Substrata-Factor Theory of Reading*, the first published theory specific to reading (Holmes, 1953). Singer (1994) writes:

> All the previous research in reading had been atheoretical. Neither Huey's (1908) book on *The Psychology and Pedagogy of Reading* nor Anderson and Dearborn's text (1952) on *The Psychology of Teaching Reading* had the term theory in the text or index (Holmes, 1953). The dominance of behaviorism with its rejection of mentalism and its emphasis on S–R psychology led educational psychologists and psychologists to avoid constructing theories about events that were not observable. (p. 895)

In contrast, the creation of Holmes's theory allowed for the genesis of hypothesis-based investigations in reading. Subsequently, Holmes proposed college-level, psychological, neurological, and developmental models of reading based on his statistical analyses and reading theory (Singer, 1994). Thus Holmes's contributions to reading have been significant both in terms of the statistical identification of the variables and subvariables that contribute to understanding reading from a cognitive perspective, and in terms of the creation of the first testable, hypothesis-driven theory of reading ability based on the factors identified in his statistical work. Holmes's theory is classified as cognitive because he was interested in explaining cognitive and neurological aspects that contribute to effective reading.

## TEACHERS' ANECDOTES:
## SUBSTRATA-FACTOR THEORY OF READING

When looking at Holmes's variables, I began to think about the differences between the higher and lower level readers in my classroom. As I thought about the higher readers as a whole, it became evident that they seem to have each of the important variables that Holmes discusses in his Substrata-Factor Theory of Reading. They each possess high cognitive abilities, evidenced by their success in all subject areas. Their verbal abilities are far more mature than those of the lower readers. They are able to speak about a topic sequentially and can explain their answers and thoughts clearly. The higher readers tend to have fine motor skills that are more advanced than those of lower readers, as they are more accurate in most hands-on activities. Finally, their personalities are such that they are motivated, determined, and strive to please. Each of these components adds up to the strong readers that they have become. On the other hand, the lower readers as a whole are weaker in each of these variables. Holmes would most likely argue that they are not as successful with reading because of their deficiencies in these areas.

—JENNIFER MORRA, second-grade teacher

I study these variables in the beginning of the year to predict how my students will perform in reading. I like to get to know all my new students and learn what their strengths and weaknesses are. I do this by reviewing their kindergarten report cards in order to assess their cognitive ability; having individual "getting to know you" conversations so I can learn more about their personality; noting their fine motor skills when they hold their pencils, crayons, and scissors; watching their eye contact when I speak; and engaging them in conversations to judge their verbal abilities. Like Holmes did, I too predict what type of student each child will be and what kind of help each child will need in order to succeed.

—JOY VALENTI, first-grade teacher

## RAUDING THEORY

Like Holmes (1953), Carver (1977) was also interested in quantifying the reading process according to its composite and most important variables. Carver created *Rauding Theory* in 1977 and it is still used by researchers today. In designing this theory Carver generated several new vocabulary terms. To him, the general term "reading ability" includes five cognitive skills in which readers engage during various reading tasks: skimming, scanning, rauding, learning, and memorizing (Carver, 1992). "Rauding" refers to "typical reading" and is contrasted with the skills of skimming, scanning, learning, and memorizing. Carver (1992) writes:

> The reading process that is typically used by most individuals is the rauding process; it proceeds at a rather constant rate and involves no studying. Individuals may be forced to shift out of their rauding process into a learning process or a memorizing process when they are given relatively hard material or when they are given extra time to reread the material. (p. 165)

In Carver's work, the concept of general reading ability is referred to as "rauding efficiency level." Within rauding efficiency level are the factors "rauding accuracy level" and "rauding rate level." *Rauding accuracy level* reflects a reader's knowledge of vocabulary. *Rauding rate level* refers to a reader's rate of typical reading (rauding). According to Carver and Leibert (1995), research strongly supports these two subfactors as *the* critical components of standardized measures of reading comprehension.

In Rauding Theory, mathematics are used to predict the amount of information that a reader can comprehend based on factors including rauding efficiency level, rauding accuracy level, rauding rate level, text difficulty, and time provided for the task. Importantly, in contrast to Schema Theory (see Chapter 4), "there are no provisions in rauding theory for the purported differential effects of prediction activities, prior knowledge, or text type" (Carver, 1992, p. 165).

Carver's work has generated two important hypotheses that have been tested in research (Carver & Leibert, 1995). The first is that reading improvement requires that readers use texts that are closely matched to their ability levels. The second is that the use of texts that are easy for readers helps them maintain an adequate reading rate. These authors suggest that when text is too easy, new vocabulary cannot be learned and therefore reading ability will not improve. When text is too difficult, however, reading rate will be laboriously slowed, which will have a negative effect on comprehension.

## GOUGH'S MODEL

In 1972, Gough proposed a model of reading based on an information processing perspective. Early cognitive models of reading such as Gough's became known as *"bottom-up" information processing models* because they depicted the cognitive processing of information as proceeding from lower order to higher order stages. Stanovich (2000) writes about the link between early information processing models and the emergence of "bottom-up" models of the reading process:

> There was a strong tendency in early cognitive theorizing to depict information processing as a series of discrete stages, each performing a specific transformation on its input and passing on the new recoded representation as an input to a subsequent stage . . . Since the sequence of processing operations proceeds from the incoming data to higher-level encodings, such conceptualizations have been termed "bottom-up" models. It is not surprising that, since these models were so influential in the early development of information processing theorizing, they were the first to be applied to reading. (p. 21)

In Gough's model (Figure 7.2), as in the general information processing perspective, the reading process is depicted as consisting of a series of discrete stages. According to Rumelhart (1994), in Gough's model the reading process begins when the eye captures the input of each letter from the printed text. This *iconic image* is held briefly as the *scanner* begins to examine the image, searching for patterns of lines and curves in an attempt to identify the image. The iconic image is identified and briefly stored as a letter in the *character register.* After the image is identified as a letter, *decoder* processing begins. A *code book* is used in this stage to attach the correct phonemes to each letter. According to Samuels and Kamil (1984), "These systematic phonemes are abstract representations of speech that are related to sounds but not the sounds themselves" (p. 195). The phoneme is then recoded as a sound in the *phonemic tape.* The sounds of the letters are put together in the *librarian*, where the search for word meaning occurs. The *lexicon* holds the meanings for all words, and the librarian attaches meaning to those words. Sentences are then constructed in the *pri-*

SUPPOSE THE EYE . . .

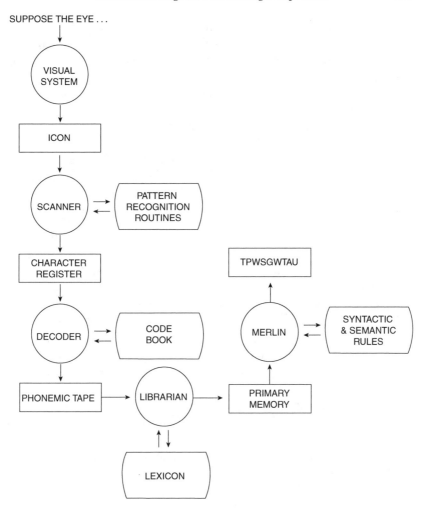

FIGURE 7.2. Gough's Model. From Pearson, Barr, Kamil, and Mosenthal (1984). Published by Allyn & Bacon, Boston, MA. Copyright 1984 by Pearson Education. Reprinted by permission of the publisher.

*mary memory.* Once a sentence is constructed, *Merlin,* the "magician," goes to work. This is where the final meaning of the sentences are construed, using the resources of the *syntactic and semantic rules processor.* Finally, sentences are shipped to *TPWSGWTAU,* "the place where sentences go when they are understood." This model was modified and renamed *The Simple View* (Gough & Tunmer, 1986). *The Simple View* suggests that reading comprehension is a result of two processes: decoding skill and language comprehension. Gough's Model is exemplary of the cognitive processing perspective applied to the field of reading due to its focus on explaining unobservable, underlying cognitive processes during the reading process. It is also exemplary of information processing theories due to its emphasis on a stage-by-stage conceptual orientation to the processing and storage of text.

---

### TEACHER'S ANECDOTE: GOUGH'S MODEL

Many of my resource room kids are very low readers who still don't know the basic sounds some letter or blends make. This deficiency breaks down the reading process at the decoder. Other students get lost at the librarian due to the limited amount of words that they have in their vocabulary. There are even a few students who can't decipher between *p, b, d,* and *g* and they get stuck at the scanner because the pattern recognizer isn't working up to par. Gough's Model is good for trying to explain all the different points at which my kids could be experiencing reading problems.

—RENEE BEN-DAVID, seventh-grade special education teacher

---

### AUTOMATIC INFORMATION PROCESSING MODEL

Another "bottom-up," cognitive processing model that emerged in the 1970s is the Automatic Information Processing Model (LaBerge & Samuels, 1974). Samuels (1994) reports that in the 1980s this model was the most frequently presented reading model in reading methods textbooks. As described by Samuels (1994), there are five major components to the Automatic Information Processing Model: visual memory, phonological memory, episodic memory, semantic memory, and attention.

In LaBerge and Samuels's model (Figure 7.3), reading begins with visual processing of text. The *visual memory* (VM) is where the graphic

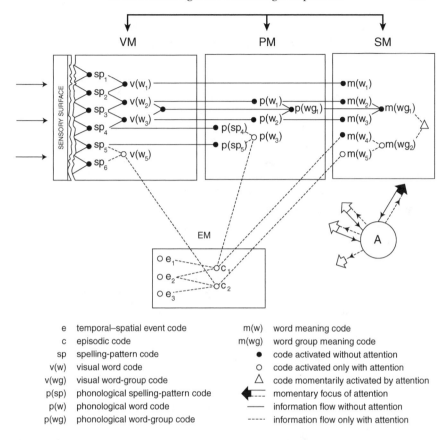

FIGURE 7.3. LaBerge and Samuels's Automatic Information Processing Model. From Pearson, Barr, Kamil, and Mosenthal (1984). Published by Allyn & Bacon, Boston, MA. Copyright 1984 by Pearson Education. Reprinted by permission of the publisher.

input from the text is processed. Features such as lines, curves, and angles are used for letter identification. LaBerge and Samuels suggested that "with exposure and practice, the visual features in stimuli like letters become unitized and then perceived as a single unit. As these units accumulate and letter perception becomes increasingly automatic, attention to early visual coding processes decreases. This decrease allows attentional resources to be reallocated to other areas" (quoted in Wolf & Katzir-Cohen, 2001, p. 214). The process through which individual letters are recognized as a single unit (the word) is known as *unitization*.

Following the visual processing of text, the LaBerge and Samuels model proposes that information is then processed in the *phonological memory* (PM), where sounds are attached to the visual images. *Episodic memory* (EM), in the LaBerge–Samuels model, is next, where the context that surrounds the target information is recorded. All kinds of other knowledge are then stored in the *semantic memory* (SM).

The fifth, and central, component of the Automatic Information Processing Model is *attention* (A). There are two types of attention: internal attention and external attention. *External attention*, the more familiar of the two, is directly observable attention—the obvious behavior of using one's eyes and ears to gather information in an efficient and effective manner. As Samuels (1994) explains, this is what a teacher means when she or he says that her or his students are or are not "paying attention."

In contrast to external attention, *internal attention* is unobservable attention. It refers to what is happening inside an individual's mind, regardless of the way the individual's external attention appears. Thus, while judging from external attention cues it may appear as though an individual is paying attention, in reality that individual's internal attention may be on a totally different topic (e.g., baseball practice or the cute girl sitting across the aisle). According to Samuels (1994), internal attention is the core of LaBerge and Samuels's model. Internal attention includes three components: alertness, selectivity, and limited capacity. *Alertness* refers to how active and vigilant the reader is in trying to decipher the message of the text. *Selectivity* refers to the process that allows the reader to decide which aspects of his or her experience he or she will attend to, and to what degree different aspects of that experience will be processed. Finally, *limited capacity* refers to the fact that humans have a limited amount of attention available for processing information. In addition to these concepts, LaBerge and Samuels applied the notion of *automaticity*, the ability to perform a task while devoting little attention to the reading task. Samuels (1994) writes, "The critical test of automaticity is that the task, which at the beginning stage of learning could only be performed by itself, can now be performed along with one or more other tasks" (p. 819). Examples of behaviors that can become "automatic" include driving, knitting, typing, and, of course, reading.

Samuels (1994) describes the ways in which these concepts relate to reading. He explains, "It is assumed in the theory—as well as by many who study reading—that getting meaning from printed words involves a two-step process: first, the printed words must be decoded; second, the decoded words must be comprehended" (p. 820). The beginning reader comprehends by switching his or her attention (of which there is a limited capacity) back and forth between the two processes of decoding and comprehending. For the beginning reader this process can be slow, laborious, and frustrating. Furthermore, the beginning reader's comprehension can often be compromised if he or she devotes too much attention to accurate decoding of the text. In contrast, the fluent reader needs little internal attention to decode text because he or she is able to decode most, or all, of the words of the text with automaticity. For the fluent reader, little or no attention is needed to decode the words, and, as a result, most or all of his or her attention is available for comprehension.

Samuels (1994) describes the usefulness of the Automatic Information Processing Model for diagnosis and remediation. He writes, "Teachers have observed that some students can recognize words accurately, but not comprehend them with ease. . . . Automaticity theory suggests that one possible reason for the students' problem is that the decoding requires so much attention that it interferes with comprehension" (p. 833). A solution to this problem is to find easier texts that require less attention for decoding. Rereading a text can also be helpful in this case. Rereading, especially with beginning readers, often allows the reader to attend to the message. Samuels continues, "Another common problem is seen when skilled readers, often college students, claim that even though they read the text with care, they cannot remember what they have read. . . . Automaticity theory suggests that instead of focusing on deriving meaning from the text, perhaps the reader's internal attention has wandered" (p. 833). In this case, an explanation of the nature of the problem to the student can be helpful, and solutions can often be reached through the application of metacognitive strategies (see Chapter 10).

Like Gough's Model, LaBerge and Samuels's Automatic Information Processing Model is reflective of the cognitive processing perspective, information processing theories, and "bottom-up" processing. It is reflective of the cognitive processing perspective because it focuses on explaining underlying, unobservable, cognitive processes. It is reflective of information processing theories because of its stage-by-stage conceptual orientation to the processing, storage, and retrieval of information. Finally, the model is reflective of "bottom-up" processing because it represents the reading process as beginning with the processing of graphic stimuli (the "bottom" of the process) and proceeding to higher levels of cognitive processing (the "top" of the process).

Beginning and low-ability readers need to use a lot of internal attention to decode words. This adversely affects comprehension. Eventually, children are able to decode automatically and all internal
attention becomes available for comprehension. This was most evident to me when I taught second grade. The students who struggled
with decoding during reading were the same students who had comprehension difficulty. As their automaticity of word recognition
increased, so did their understanding of what they read.

—LU ANNE TOYE, fourth-grade teacher

## INTERACTIVE MODEL

With support of the contributions of Posner and Snyder's (1975a,
1975b) Theory of Expectancy regarding context facilitation effects,
Rumelhart (1977, 1994) proposed the first nonlinear model of the reading process. Rumelhart noticed that both Gough's (1972) and LaBerge
and Samuels's (1974) models were *linear*, meaning that information
could only be passed in one direction, from lower level processing to
higher level processing. As stated previously, models that depict information as only flowing from lower level to higher level processing are also
known as "bottom-up models." Rumelhart realized that linear, bottom-
up models of reading that did not conceptually allow for higher level
thinking to influence lower level processing had serious flaws. He
observed that during the reading process there are many times in which
higher level processing (such as comprehending the meaning of a sentence) assists in lower level functions (such as word identification). In
reality, there are a variety of ways that words are identified during reading; word identification is not limited to "bottom-up" decoding identification processes. Rumelhart argued that an accurate model of the reading process needed to reflect such real-life phenomena; as a result, he
created his Interactive Model. In Rumelhart's Interactive Model (Figure
7.4), the reading process is still initiated by a visual text input, as
Gough (1972) and LaBerge and Samuels had suggested. However, in
Rumelhart's Interactive Model, a variety of processors converge on
visual information simultaneously, rather than in a linear process. The
simultaneous processing of syntactic information (referring to word

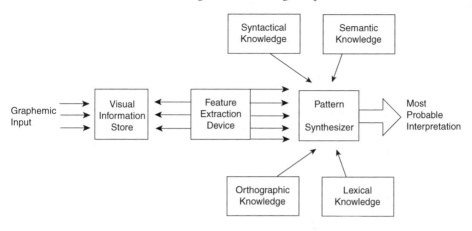

FIGURE 7.4. Rumelhart's Interactive Model. From Pearson, Barr, Kamil, and Mosenthal (1984). Published by Allyn & Bacon, Boston, MA. Copyright 1984 by Pearson Education. Reprinted by permission of the publisher.

order within sentences), semantic information (related to message construction), orthographic information (related to visual input), and lexical information (referring to word knowledge) allows for higher level and lower level processes to simultaneously interact on the visual input. The result, according to Rumelhart's model, is the most probable interpretation of the message.

Rumelhart's Interactive Model (1977, 1994) is consistent with the cognitive processing theoretical orientation to reading because it hypothesizes about unobservable, underlying cognitive processes that take place during the reading process. The model is also consistent with information processing theories because it uses a stage-by-stage conceptualization of the reading process. Rumelhart's model is considered interactive rather than "bottom-up," however, because it depicts multiple processors converging on visual input simultaneously, rather than in a linear, sequential manner.

---

TEACHER'S ANECDOTE: INTERACTIVE MODEL

Rumelhart stated that the reading process is neither bottom-up nor top-down, but interactive. His Interactive Model shows four processors converging simultaneously on data to create the most probable word interpretation, with syntactic, semantic, orthographic, and lexical knowledge working together. Rumelhart believed that models could not be linear because, in reality, during reading there are instances in which lower order processing affects higher order processing, just as there are instances in which higher order processing affects lower order processing. I teach my kids that there are many ways to identify a word: sight, decoding, word families, and context clues. When I teach my kids to identify a word using sight, decoding, and word family strategies, I am teaching them to use bottom-up approaches. However, when I teach my kids to use context clues, I am teaching them to use a top-down approach. The Interactive Model suggests that when students are actually reading both bottom-up and top-down processes will help the kids identify words.

—RENEE BEN-DAVID, seventh-grade special education teacher

## CLASSROOM APPLICATIONS

The cognitive processing models of the 1950s–1970s still hold implications for classroom instruction today. Most notably, the models are extremely useful for suggesting how the reading process works and the ways in which this process can break down. As a result, the models can be viewed as valuable for diagnostic purposes. For example, using the Information Processing Model perspective, teachers can consider students' perceptual abilities, short-term and long-term memory capabilities, and executive control processes. While all of these skills can be assessed with formal diagnostic instruments, students' perceptual abilities can also be evaluated through informal procedures in which students are asked to replicate drawn shapes and repeat auditory stimuli. Similarly, students' short-term memories can be informally assessed by asking students to repeat a list of items or to follow multistep directions. Students' long-term memory abilities can be informally assessed by observing their day-to-day retention of learned material. Classroom teachers who are examining children's abilities in these realms are urged to inform school specialists if they are especially concerned about a child's performance in one or more of these areas.

Holmes's Substrata-Factor Theory of Reading and Gough's Model are also valuable lenses for considering areas of deficit and strength in readers. The Substrata-Factor Theory of Reading suggests that cognitive, verbal, and fine motor skills all contribute to children's successful reading. Gough's Model identifies letter perception, the ability to attach sounds to letters, children's knowledge of word meanings, and the ability to construct messages during reading as critical components of the reading process. As stated above, classroom teachers and other learning specialists can formally or informally evaluate all of these skills. If deficits are revealed, instruction can be tailored accordingly.

The Automatic Information Processing Model also has clear diagnostic and intervention value. The model suggests that if a student is reading a text without comprehension, it may be because that student is experiencing too much of a cognitive load. This would be the case if the reader needs to allocate an excessive amount of cognitive energy to decoding words. If decoding uses all of the reader's internal attention, there will not be adequate cognitive resources remaining to devote to message construction (comprehension). In such cases the correct intervention is to lower decoding demands by giving the reader an easier text to read. When readers can decode automatically, or nearly automatically, then their internal attention can be devoted to understanding the message of the text.

One of the best ways to monitor children's reading skills and development is to include guided reading instruction as a part of a classroom literacy program. Although guided reading did not become a popular classroom practice until the 1990s, many of the skills identified as important to reading success by the cognitive processing models of the 1950s to 1970s can be examined through this powerful instructional activity.

Three characteristics identify a reading activity as guided reading. First, the reading instruction must take place in a small group. A teacher and five to seven students is the ideal group size for guided reading instruction. Through small-group instruction a teacher can learn much more about his or her students' strengths and weaknesses than he or she can learn when working with an entire class at once. Second, all of the students in the group must be of similar reading ability. While children should not be homogeneously grouped for *all* language arts activities *all* day long, it is important that they are homogeneously grouped for guided reading. Ability-based grouping is necessary for providing students with reading materials that are on their correct reading level; this is the third characteristic of guided reading. Books in which students can correctly decode approximately 95% of all words on a page and adequately comprehend what they are reading should be used for guided reading. The second and third characteristics of guided reading are closely related: when children are grouped according to their reading ability, it is possible to provide them with texts that are at the ideal instructional level.

A wide variety of reading materials are suitable for guided reading. Some teachers and schools purchase *leveled readers*, small storybooks written expressly for the purposes of guided reading. Some teachers use high-quality children's literature and novels, calculating the match between the texts and the students themselves. Supplemental materials such as newspaper, magazine, and Internet articles can also be used. Finally, even basal series materials can be used for guided reading as long as the texts provided to the students are on their correct instructional levels. Regardless of the type of reading material chosen, teachers will need five to seven copies of each text (i.e., a copy for each student) to use for the guided reading experience.

It can be useful for teachers to plan their guided reading lesson in three phases: before reading, during reading, and after reading. In the *before-reading phase*, teachers should help their students prepare to comprehend the upcoming reading material. Activities that focus on building and activating children's prior knowledge and strengthening children's knowledge of key vocabulary are frequently used. In the *during-reading phase*, instruction focuses on increasing comprehension. Teachers often have students make predictions about upcoming text, and then read to verify their predictions. Sometimes teachers provide word identification, vocabulary, and metacognitive instruction as part of the during-reading phase. While a portion of this phase of the lesson can be devoted to children reading aloud, it is important that guided reading does not become old-fashioned "round-robin" reading. This problem can be avoided by emphasizing students' silent reading followed by group discussion during this part of the lesson. Students can go back and reread aloud particularly important passages for verification or clarification. The *after-reading phase* can be completed while the small group is still assembled, or even when students return to their regular seats. The after-reading activities are designed to reinforce and extend learning that has transpired during the guided reading experience.

Assessment is an important part of guided reading instruction. Teachers who employ guided reading become skilled in recording students' occasional oral reading performances using a format called "running records." Teachers can also take free-form anecdotal notes during guided reading. Such running records and notes can be added to students' files and used to document their reading growth. This information can also be shared with parents during parent–teacher conferences.

Guided reading is a very important instructional activity that should be part of literacy instructional programs. The small-group size inherent in guided reading allows teachers to monitor many of the components of reading identified as central by the cognitive processing models of the 1950s–1970s. Educators interested in learning more about guided reading are urged to read Fountas and Pinnell's (1996) *Guided Reading*, the seminal text in this area.

## RESEARCH APPLICATIONS

### Research Application Example: Information Processing Theories

Theories of cognitive processing are used to describe unobservable learning events. Educators cannot look into the human mind and see it at work unless highly sophisticated, state-of-the-art technology is used (see Chapter 11). In the absence of state-of-the-art equipment, the cognitive theories of the 1950s to 1970s can only be used as hypothetical descriptions of what *might* be occurring during any individual's reading experience. Nonetheless, researchers and graduate students can choose to frame their research within an information processing theoretical lens. This model can be particularly useful for explaining individual reading differences.

Wolf and Katzir-Cohen (2001) used an information processing perspective as one of the theoretical lenses framing their research in the area of reading fluency and interventions to improve fluency. In their work, 200 second- and third-grade children with severe reading disabilities participated in a program designed to strengthen their skills in the areas of visual and auditory recognition, orthographic pattern recognition, lexical retrieval, and semantic activation processes. The effectiveness of the intervention, entitled RAVE-O, was measured by children's achievement in the areas of word identification, word attack, and comprehension. Preliminary results of the study revealed that significant gains were achieved in all of these areas following 70 sessions of the RAVE-O program. Although Wolf and Katzir-Cohen used multiple theoretical perspectives to contextualize their research, their fundamental perspective is rooted in the foundational components of information processing theory.

## Research Application Example:
## Substrata-Factor Theory of Reading

Researchers and graduate students may want to include Holmes's Substrata-Factor Theory of Reading in historical discussions regarding the identification of individual factors that contribute to reading achievement. Although several of the factors identified by Holmes are no longer considered to have a significant effect on students' reading performance, the Substrata-Factor Theory of Reading remains notable because of its historical place in the evolution of reading theories.

According to Singer (1983), Katz (1980) tested the substrata-factor hypothesis. Katz trained first-grade teachers to provide supplemental reading instruction to students in one of four areas: graphophonemics, morphophonemics, semantics, and syntax. After 10 weeks of instruction, Katz tested the students' reading abilities and determined that "methods of instruction interact with students' capabilities to differentially develop subsystems underlying reading achievement. The subsystems of graphophonetics, syntax, and semantics developed at the first-grade level are initially functionally related to differences in methods of instruction" (Singer, 1983, p. 19).

## Research Application Example: Rauding Theory

A study composed of three investigations examined the effect of reading library books at different levels of difficulty on reading achievement (Carver & Leibert, 1995). In the work, students in grades three, four, and five read library books that were either slightly above or slightly below their reading levels as part of a 6-week summer reading program. Books that were slightly easy for the students were judged to produce easy rauding, while books that were slightly difficult for the students were judged to produce matched rauding. The results of the first study demonstrated that neither group gained in reading/rauding ability during the 6-week study period; however, results of the second and third investigations revealed that, in fact, the books had not been correctly evaluated with regard to difficulty. The researchers' overall conclusion was that reading easy material did not produce gains in AL (rauding accuracy level), RL (rauding rate level), or EL (rauding efficiency level) for the students in this program.

**Research Application Example: Gough's Model**

Like Holmes's Substrata-Factor Theory of Reading, Gough's Model retains most of its usefulness because of its place in the historical development of more current theories of the reading process. Researchers and graduate students may want to refer to this model as one example of how we once understood the reading process to occur.

Cardoso-Martins (2001) refers to Gough's work in the area of word recognition in her study of the beginning reading skills of Brazilian Portuguese children. Cardoso-Martins arranged for two groups of 5- to 6-year-old children to receive two different types of reading instruction. The first group received instruction that began with a whole-word approach and then switched to a syllabic approach. The second group received instruction that emphasized only a phonics approach. The children participated in the two instructional groups for a period of a year during which time a variety of measures were collected on the development of their reading skills. The study showed that children in the whole-word first condition did not develop phonics skills until instruction in the syllabic approach began. This finding supported the belief that children's early reading development is closely tied to the reading instruction that they receive. Cardoso-Martins used Gough's work for the presentation of foundational understandings regarding word recognition processes.

**Research Application Example:
Automatic Information Processing Model**

Although LaBerge and Samuels's Automatic Information Processing Model is as old as several of the other theories presented in this chapter, certain elements of the model still have great value. Although researchers will probably not want to use the entire model as a contextual framework, LaBerge and Samuels's conceptualization of internal attention, external attention, and automaticity are still highly applicable to contemporary understanding of the reading process. They are as viable in the 21st century as when they were presented in the early 1970s. As a result, researchers and graduate students seeking to examine individual differences in reading achievement, particularly in the area of comprehension, may choose to use these concepts when framing and interpreting their research.

Fuchs, Fuchs, Hosp, and Jenkins (2001) examined several different theories that support the position that oral reading fluency is a reflection of overall reading competence. They note that "LaBerge and Samuels's (1974) automaticity model of reading is probably most frequently invoked as a framework for conceptualizing oral reading fluency as an indicator of overall reading competence" (p. 241). The authors explain that LaBerge and Samuels's model was and is significant because it was the first to recognize that "skilled reading involves the reallocation of attentional capacity from lower level word identification processing to resource-demanding comprehension functions" (p. 241). Although Fuchs et al.'s paper is a theoretical and historical analysis of oral reading fluency, it is interesting to note that the authors perceive the contributions of LaBerge and Samuels's Automatic Information Processing Model as still valuable.

### Research Application Example: Interactive Model

Subsequent to the presentation of their Interactive Model in 1977, Rumelhart and colleagues introduced a refined version of that model called the Parallel Distributed Processing Model in 1989 (see Chapter 8). The key components of the Interactive Model were expanded and polished in the Parallel Distributed Processing Model. Thus, while the Interactive Model remains historically significant for its contributions, researchers seeking to contextualize their research from this perspective would most likely choose the most current version of the model.

Wolf and Katzir-Cohen's (2001) paper on reading fluency and interventions to improve reading fluency was previously presented as a research example that used information processing theory as one of its theoretical lenses. It is presented here as well because the authors also used the Parallel Distributed Processing Model as another of its theoretical lenses. In fact, Wolf and Katzir-Cohen used many theoretical perspectives to present different views of reading fluency. These authors' use of multiple theoretical lenses to study the topic of reading fluency is consistent with the present text's use of multiple theoretical lenses to study the whole field of reading instruction and reading research.

### SUMMARY

This chapter presented six cognitive processing theories relevant to reading that were prominent from about 1950 to 1970. Atkinson and Shiffrin's (1968) Information Processing Model presented the general outline of information processing theory. This widely accepted model suggests that information moves through different stages, or storage systems, as it is processed by the brain. These stages include the sensory register, short-term memory, the articulatory loop, and long-term memory. The Substratra-Factor Theory of Reading (Holmes, 1953) was the first theory based on information processing that specifically addressed reading. In his work Holmes used subvariables in the categories of cognitive ability, verbal ability, fine motor skills, eye movements, and personality factors to predict the speed and power of an individual's reading ability. Rauding Theory (Carver, 1977) argues that the rauding process is the typical reading process used by most readers when they are reading material that is at a comfortable level of difficulty. It states that rauding accuracy level (vocabulary knowledge) and rauding rate (reading rate) are the two critical components of standardized measures of reading comprehension. Gough's Model (1972) is famous for being the first reading model to incorporate the stage theory of the information processing perspective. These stages include the scanner, the character register, the decoder, the code book, the phonemic tape, the librarian, the primary memory, and TPWSGWTAU, the place where sentences go when they are understood. The Automatic Information Processing Model (LaBerge & Samuels, 1974) integrated the concepts of internal attention, external attention, and automaticity into the information processing perspective of reading. The Interactive Model (Rumelhart, 1977) proposed the first nonlinear representation of the reading process in which four cognitive processors (orthographic, semantic, syntactic, and lexical) simultaneously converge to create the most probable interpretation of text. Although the theories and models presented in this chapter are at least several decades old, and our understanding of cognitive processing has progressed since their publication (see Chapters 8 and 9), many of these models and theories retain value for their central components which are still relevant to practice and research, and all retain value for the historical contributions they have made to our current understanding of reading.

# CHAPTER 8

# Information/Cognitive Processing Perspectives, Continued

## *(1980s)*

A cognitive processing perspective on reading seeks to describe the workings of the mind during the reading process. The cognitive processing perspective emerged in the middle of the 20th century. Prominent cognitive processing theories and models from the 1950s to the 1970s related to reading were covered in the last chapter. They include the Information Processing Model (Atkinson & Shiffrin, 1968), the Substrata-Factor Theory of Reading (Holmes, 1953), Rauding Theory (Carver, 1977), Gough's Model (Gough, 1972), the Automatic Information Processing Model (LaBerge & Samuels, 1974), and the Interactive Model (Rumelhart, 1977, 1994). In the present chapter, prominent cognitive theories and models from the 1980s are presented. They include the Interactive–Compensatory Model (Stanovich, 1980), the Orthographic Processing Perspective (Ehri, 1980), the Verbal Efficiency Theory (Perfetti, 1985), the Construction–Integration Model (Kintsch, 1994), and the Phonological–Core Variable Difference Model (Stanovich, 1988).

## INTERACTIVE–COMPENSATORY MODEL

In 1980, Stanovich published an article entitled "Toward an Interactive–Compensatory Model of Individual Differences in the Development of Reading Fluency." In the article, Stanovich began by reviewing the concepts of "bottom-up," "top-down," and interactive models of the reading process. To summarize, "bottom-up" models are those that depict the reading process as a series of discrete stages through which information passes. By definition, "bottom-up" models present reading as progressing from the processing of lower levels of information, such as letter identification, to the processing of higher levels of information, such as the construction of the meaning of messages. In a "bottom-up" model of reading, first letters are identified, then sounds are attached to them, the word meaning is added, and finally—after all the words are processed—the sentence's meaning is understood. The models of Gough (1972) and LaBerge and Samuels (1974) presented in Chapter 7 are illustrative of "bottom-up" models of reading.

"Bottom-up" models of the reading process contrast with "top-down" models. "Top-down" models are built on the assumption that the reading process is primarily driven by what is in the reader's head rather than by what is on the printed page. "Top-down" models of reading emphasize the importance of a reader's background knowledge during the reading process. This background knowledge includes information from many sources: knowledge about the topic, knowledge of text structure, knowledge of sentence structure, knowledge of word meanings (vocabulary), and knowledge of letter–sound correspondences. According to "top-down" models, readers use all of these sources of information to make predictions and hypotheses about upcoming text. When the upcoming text is consistent with a reader's hypotheses and predictions, the reading process progresses rapidly and smoothly, with the reader sampling the text and confirming his or her hypotheses and predictions. However, when the upcoming text is inconsistent with the reader's expectations, reading is slowed, and the reader attends more closely to the actual printed text. The term "top-down" is derived from this heavy reliance on the reader (rather than the text) during the reading process. Psycholinguistic Theory (Goodman, 1967; Smith, 1971), described in Chapter 4, is the theoretical model of reading most closely aligned with a "top-down" model.

Stanovich (1980) also reviewed interactive models of reading (Rumelhart, 1977). As described in Chapter 7, the central characteristic of an interactive model is that the reader uses information that is simultaneously provided from multiple sources during the reading process. The simultaneous processing of syntactic information (referring to word order within sentences), semantic information (related to message construction), orthographic information (related to visual input), and lexical information (referring to word knowledge) allows for higher level and lower level processes to mutually interact during the reading process in ways that are neither exclusively "bottom-up" nor "top-down." The result is the most probable interpretation of the message. Rumelhart's (1977) Interactive Model, discussed in Chapter 7, was the first model of reading to propose a nonlinear, simultaneous view of information processing.

In addition to summarizing the key points of "bottom-up," "top-down," and interactive models of reading, Stanovich (1980) extended Rumelhart's (1977) Interactive Model to include the idea that not only are text processors interactive and nonlinear, but that they are also *compensatory*. By this Stanovich meant that if one processor is not working well, or has insufficient data, the other processors compensate for it. For example, if an individual is reading a note that is written in ink and part of the note is wet, some of the print may be blurred (insufficient data). Therefore the orthographic processor would not be able to work effectively. In this case, the individual's other processors would compensate. For instance, the syntactic processor, responsible for constructing the meaning of sentences and passages, would aide in word identification by suggesting the word that makes the most sense. In this example, the syntactic processor compensates for problems in the orthographic processor. Stanovich used the concepts of the Interactive–Compensatory Model to theorize on the differences in individuals' reading abilities. Like Rumelhart's (1977) Interactive Model, Stanovich's (1980) Interactive–Compensatory Model is compatible with both cognitive processing and information processing orientations to reading.

---

TEACHER'S ANECDOTE:
INTERACTIVE–COMPENSATORY MODEL

In 1980, Stanovich added to Rumelhart's Interactive Model, creating the Interactive–Compensatory Model. He believed that not only do the processors interact, but that when one processor is weak, the other processors will compensate. One way that this model is apparent in the classroom is seen during a cloze exercise. Can the students use the clues surrounding a blank in order to fill it in? Can they make up for the lack of the graphic information available for input? When they are able to do so, it proves that Stanovich's theory is correct. When information for one processor is inadequate (in this example graphic information is missing), another processor (in this example the syntactic processor) is able to compensate. The result is that the student is able to figure out the missing word even though there is no graphic information present at all.

—RENEE BEN-DAVID, seventh-grade special education teacher

## ORTHOGRAPHIC PROCESSING PERSPECTIVE

In the same year that Stanovich (1980) published the Interactive–Compensatory Model, Erhi (1980) published an article that articulated the ways in which the brain processes orthographic information (visual, printed text) during the reading process. Ehri identified the way in which orthographic forms (words) are captured in memory. She reported, "This written unit is thought to be incorporated not as a rotely memorized geometric figure but rather as a sequence of letters bearing systematic relationships to phonological properties of the word" (p. 313).

In 1992 Ehri explained the process through which readers see a printed word and connect it to its pronunciation stored in memory. She called a key early step in this process "recoding." During recoding printed letters are connected to their pronunciations through the use of letter–sound rules. More familiar terms for Ehri's "recoding" are "decoding" and "sounding out." Ehri (1992) writes:

> This [recoding] begins the process of setting up a visual–phonological route for that word leading from its spelling directly to its pronunciation in memory. Once such routes are set up, readers can look at spellings and immediately retrieve their specific pronunciations without resorting to translation rules and recoding. . . . The matter of connections is a crucial one, for this is what determines how easy it is for readers to retrieve words in memory from the visual forms that they see. (p. 114)

More recently, Ehri (2000) has been stressing the importance of graphophonemic awareness. "Graphophonemic awareness" refers to the reader's ability to connect printed text (graphemes) to sounds (phonemes). In lay language, graphophonemic awareness is the knowledge that underlies decoding skill. Ehri emphasizes that graphophonemic awareness is critically important to successful early reading.

## VERBAL EFFICIENCY THEORY

In 1985, Perfetti wrote an influential book entitled *Reading Ability*. In this text Perfetti outlined a theory of the reading process that attempted to explain individual differences in reading ability. Entitled the Verbal Efficiency Theory, the theory was built on three assumptions (Kuhara-Kojima, Hatano, Saito, & Haebara, 1996). The first, and most general, assumption is that word recognition skills during reading are related to *speech access*. This means that as the reader reads, the sound of the word (the phonological code) is activated as the word is read (the lexical access). Thus the first general assumption of the Verbal Efficiency Theory is that one's reading of printed text is related to one's internal hearing of it.

The second assumption of the Verbal Efficiency Theory is that the amount of time it takes the reader to read an isolated word aloud is indicative of how well the reader knows the word. The amount of time it takes to read an isolated word aloud is known as *vocalization latency*. How quickly the reader can identify a printed word is also known as *word recognition automaticity*. Thus the second assumption of the Verbal Efficiency Theory is that "vocalization latencies to single printed words represent the extent of automaticity of word recognition" (Kuhara-Kojima et al., 1996, p. 158). Perfetti and his colleagues have demonstrated that more skilled comprehenders have faster automatic word recognition than less skilled comprehenders (Hogaboam & Perfetti, 1978). The Verbal Efficiency Theory suggests that faster word recognition is associated with improved reading because automatic word recognition requires less cognitive energy than decoding, thus freeing up cognitive capacity for comprehension processing (Wolf & Katzir-Cohen, 2001).

The third assumption of the Verbal Efficiency Theory is that a reader's decoding skill is the major source of variation in his or her vocalization latency. In simpler terms, how well a reader can decode will determine how quickly he or she can identify words when reading isolated words. The reading of isolated nonsense words is often used as a measure of decoding skill since this condition eliminates the readers' ability to use context or whole-word recognition skills for word identification. Indeed, Stanovich (1980) has reported that "the speed of naming pronounceable non-words is one of the tasks that most clearly differentiates good from poor readers" (p. 62).

In summarizing the importance of Perfetti's Verbal Efficiency Theory, Kuhara-Kojima et al. (1996) state that Perfetti's "assumptions about vocalization latencies as a measure of automaticity of word recognition and about decoding skill as the major source of variations in the latencies have been accepted virtually unanimously in the North American reading research community" (p. 161). Perfetti's Verbal Efficiency Theory is reflective of a cognitive processing orientation toward reading because it tries to explain the cognitive functioning of readers of differing ability.

---

### TEACHER'S ANECDOTE: VERBAL EFFICIENCY THEORY

I currently tutor a student who is working on building his sight word vocabulary. He is creating flashcards with the sight words he is learning. When he practices the words independently I tell him to test himself by reading each word to himself and if he can flip the cards without a long pause then he knows the word. However, if he has to stop at a card, then that is a word he needs to practice some more. Sometimes he asks why he has to do this and I explain to him that it will help him when he reads because he will not have to stop to figure out the words. As a result he will be able to enjoy the book and read harder books. With this student I am basing my teaching on Perfetti's second assumption because I want the sight words he is working on to become automatic for him. This way when he sees a word he will also be able to hear it and read it.

—PATRICIA POLLAK, elementary special education teacher

---

## CONSTRUCTION–INTEGRATION MODEL

According to the Construction–Integration Model, when readers read they construct representations, or understandings, of what they have read in their heads. The Construction–Integration Model (Kintsch, 1994) aims to articulate the ways in which these text representations are constructed when readers read, and also the ways in which the cognitive processes that construct them work.

The Construction–Integration Model suggests that during reading, representations occur at several levels: the *linguistic level* (a representation of the words themselves), the *conceptual level* (a representation of what the words and sentences mean), and the *situational level* (a representation of the text integrated with the general knowledge in the person's mind). Additionally, the model suggests that two primary cognitive processes are used to construct the linguistic-, conceptual-, and situational-level representations. The first process is *construction* in which "a text base is constructed from the linguistic input as well as from the comprehender's knowledge base" (Kintsch, 1994, p. 953). The second process is *integration* in which the understanding of the text is integrated into the reader's general knowledge base.

Kintsch (1994) elaborates on both of these primary processes. Regarding the *construction* process, he writes:

> The steps in constructing a text base according to the construction–integration model involve: (a) forming the concepts and propositions directly corresponding to the linguistic input; (b) elaborating each of these elements by selecting a small number of its most closely associated neighbors from the general knowledge net; (c) inferring certain additional propositions; and (d) assigning connection strengths to all pairs of elements that have been created. . . . The result is an initial, enriched, but incoherent and possibly contradictory text base, which is then subjected to an integration process to form a coherent structure. (p. 956)

Following the construction phase, the reader moves into the *integration* phase. Of this second primary cognitive process, Kintsch (1994) writes:

> Text comprehension is assumed to be organized in cycles, roughly corresponding to short sentences or phrases. . . . In each cycle a new net is constructed, including whatever is carried over in the short-term buffer from the previous cycle. Once the net is constructed, the integration process takes over: [connectionist] activation is spread around until the system stabilizes. . . . Usually, the system finds a stable state fairly rapidly; if the integration process fails, however, new constructions are added to the net, and the integration is attempted again. . . .

Thus, there is a basic, automatic construction-plus-integration process that normally is sufficient for comprehension. This process is more like perception than problem-solving, but when it fails, rather extensive problem-solving activity might be required to bring it back on track. (p. 963)

To summarize, the Construction–Integration Model suggests that readers construct three levels of representations during reading: linguistic, conceptual, and situational. Furthermore, the model hypothesizes that there are two primary cognitive processes in which readers engage during reading: a *construction phase* in which information from a variety of sources is collected, and an *integration phase* in which the information is synthesized. The Construction–Integration Model is consistent with a cognitive processing perspective because of its heavy emphasis on articulating the ways in which the brain is seen as functioning during reading. The model is also consistent with a constructivist perspective on reading (see Chapter 4).

## PHONOLOGICAL–CORE VARIABLE DIFFERENCE MODEL

In the 1980s the cognitive processing perspective was also used in the identification and treatment of reading disabilities. One of the major issues examined in this realm was the definition of the term "dyslexia." For years, controversy had existed about the term "dyslexia." One popular conceptualization was that there were two kinds of poor readers: "garden-variety" poor readers and "IQ-discrepant" poor readers (Stanovich, 1988). According to Stanovich, the term "garden variety" had been used to describe poor readers whose reading performance was consistent with their IQ. In contrast, "IQ-discrepant" readers were those whose reading performance was significantly below what their IQ would predict. Frequently, these readers were identified as "dyslexic" for purposes of research and treatment. Although this dichotomy has since been demonstrated to be false (Stanovich & Siegel, 1994), unfortunately the criterion is still often used for classifying students (Stanovich, 2000).

Stanovich's research (2000) demonstrated that IQ discrepancy was not an accurate way of identifying dyslexic readers. Instead, in his Phonological–Core Variable Difference Model (1988) he argued that the primary difference between normal and dyslexic individuals was determined by deficits in the phonological realm of cognitive functioning. As has been described earlier, phonological capabilities refer to an individual's awareness and ability to hear and manipulate sounds within words. Stanovich (1988) argued that dyslexia is a type of learning disability characterized by problems related to literacy learning in the absence of problems in other areas of cognitive functioning. Furthermore, he emphasized that the locus of these literacy learning problems was a phonological processing deficit.

In addition to using the cognitive processing lens to clearly define dyslexia, Stanovich (1986) wrote extensively about the academic consequences of being dyslexic. He published a seminal paper entitled "Matthew Effects in Reading: Some Consequences of Individual Differences in the Acquisition of Literacy." Stanovich argued that research demonstrates that children with phonemic awareness deficits are slower to break the sound–symbol code of reading. As a result of this delay in the development of decoding skills, these children are exposed to less text in school. The exposure to less text in school leads to fewer opportunities for vocabulary and syntactic development, fewer opportunities to practice reading, and less exposure to content knowledge in general. These cognitive problems are then compounded by motivational issues because when children are less successful with early reading they are less likely to want to read. Reading less further exacerbates the cognitive differences between the reading-disabled students and their nondisabled peers. Ultimately, the reading-disabled children develop generalized cognitive deficits when compared to their nondisabled peers. The Matthew Effects have been justly described as "fan-spread effects" because the reading-disabled child's problems are initially specific to the area of phonemic awareness, but then "fan out"—that is, they become more generalized and widespread over time. The concept of Matthew Effects has tremendous implications for the importance of early identification and treatment of children with phonemic awareness problems.

In sum, during the 1980s when extensive research was devoted to investigating the concept of dyslexia, Stanovich (1988) argued that phonological deficits were central to dyslexic readers' cognitive difficulties. He articulated this position in his Phonological–Core Variable Difference Model (1988). Stanovich's early emphasis on the area of phonological deficits as the primary issue characterizing dyslexia would prove to be an important key to future efforts to understand and treat at-risk readers (Shaywitz et al., 2004). The Phonological–Core Variable Difference Model is classified as a cognitive processing model because the central feature of the model is a deficit in the phonological processor.

## TEACHER'S ANECDOTE: PHONOLOGICAL–CORE VARIABLE DIFFERENCE MODEL

Reading Recovery is used in the first grade to help struggling readers progress to at least the middle achievement level of their class. I break the reading process down into steps that are easier for these struggling students to understand. I can see if we have any dyslexic students so that our program can remediate their problems. When the students read and write, I encourage them to "say the words slowly" to try to hear each sound and put them together to make words. I use sound boxes in writing to help them visualize each individual sound in a word that may be troubling them.

I think the Reading Recovery program in our school also counteracts Matthew Effects. The students receive the same 90-minute reading block as their peers in their classroom and then receive an additional 30 minutes working with me. The first 10 days of our program I work with what the students know and allow them to read as many books as possible. Yes, they are easy to read, because they need to build their confidence, but they are exposed to many different writing styles and vocabulary. During the lessons I always try to keep their reading at an instructional level. The children are learning to build their confidence in reading as well as learning strategies to help them read more difficult text. It seems like it might be easier in Reading Recovery to make sure struggling readers are appropriately challenged because we are working with them one on one. Hopefully the classroom teachers can take a step back and recognize how to challenge each individual student in their classes, regardless of his or her reading abilities.

—ANDREA EDWARDS, Reading Recovery teacher

## CLASSROOM APPLICATIONS

The Interactive–Compensatory Model suggests that there are four primary processors used during reading: the orthographic processor that handles visual input, the syntactic processor that handles word order within sentences, the lexical processor that handles word meanings, and the semantic processor that is responsible for overall message construction. Additionally, the Interactive–Compensatory Model suggests that these processors are interactive, nonlinear, and compensatory. One classroom application idea related to the Interactive–Compensatory Model is teaching children to be flexible readers. Flexible readers know that there are many ways to figure out words and word meanings when reading. Sometimes words can be identified immediately because they are in the reader's sight vocabulary. Sometimes word families can be used to help identify a word or a word can be sounded out based on its phonetic clues. Sometimes a reader can figure out the meaning of an unknown word because he or she understands the meaning of a sentence. When readers process text in these flexible ways they are intuitively, but unconsciously, using their reading processors in interactive and compensatory ways. When teachers provide instruction on how to be a flexible reader, they are providing instruction consistent with the Interactive–Compensatory Model. Teaching children how to use context clues when reading is a popular and effective instructional activity associated with this model.

Verbal Efficiency Theory emphasizes the central role of language ability in the reading experience. Classroom activities that acknowledge and reinforce the link between oral language development and reading are consistent with this perspective. Activities known to strengthen children's oral language include listening to stories read aloud, listening to books on tape, creating language experience charts, buddy reading, engaging in dramatic play, storytelling, and cooking activities. One specific idea to build children's language is a monthly poetry recital (Morrow, 2005). For this activity the teacher selects a poem that will be used in class for about a month and copies it onto a large piece of chart paper. The teacher reads the poem to the students and encourages students to read along for several days. Then students create props to go with the poem. After the poem has been practiced with the props the students can present their poem to children in other classes in the school. After the students have completed their presentations a new poem is introduced. This fun activity is a great way to expand children's oral language abilities, and ultimately their reading skills as well.

Since Stanovich's (1988) identification of phonological deficits as central to reading difficulties in the Phonological–Core Variable Difference Model, the term "phonemic awareness" has gained prominence. *Phonemic awareness* refers to a child's understanding that words are comprised of individual sounds. Children who acquire this ability are able to hear rhyming words and can segment individual sounds out of words and blend them together again. Phonemic awareness is developed over time and through practice (Juel, 1991). When children are phonemically aware, they know that a word such as *bug* is composed of three sounds that can be segmented into the sounds /b/u/g/. They also know that the sounds can be blended together again and that the individual sounds make the spoken word *bug*. Phonemic awareness does not involve associating the visual letter symbols with the sounds of the letters; it is simply hearing that there are different sounds in words and being able to segment the sounds, say them, and then blend them together.

There are many ways to strengthen children's phonemic awareness skills. Children can listen to rhyming books and nursery rhymes and play rhyming games. They can also play linguistic games in which speech sounds are manipulated. Researchers have suggested that children should study larger word unit sounds (e.g., compound words and syllables) before learning about the more abstract segmenting and blending of individual sounds (Yopp & Yopp, 2002).

## RESEARCH APPLICATIONS

### Research Application Example:
### Interactive–Compensatory Model

Schraw (1996) reported that the results of three studies indicated that students "spontaneously adopted an interactive, compensatory strategy" (p. 55) during reading. In these investigations Schraw examined the effects of text-based versus task-based information on students' reading. *Text-based information* was described as information central to the contents of the reading passage. *Task-based information* was described as information central to performing the job of reading, such as following directions. In the work, Schraw studied undergraduates as they were engaged in reading tasks. The results showed that while students were using an Interactive–Compensatory Model approach to reading, "task-based importance superceded text-based importance" (p. 55).

### Research Application Example:
### Orthographic Processing Approach

Booth, Perfetti, and MacWhinney (1999) reported that during reading rapid and accurate access to both orthographic and phonological information stored in the brain probably plays a central role in reading acquisition. Specifically, these researchers demonstrated that older and better readers access both orthographic and phonemic information sooner and more effectively than do younger and less able readers.

Foorman, Francis, Fletcher, and Lynn (1996) demonstrated that more able readers use orthographic information better than less able readers when they are very young. However, these authors also found that as less able readers mature, they become surprisingly good at orthographic processing. Foorman et al. interpreted their findings as supportive of a compensatory mechanism. They suggest that less able readers made extensive use of their orthographic processing skills as a compensation for their persistent phonological processing deficits.

In short, investigations into the topic of orthographic processing suggest that it is an important variable contributing to early reading ability. Booth et al. (1999) and Foorman et al. (1996) examined the role of orthographic processing in comparison to phonological processing in reading acquisition, while Ehri (1980, 1992, 2000) has articulated the connections between orthographic and phonological processing in early reading.

## Research Application Example: Verbal Efficiency Theory

Perfetti (1985) put forth the Verbal Efficiency Theory in his text *Reading Ability*. To briefly summarize, the theory is built on the assumptions that (1) word identification during reading is related to internal phonological access; (2) the speed with which a reader vocalizes an isolated word is a measure of how well the reader knows that word; and (3) a reader's decoding skill is the major source of variation in his or her vocalization latency. Kuhara-Kojima et al. (1996) implemented a series of studies to determine if these assumptions, which are widely accepted regarding the processing of the English language, are also applicable to two types of script used in the Japanese language. The two types of scripts examined were hiragana and kanji. *Hirigana* is a script based on 71 characters, with each character representing a syllable. *Kanji* is a script consisting of approximately 2,000 characters, each of which has its own meaning (morpheme) and often multiple pronunciations. Fifth-grade Japanese students participated in three studies of isolated word reading in differing conditions. The results of the research supported a universal application of the first two assumptions of the Verbal Efficiency Theory, but not the third. The authors concluded that the well-established relationship between decoding ability and reading comprehension is specific to languages built on the use of alphabetic systems, but not generalizable to all languages.

## Research Application Example:
## Construction–Integration Model

Caillies, Denhiere, and Kintsch (2002) implemented a research project to investigate the effects of prior knowledge on text understanding. The research was also designed to evaluate the usefulness of Kintsch's (1994) Construction–Integration Model for interpreting data related to this question. Fifty-four adult subjects with varying levels of background knowledge of Microsoft's Word and Excel software were given six sets of texts to read on these topics followed by a primed recognition task (in which they had to determine whether or not they had previously read target information). The subjects were also given follow-up comprehension questions. The Construction–Integration Model predicted that readers with the least amount of prior knowledge of Word and Excel would take the longest to read the sentences and have the lowest accuracy on comprehension questions. Similarly, the model predicted that readers with the most amount of prior knowledge would read most quickly and accurately, and subjects with intermediate levels of prior knowledge would perform accordingly. Using measures of reading rate and comprehension scores, the research supported the model's predictions. Surprisingly, however, results from the primed recognition task showed that beginners read primed sentences more quickly than did intermediate and advanced readers. The authors interpreted this finding as an indication that beginning readers responded to surface aspects of the primed sentence while intermediate and advanced readers responded to a deeper level reading of the sentence. The finding that intermediate and advanced readers outperformed beginning readers in the area of comprehension accuracy was consistent with this interpretation. In sum, the investigation demonstrated that prior knowledge has an effect on comprehension, as judged by reading speed and comprehension accuracy, and that Kintsch's (1994) Construction–Integration Model was a useful lens for examining these phenomena.

## Research Application Example:
## Phonological–Core Variable Difference Model

In 1994, Stanovich and Siegel investigated the role of the Phonological–Core Variable Difference Model in discriminating between types of reading-disabled students. Of paramount interest in the investigation was an examination of the differences, or lack of differences, between IQ-discrepant and IQ-nondiscrepant disabled readers. As explained previously, at that time if a student's reading abilities were substantially below what his or her IQ would predict, he or she would be labeled "IQ-discrepant" and qualify for a diagnosis of dyslexia. In contrast, if a child's IQ was not discrepant with his or her reading ability, then that child was considered to be a "garden-variety" poor reader. In several well-designed research trials Stanovich and Siegel (1994) demonstrated that there were no statistical differences between IQ-discrepant and IQ-nondiscrepant disabled readers on reading tasks specifically related to phonemic abilities. On tasks that were not specific to phonemic aware-ness, however, reading-disabled children with higher IQs outperformed reading-disabled students with lower IQs. Stanovich and Siegel inter-preted the results of their work as showing strong support for the Phonological–Core Variable Difference Model because it demonstrated the role of phonemic processing difficulties in all reading-disabled chil-dren. Equally important, the research proved false the long-held popular belief that IQ discrepancy was the key criterion on which to discriminate dyslexic readers. Instead, as a result of Stanovich and Siegel's research, the role of phonemic processing deficits as the central area of deficit in the reading problems of all disabled students was further underscored, and dyslexia was redefined as a learning disability specific to the realm of language learning, whether or not an IQ discrepancy was present.


## SUMMARY

Cognitive processing perspectives on reading seek to describe the work-ings of the mind during the reading process. In the present chapter, prominent cognitive theories and models related to reading from the 1980s are presented. They include the Interactive–Compensatory Model (Stanovich, 1980), the Orthographic Processing Perspective (Ehri, 1980), the Verbal Efficiency Theory (Perfetti, 1985), the Construction–Integration Model (Kintsch, 1994), and the Phonological–Core Variable Difference Model (Stanovich, 1988). In his Interactive–Compensatory Model, Stanovich (1980) extended the Interactive Model presented by Rumelhart in 1977 (see Chapter 7) by arguing that text processors are not only interactive and nonlinear, but also compensatory. By this he meant that if one processor is not working well, or has insufficient data, the other processors compensate for it. Ehri (1980) identified the way in which orthographic forms (words) are captured in memory, and reported that words are encoded as separate letters "bearing systematic relationships to phonological properties of the word" (p. 313). Perfetti

(1985) outlined the Verbal Efficiency Theory that attempted to explain individual differences in reading ability. The theory is based on three assumptions: (1) that word recognition skills during reading are related to speech access; (2) that the amount of time it takes to read an isolated word aloud is an indication of how well the reader knows the word; and (3) that a reader's decoding skill will determine how quickly he or she can identify words when reading isolated words. The Construction–Integration Model (Kintsch, 1994), suggests that during reading, representations occur at several levels: the *linguistic level* (a representation of the words themselves), the *conceptual level* (a representation of what the words and sentences mean), and the *situational level* (a representation of the text integrated with the general knowledge in the person's mind). Additionally, the model indicates that two primary cognitive processes are used to construct these representations: a construction process and an integration process. Stanovich's (1988) Phonological–Core Variable Difference Model presents the primary difference between normal and dyslexic individuals as determined by deficits in the phonological realm of cognitive functioning.

# CHAPTER 9

# Information/Cognitive Processing Perspectives

*State of the Art (1989–Present)*

## PARALLEL DISTRIBUTED PROCESSING MODEL

One approach to the cognitive processing perspective of reading that is receiving widespread attention is the Parallel Distributed Processing Model (Rumelhart & McClelland, 1986; Seidenberg & McClelland, 1989). Rumelhart and McClelland proposed an early version of the model in 1986, but the Seidenberg and McClelland (1989) version of the model has received the most research attention (Berninger et al., 2000). The model is regularly updated; the Plaut and McClelland (1993) version is currently prominent.

Researchers that conduct computational research in reading build computers that can "read" text. The researchers build the computers in ways that they believe reflect the cognitive process of reading.

Two central features of the Parallel Distributed Processing Model are (1) that all cognitive information is stored as a series of *connections* between units, and (2) that these connections between units becomes stronger and faster with repeated pairings. The conceptualization of storing information in the brain as a series of connections of differing strength is known as *Connectionism*. Accordingly, the Parallel

164

Distributed Processing Model is a *connectionist* theory of reading. Connectionism can be thought of as a system of cognitive processing built on weighted relationships. As pairings become more frequent, the strength (i.e., the weight) of the connection increases. Connectionism theorizes that neural networks are capable of "learning." This means that connections between different units continue to change over time based on the experience of pairings.

Explained in great detail in Adams's (1990) *Beginning to Read*, the Parallel Distributed Processing Model suggests that four primary processors are central to the reading process: the orthographic processor, the meaning processor, the context processor, and the phonological processor (see Figure 9.1). According to the model, the reading process begins in the *orthographic processor* where print recognition occurs. The orthographic processor can be thought of as a storehouse of orthographic knowledge (Byrnes, 2001). This processor holds knowledge about lines, curves, angles, and space, all associated with the information needed for letter (and number) identification.

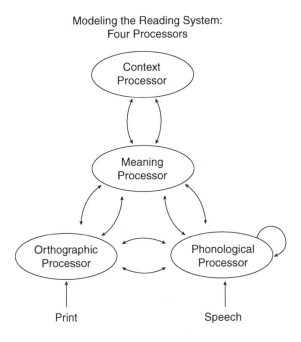

FIGURE 9.1. The Parallel Distributed Processing Model. From Adams (1990). Copyright 1990 by the MIT Press. Reprinted by permission.

In the case of letter identification, the connections between the units comprising any single letter become stronger with repeated exposure. For example, the associations between the straight line and the small curve in the letter *b* become stronger with repeated exposure to the letter *b*. The same kind of processes occurs for all letters and numbers. As individuals have repeated practice with print, they make stronger and faster connections between the separate units within letters and numbers (the lines, curves, angles, and space). Eventually, they experience letter and number identification as automatic. The concept of Connectionism applies to the strength of the associations between letters within a word, as well as to the strength of the associations of lines, curves, angles, and space within a letter. Connections between letters form when letter patterns frequently occur together in words. For example, in the English language the letter *t* is frequently followed by the letter *h*, and rarely followed by the letter *q*. According to the Parallel Distributed Processing Model, as a result of the frequency of these two letters occurring together, the connection between the letters *t* and *h* is much stronger and faster than the connection between the letters *t* and *q*. The model suggests that during the reading process the orthographic processor uses the strength of the connections between letters to activate letters that are likely to follow the initially identified letter and to suppress letters that are unlikely to follow the initially identified letter. This process, known as the "interletter associational unit system," assists readers in gradually building rapid word identification skills.

Adams (1990) underscores a critical element of the interletter associational unit system: letter recognition must be automatic for the system to operate.

> If it takes more than a moment to resolve the visual identities of successive letters in a word, then the stimulation of the visual recognition unit for the first will have dissipated by the time that the second has been turned on. Unless the units are active at the same time, there is no way for the system to learn about the conjoint occurrence of their letters. (p. 112)

In other words, activation of the interletter associational system, the system built on connections between letters and designed to activate and suppress upcoming letters based on the strength of those connections, will not function if letter identification is not extremely fast and automatic. In its absence, readers are forced to read one letter at a time, greatly slowing the reading process and decreasing the likelihood of adequate comprehension.

The second processor in the Parallel Distributed Processing Model is the *meaning processor*. The meaning processor attaches the meaning (vocabulary) to words identified in the orthographic processor. As in the orthographic processor, the meanings of vocabulary words are organized according to connectionist principles, with any individual's personal experiences determining which associations are made and the strength and speed of those associations. For example, regarding the target word *swimming*, one child might immediately think of a community pool, while another would picture a lake in the country. This processor also functions to enable likely word meanings to be activated as unlikely word meanings are suppressed. The totality of a person's knowledge of any topic is his or her *schema* (described in Chapter 4); the strength and speed of the connections among the units within a schema, or between schemas, are, according to this model, connectionist in nature. The Parallel Distributed Processing Model suggests that as individuals progress through life, they acquire an ever greater number of schemas that are organized, within and between, by connectionist principals. These schemas are the sources of word meaning as readers engage in the reading process.

The third processor in the Parallel Distributed Processing Model is the *phonological processor*. The phonological processor is where the sounds associated with words are processed. In the English language, the smallest unit of sound is known as a *phoneme*. In the phonological processor, each phoneme is considered a unit. As with the orthographic and meaning processors, the units within the phonological processor are linked according to the rules of Connectionism. This means that sounds that frequently occur together have stronger and faster connections with each other than sounds that rarely occur together. Based on this construction of connections, the phonological processor activates sounds that are likely to follow each other while suppressing sounds that are unlikely be adjacent.

Adams (1990) and Byrnes (2001) summarize two additional benefits offered by the phonological processor. First, the phonological processor provides a redundancy system to the orthographic processor known as the *alphabetic backup system*. This aspect of the phonological processor becomes activated when a person has an auditory familiarity with a word but has never seen it printed. In this case the reader "sounds out" the word and uses the sounds of the word to aid in accessing word identification and meaning. The second benefit of the phonological processor is its *running memory capability*. This feature provides an "inner voice" when one is reading, allowing words to be briefly held in working memory and available for further processing as they are read.

The fourth processor in the Parallel Distributed Processing Model is the *context processor*. The context processor is where the reader constructs and monitors the meanings of phrases, sentences, paragraphs, and full texts during the reading process. When the reading experience is progressing smoothly, the outcome of the context processor is a coherent message to the reader. As with the other processors, the organization of the context processor is connectionist in nature, with knowledge of the topic, language, and text all providing units of information for synthesis. Furthermore, like the other processors, the context processor both receives and delivers information. In the Parallel Distributed Processing Model the context processor receives and delivers information to and from the meaning processor. As a message is being constructed in the context processor, information is being shipped to the meaning processor regarding words that are likely to occur next in the text. As words are being given meaning in the meaning processor, they are shipped to the context processor for use in the message construction. As shown in Figure 9.1, the orthographic, phonological, and meaning processors function in a circular pattern, while the pattern between the meaning and context processors is bidirectional. The meaning processor is the only processor in the model that both receives and delivers information to all the other processors.

In summary, according to the Parallel Distributed Processing Model, successful reading is dependent on a reader's abilities in four areas: automatic letter recognition, accurate phonemic processing, strong vocabulary knowledge, and the ability to construct meaningful messages during reading. The information within and between each of these processors is organized according to connectionist principles. Furthermore, the processors are all interactive and compensatory. These aspects of the Parallel Distributed Processing Model are directly derived from earlier work by Rumelhart (1977) and Stanovich (1980). The Parallel Distributed Processing Model is also consistent with the work of LaBerge and Samuels (1974) suggesting that when too much internal attention is used in lower level processing (in this case, the orthographic, meaning, and phonological processors), comprehension in higher-level processing (in this case, the context processor) will suffer. The model is representative of a cognitive processing perspective because it explains cognitive structures and systems inherent in reading.

TEACHER'S ANECDOTE:
PARALLEL DISTRIBUTED PROCESSING MODEL

When my students read rapidly and accurately I know they are using their orthographic processor to do so. When my high reading students come across a word that is extremely difficult I find that most of the time they will get the word right. I now know that is because these children are activating likely letter patterns and suppressing unlikely ones. In contrast, my slower readers often incorrectly read an unfamiliar word. I feel this may be because their letter recognition is not fast enough and, as a result, their brains are not searching for common letter patterns.

I also see the students using their context processors when they read. When we review stories I ask the children which words were difficult for them and how they figured them out. Most of the time I find that they came up with the meaning due to the message in the sentence or paragraph. I am delighted to see that they are using their context processors to help them identify words and figure out word meanings.

—DAWN SPRINITIS, reading specialist

## DUAL-ROUTE CASCADED MODEL

In 1993, Coltheart, Curtis, Atkins, and Haller published a research article that contrasted the Parallel Distributed Processing Model (Seidenberg & McClelland, 1989), described above, with their model of reading, the Dual-Route Cascaded Model. According to Coltheart et al. (1993), the Parallel Distributed Processing Model and the Dual-Route Cascaded Model are similar in that both are computer-based models that encode text and output sound. The primary difference between the two models is in the way word identification is conceptualized to be handled by the computer architecture. In the Parallel Distributed Processing Model all words and nonwords (i.e., words that are made up for experimental purposes) are "read" by the computer in a single path that exists for turning print into sound. As described earlier, this path is based on a system in which the principles of Connectionism (connections are weighted according to frequency of pairings) govern relationships.

In contrast to the Parallel Distributed Processing Model, the Dual-Route Cascaded Model computer architecture has two routes for processing text input: one path for handling words that are already known to the reader/computer and another path for handling unknown words and nonwords. In the Dual-Route Cascaded Model, familiar words are read by a dictionary look-up system known as the "lexical route." The *lexical route* first identifies a word as familiar, and then processes the word as a whole, immediately providing the reader/computer with the word's correct meaning and pronunciation. In simple terms, the lexical route can be thought of as a "whole-word" or "sight-word" approach to reading in which words are automatically recognized rather than broken down according to sound–symbol relationships.

The second route of the Dual-Route Cascaded Model is called the "nonlexical route" or the "sublexical route." The *nonlexical route* is based on a letter-to-sound rule procedure. In the Dual-Route Cascaded Model, this path is only used for words and letter strings that are unfamiliar to the reader. One hundred and forty-four grapheme–phoneme correspondence rules govern the computer architecture of the Dual-Route Cascaded Model. These rules are applied to incoming letter strings (words and nonwords) as the computer "reads." The degree to which the computer is able to correctly pronounce the letter strings that are presented is judged to be an indicator of the effectiveness of the model in representing human cognitive processing during reading. The Dual-Route Cascaded Model argues that acquisition and knowledge of rules is one feature that distinguishes better and poorer readers: better readers have a greater grasp of the rules that govern letter–sound relationships, while poorer readers have a weaker grasp of this information.

In short, the foundational differences between the Parallel Distributed Processing Model approach and the Dual-Route Cascaded Model processing approach are the use of two processing routes and a "rules-based" system in the latter, while the former postulates a single processing route organized according to principles of Connectionism based of weighted relationships. Additionally, in the Dual-Route Cascaded Model the term "cascaded" refers to the speed with which levels of the model within the two routes are activated during the reading process. In this model information is passed from one level to the next without waiting for full processing. The Dual-Route Cascaded Model is described very briefly here. For further information readers should see Coltheart and Rastle (1994) and Coltheart, Rastle, Perry, Langden, and Ziegler (2001).

## TEACHER'S ANECDOTE:
## DUAL-ROUTE CASCADED MODEL

I can tell which branch of the Dual-Route Cascaded Model a student is using when she answers comprehension questions after orally reading a new story or passage. If an on-level reader can decode a passage with basic, grade-level vocabulary words both quickly and accurately, I know that she has used the lexical route. Her use of the lexical route is further proved when the student reads with fluency and does not need to sound out a word. I also know that a student is employing her lexical route if she correctly answers comprehension questions about full text or individual word meaning without having to refer back to the passage.

Contrarily, a student employs different reading behaviors when she uses the letter-to-sound route. When a student quickly mumbles, or cascades, over an unfamiliar word and cannot explain the meaning of the sentence or passage, I know that she has used the letter-to-sound route. Upon observing this type of behavior, I know as a teacher that I need to reread the sentence with my student and explain a word's meaning so that she can fully process the information.

—MICHELLE HILKE, third-grade teacher

## DOUBLE-DEFICIT HYPOTHESIS

Wolf and Bowers (1999) proposed the Double-Deficit Hypothesis to explain the cause of reading disabilities. Wolf and Bowers argue that the Phonological–Core Variable Difference Model (Stanovich, 1988), in which a phonological deficit is viewed as the primary cause of reading disability (see Chapter 8), is incomplete. According to the Double-Deficit Hypothesis, many reading-disabled children also suffer from a deficit in rapid naming skill. Children with this deficit are less able to rapidly recite names of colors when shown pictures of colored blocks, less able to rapidly name objects when shown pictures of objects, and less able to rapidly name letters and numbers when shown strings of such print. According to Wolf and Bowers's model, reading-disabled children fall into one of three categories: children for whom phonological deficits are the core of their reading disability, children for whom naming speed deficits are the core of their reading disability, and children for whom both phonological deficits and naming speed deficits are problematic. The children who fall into the last category, those with a "double deficit," are also those whose reading impairment is most severe.

Wolf and Bowers acknowledge that many researchers recognize that naming speed is a deficit among disabled readers, but also note that others categorize the naming speed deficit as a subarea of the phonological deficit. In contrast, their Double-Deficit Hypothesis views naming speed as a distinct and separate entity uniquely contributing to reading failure. Those who believe in the Double-Deficit Hypothesis argue that educational interventions ideally matched to the different subtypes of disabled readers are needed.

## TEACHER'S ANECDOTE: DOUBLE-DEFICIT HYPOTHESIS

Knowing about the continuing debate on Rapid Automatized Naming Test (RAN) and phonemic awareness (PA) has produced a number of changes in my interactions with my students, their parents, and their classroom teachers. First, I use RAN scores to help me determine which children are most at risk for difficulty learning to read in first grade. Second, I have discussed the significance of both the RAN and phonemic awareness scores with kindergarten teachers. They, in turn, have become better at identifying which children have poor RAN and/or PA scores and which have other issues. Third, after I have discussed the scores with parents, they have tended to become more actively involved in providing reading support for their child. They are less likely to dismiss the child's difficulties as something the child will grow out of by the third grade. Fourth, both parents and the first-grade teachers are less likely to say that the child doesn't "know" phonics, and more likely to understand that the child is having great difficulty saying what she does know. Fifth, sometimes the child can appreciate that he knows what he is doing when he reads. He may be slow now, but he will get faster with time and effort. This self-awareness produces a much better attitude than the too common ones of discouragement and defeat. Sixth, I scour the reading research literature for articles on RAN and better ways to teach my students. My knowledge of the problem has led to my "ownership" of the problem. I keep looking for ways to provide my students with the best support available.

—CHARLOTTE KANTZ, ESL/reading teacher

## NEUROSCIENCE AND EDUCATION

As stated earlier, the cognitive processing perspective, also called cognitive science, is a theoretical and conceptual lens used to describe how people think, or, in the current text, how people read. The roots of the cognitive processing/cognitive science prospective grow out of linguistics.

Neuroscience also studies cognition, but it is rooted in biology. Neuroscience is concerned with the study of neurons and cells. According to Goswami (2004), neuroscience is "the processes by which the brain learns and remembers, from the molecular and cellular levels right through to the brain system" (p. 1). Goswami writes:

> Brain cells (or neurons) transmit information via electrical signals that pass from cell to cell via the synapses, triggering the release of neurotransmitters (chemical messengers). There are around 100 billion neurons in the brain, each with massive connections to other neurons. Understanding the ways in which neurotransmitters work is a major goal of neuroscience. (p. 1)

In contrast to the terms "cognitive science," which is theoretical in nature, and "neuroscience," which is biological in nature, the term "cognitive neuroscience" refers to the study of higher patterns of brain functioning through brain imaging technology (Goswami, 2004). Goswami explains:

> Patterns of neural activity are thought to correspond to particular mental states or mental representations. Learning broadly comprises changes in connectivity, either via changes in potentiation at the synapses or via the strengthening or pruning of connections. Successful teaching thus directly affects brain functioning by changing connectivity. (pp. 1–2)

Patterns of brain activity, which are believed to reflect mental states, mental representations, and learning, can be viewed in a number of ways (Goswami, 2004). This viewing of brain activity is known as "neuroimaging." Neuroimaging can be done through positron emission tomography, functional magnetic resonance imaging, and event-related potentials.

*Positron emission tomography* (PET) is a technique in which radioactive tracers are injected into experimental subjects or patients who subsequently perform tasks. The PET technology identifies the areas of neural activity by following the tracers. The PET procedure is invasive and not appropriate for children.

*Functional magnetic resonance imaging* (fMRI) is a noninvasive neuroimaging procedure. In fMRI, participants lie in a large machine designed to monitor the magnetic resonance signal, which is created by the amount of water in neural cells. When activity in a particular brain area occurs, blood flow increases there, bringing with it a charge in the magnetic resonance signal. The fMRI measures changes in the magnetic resonance signal. fMRIs are also difficult to use with children because subjects must remain very still within the fMRI machine that can be noisy and frightening. Goswami (2004) reports that as technology advances fMRI machines that are more suitable for use with children are being developed.

A third neuroimaging technique is *event-related potentials* (ERPs). In ERP monitoring electrodes are attached to specific areas of the skull with a putty-like substance. After the electrodes are in place the subject is asked to perform a variety of tasks. In ERPs, the timing (rather than the location) of brain activity is recorded. This technique allows researchers to determine how quickly or slowly visual and auditory stimuli are perceived. ERPs can also document brain activation before, during, and after stimuli presentation.

Goswami (2004) reports several neuroscientific findings related to reading. For example, she states that neuroimaging has confirmed earlier beliefs that the left side of the brain handles the primary systems involved in the reading process. Specifically, she summarizes work by Pugh et al. (2001), who found that the occipital, temporal, and parietal areas are largely responsible for processing print. She also discussed Shaywitz et al.'s (2002) findings that as reading skill improves it is accompanied by increased activation in the temporal–occipital region of the brain. Additionally, children diagnosed with developmental dyslexia showed decreased activity in this region when compared with normally functioning peers. Goswami also reviews the work of Simos et al. (2002), who found the temporal–parietal junction to be central to phonological processing, letter–sound recoding, and spelling dysfunction. Simos et al. (2002) reported that dyslexic children showed impaired neuroimaging performance, compared to normally developing readers, during a task related to rhyming. Impressively, these authors also demonstrated that, following a remedial intervention, the dyslexic children's neuroimaged performances improved. Finally, Goswami discusses the results of Heim, Eulitz, and Elbert (2003), who have shown that neuroimaging of dyslexic children reveals atypical organization of the right side of the brain consistent with the development of compensation strategies.

Although neuroscience currently has few classroom applications, Goswami (2004) believes that neuroscience will be an important part of the future of research in education. She predicts that it will be used increasingly for the early diagnosis of children in need of special education and in the study of the effects of varying interventions on learners of all ages and abilities.

---

## TEACHER'S ANECDOTE: NEUROSCIENCE AND EDUCATION

I recently taught a third-grade student who was at the preprimer reading level. Classified with a learning disability in reading, she had trouble with basic rhyming tasks, she could not identify short vowel sounds, and she had trouble representing sounds with the correct letters.

As the majority of her classmates were at or above grade level in reading when they entered my classroom, it was difficult for me to understand or to determine why she had such discrepancies in her reading ability.

I now realize that she probably has impairments in the occipital, temporal, and parietal areas of her brain, where print processing occurs. She has had intense remedial reading instruction for 3 years. It would be interesting to learn if a postremediation neuroimage would display any improvement in the print processing areas of her brain.

—MICHELLE HILKE, third-grade teacher

---

## CLASSROOM APPLICATIONS

The Parallel Distributed Processing Model suggests that four key processors are used during reading: the orthographic processor that handles visual input, the phonemic processor that links sounds to print, the meaning processor that provides meanings for vocabulary words, and the context processor that is responsible for constructing and maintaining a coherent message during the reading experience. Additionally, the model is connectionist in nature, meaning that information is portrayed as being stored in the brain as a series of connections of differing strengths. As the frequency of any connection increases, so does the strength of the connection. Within the field of reading, Connectionism implies that there are stronger associations between letters and words that frequently follow each other than those that don't.

In terms of classroom application, the Parallel Distributed Processing Model suggests that reading is dependent on automatic letter recognition and that unless letter identification is automatic the interletter associational unit system will not initiate, greatly impairing reading fluency (Adams, 1990). Thus classroom instruction that develops rapid letter identification is essential. Carnine et al. (2004) offer four guidelines for effective letter instruction: (1) initially introduce only the most common sounds associated with each letter, (2) teach separately letters that are highly similar in sound or print, (3) teach letters that are most frequent first, and (4) teach lowercase letters before uppercase letters. These authors assert that the pace at which letters are taught should be determined by the students' success rate. Carnine et al. suggest that letter instruction should begin with an introductory phase based on modeling and student repetition, and be followed by a discriminatory phase in which students' knowledge of newly learned letters is tested against their knowledge of previously learned letters.

The Parallel Distributed Processing Model also indicates that helping students learn to read by using *word families* (frequent letter combinations such as the *ate* family and the *in* family) is highly effective because this approach reinforces connections between letters that frequently occur together (Adams, 1990). There are a wide variety of activities based on word families. These include matching games, sorting games, and activities that keep the word family ending and change the initial letter. For example, students can create small books containing words and pictures for each of the major and minor word families. When students are taught to read using word families their knowledge of common letter patterns within words is strengthened. According to the Parallel Distributed Processing Model, such learning will positively contribute to overall reading proficiency (Adams, 1990).

The Dual-Route Cascaded Model (Coltheart et al., 1993; Coltheart & Rastle, 1994) suggests that readers process text through two routes: one for handling words that are already known and another for words that are unknown. In this model, familiar words are read by sight using a dictionary, whole-word, look-up system, and unfamiliar words are decoded according to a rules-based system. Thus the Dual-Route Cascaded Model emphasizes the importance of automatic, sight-word recognition.

Carnine et al. (2004) dedicate a chapter of their text to sight-word instruction. In sight-word reading students do not sound out words; rather, they look at them and pronounce them automatically. *Highfrequency words* (those that occur with the greatest frequency in the English language) are often taught as sight words because there is a great payoff for the reader in knowing very common words. Additionally, high-frequency words (e.g., *the, this, through*, and *there*) are often phonetically irregular and therefore well suited to sight-word instruction. Carnine et al. suggest that sight-word instruction begin with lists and then progress to application in paragraphs. Introductory lessons can start when students know four words. When students are able to read each word in 2 seconds or less, new sight words can be added to the list, although it is recommended that word lists do not exceed 15 words. When students are able to read approximately 15 sight words on a list at a pace of 2–3 seconds per word, paragraphs that are based on the sight words, combined with easily decodable words, should be provided for students. Young readers need much practice in reading sight words in text. As they practice known sight words during text reading new sight words can be introduced and practiced in lists. Lists of high-frequency words as well as other words ideal for teaching by sight can be found in Fry and colleagues' (2000) classic book, *The Reading Teacher's Book of Lists*.

The Double-Deficit Hypothesis (Wolf & Bowers, 1999) suggests that there are two distinct areas of cognitive deficit in the most disabled dyslexic readers: phonological processing and rapid naming. Wolf et al. (2000) created and evaluated the RAVE-O program (Retrieval, Automaticity, Vocabulary, Elaboration, Orthography) specifically to address the needs of readers believed to have double deficits in their cognitive processing. As summarized by Wolf and Katzir-Cohen (2001), the program's goal is to increase readers' speed in the areas of auditory processing, visual pattern recognition, word identification, and vocabulary. The program, taught in conjunction with a high-quality phonological program, teaches a specific set of words each week that "exemplify critical phonological, orthographic, and semantic principles" (p. 231). Wolf and Katzir-Cohen write, "Each core word is chosen on the basis of (a) shared phonemes with the phonological treatment program, (b) sequenced orthographic patterns, and (c) semantic richness (e.g., each word has at least three different meanings)" (p. 231). The RAVE-O program emphasizes rapid identification of the most common orthographic patterns/word families in the English language and rapid vocabulary retrieval. Every core word in the program is taught daily. Metacognitive strategies are also emphasized. The RAVE-O program is suitable for small-group instruction in classrooms, and preliminary data support its effectiveness (Wolf et al., 2000).

## RESEARCH APPLICATIONS

Many of the studies in the literature that use the Parallel Distributed Processing Model as a theoretical lens contrast it with the Dual-Route Cascaded Model. Researchers who are affiliated with promoting one or the other of the competing computational theories often conduct these studies. Such is the case in the work of Seidenberg, Plaut, Peterson, McClelland, and McRae (1994), who used an updated version of the Parallel Distributed Processing Model (Plaut & McClelland, 1993) and the Dual-Route Cascaded Model (Coltheart et al., 1993) to examine college-age subjects' reading of nonwords. *Nonwords* are text stimuli that contain letter patterns found in the English language (e.g., -ANT, -OWN, -ANCE) but are preceded by consonant onsets that don't make real words (e.g., BANT, COWN, FANCE). An understanding of how subjects process nonwords during word recognition tasks has been a central issue for researchers who strive to create computational (computer-based) word recognition models.

Seidenberg et al. (1994) gave 24 university undergraduates 590 nonwords to read aloud in an experimental setting. The subjects were informed that the stimuli were nonwords but instructed to read them aloud as though they were real words. The nonwords were presented via a computer that also recorded the latency of the subjects' responses (i.e., the length of time it took them to pronounce the nonword). Study results indicated much agreement in subjects' reading of nonwords: subjects pronounced 83.7% of all nonwords similarly. The length of time it took a subject to read a nonword (i.e., the naming latency) varied with the number of pronunciations produced by the group of subjects and how often the subjects used the pronunciation. For example, nonwords that had two likely pronunciations (e.g., BAVE) took longer to read than those that had just one likely pronunciation (e.g., FEN). Pronunciations that were used more frequently by subjects (BAVE pronounced similarly to RAVE rather than like HAVE) also had shorter latencies.

In the discussion section of their paper the authors described the ways in which the Parallel Distributed Processing Model versus the Dual-Route Cascaded Model would explain the findings of the study. In general, the authors found that the Dual-Route Cascaded Model would explain the findings by reiterating that the subjects used rules to govern how they would pronounce each nonword, while the Parallel Distributed Processing Model would suggest that the subjects' pronunciations were a function of preexisting weighted associations that led them to generalize the pronunciation of the words in one way rather than another. The finding that the subjects took longer to read nonwords that contained patterns used in multiple pronunciations (e.g., BAVE) than those that had single pronunciations (e.g., FEN) was judged by the authors to be more supportive of the Parallel Distributed Processing Model. The authors argued that a single processing path would take longer to process ambivalent stimuli (nonwords with multiple likely pronunciations) than to process nonambivalent stimuli. Conversely, they argued that the finding of the longer latencies for ambivalent nonwords would not be predicted by the Dual-Route Cascaded Model because it suggests that all unknown words are handled equally by a second processing path. It is important to note, however, that Seidenberg, Plaut, Peterson, McClelland, and McRae are advocates of the Parallel Distributed Processing Model and that much of their research is designed to highlight the superiority of this model over the Dual-Route Cascaded Model conceptualization of cognitive processing during reading.

In a study framed by the Double-Deficit Hypothesis, Cardoso-Martins and Pennington (2004) examined the relationships between phoneme awareness, rapid naming skills, developmental period, and reading ability. Their longitudinal study followed the literacy development of 124 children. Sixty-seven children were categorized as high risk based on the fact that at least one parent had experienced great difficulty in learning how to read. Fifty-seven children were categorized as low risk because their parents had not experienced reading difficulty. The children's literacy development was followed over a period of 3 years during which all children were tested four times a year with a battery of literacy assessments. Overall, the results showed that both phonemic awareness and rapid naming play important roles in learning to read. However, Cardoso-Martins and Pennington (2004) write:

Nonetheless, relative to phoneme awareness, rapid naming seems to play a modest role in early alphabetic literacy acquisition. In particular, its effect is stronger in lower ability readers and is restricted to particular literacy outcomes, whereas phoneme awareness has a robust predictive relationship across ability levels and literacy outcomes. (p. 47)

The results of Cardoso-Martins and Pennington's (2004) study support the Double-Deficit Hypothesis because both phonemic awareness and naming speed were found to be important variables in reading development. According to this study, phonemic awareness skill has a robust effect on the reading development of all readers. In contrast, rapid naming speed ability appears to be a significant factor only for children who are less able readers.

In an exciting application of neuroscience to education, 77 children ages 6.1–9.4 years old participated in a study of the effects of varied reading interventions on their reading fluency and brain activation patterns, as measured by fMRIs (Shaywitz et al., 2004). The criteria for classification as a reading-disabled student included performance below the 25th percentile on either the Word Identification or Word Attack subtests of the Woodcock Reading Mastery Tests (Woodcock, 1987) and performance below the 25th percentile on the average of both tests.

The 77 children were divided into three groups. Thirty-seven children in the experimental intervention (EI) received, on average, 105 hours of an instructional intervention during an 8-month period (September–May). The instruction, which was highly structured, explicit, and systematic, was designed to focus children's attention on letter–sound relationships and the sounds of letters within words. Daily opportunities to apply this instruction to meaningful text reading were also provided. Students in the EI condition received their regular classroom reading instruction in addition to their EI instruction, but did not receive any other educational support such as supplemental resource room help, basic skills training, or private tutoring.

Twelve children participated in the community intervention (CI). These children received their regular classroom reading instruction as well as a range of educational services normally offered to students with learning difficulties (e.g., remedial reading instruction, resource room support, and private tutoring). Eighty-three percent of these students received more than one form of educational support. Unfortunately, the average amount of time that the students received support was not reported.

Twenty-eight children served as subjects in the community control (CC) condition. None of these students had reading difficulties, scoring at or above the 39th percentile on the previously mentioned measures. These children received only their regular classroom reading instruction during the course of the study.

All students were pretested on the previously mentioned tasks and given an fMRI prior to the outset of the research project. The fMRI was used to examine students' brain activation patterns during a letter identification task. At the conclusion of the 8-month project all measures were repeated. The results of the research indicated that students in the EI condition had significantly greater gains on measures of reading fluency (as determined by performance on the Gray Oral Reading Test) than did students in the CI condition. Additionally, results from the fMRIs indicated that both the EI and CC subjects showed increased activation in areas of the brain judged to be critical during the reading process. Subjects in the CI condition did not demonstrate this growth. Furthermore, when EI subjects were subsequently tested 1 year later, statistically significant increases in brain activation in these areas remained.

This study was very important for a number of reasons. First, the results of the investigation revealed that different reading interventions differentially affect reading-disabled students in both their behavioral performances (e.g., reading fluency as measured by an educational test) and their brain activation patterns as measured by fMRIs. Second, the results suggest that the increases in brain activation patterns are long lasting. This research suggests that fMRIs could someday be a part of routine educational assessment, allowing educators to better understand students' cognitive profiles and the effects of specific interventions on those profiles.

## SUMMARY

This chapter presents four prominent, current, cognitive processing lenses on reading: the Parallel Distributed Processing Model lens (Rumelhart & McClelland, 1986; Seidenberg & McClelland, 1989), the Dual-Route Cascaded Model lens (Coltheart et al., 1993; Coltheart & Rastle, 1994), the Double-Deficit Hypothesis lens (Wolf & Bowers, 1999), and the neuroscientific lens (Goswami, 2004). According to the Parallel Distributed Processing Model (Rumelhart & McClelland, 1986; Seidenberg & McClelland, 1989), successful reading is dependent on a reader's abilities in four areas: automatic letter recognition, accurate phonemic processing, strong vocabulary knowledge, and the ability to construct meaningful messages during reading. The information within and between each of these processors is organized according to connectionist principles. Furthermore, the processors are all interactive and compensatory. In contrast to the Parallel Distributed Processing Model, the Dual-Route Cascaded Model (Coltheart et al., 1993; Coltheart & Rastle, 1994) suggests two routes for processing text input: one path for handling words that are already known to the reader/computer and another path for handling unknown words and nonwords. In the Dual-Route Cascaded Model, familiar words are read by a dictionary, whole-word, look-up system, known as the lexical route. The second route of the Dual-Route Cascaded Model, called the nonlexical or sublexical route, is based on a letter-to-sound rule procedure. Wolf and Bowers's (1999) Double-Deficit Hypothesis is a theory used to explain the cause of reading disabilities. According to Wolf and Bowers's model, reading-disabled children fall into one of three categories: children for whom phonological deficits are the core of their reading disability, children for whom naming speed deficits are the core of their reading disability, and children for whom both phonological deficits and naming speed deficits are problematic. The children who fall into the last category, those with a double deficit, are also those whose reading impairment is most severe. The neuroscientific lens examines patterns of brain functioning during reading through the use of brain imaging technology (Goswami, 2004).

# CHAPTER 10

# Putting It All Together

The anecdote about 8-year-old Sara, which launched this text (see Chapter 1, p. 1), can now be reconsidered. The chapters in this book suggest that theories and models can be used as lenses to understand situations such as Sara's. Furthermore, the book suggests that each of these lenses gives rise to directions for intervention and research. This chapter explores the feasibility of using each of the theories and models in this text as a lens to explain Sara's reading difficulty and as a tool to provide direction for her teacher's intervention.

## EARLY ROOTS

According to Mental Discipline Theory (Plato, Aristotle), Sara's weakness in reading would be attributed to a lack of practice. Mental Discipline Theory presents the brain as a muscle that needs to be strengthened, much like a muscle in the body needs to be strengthened in order to succeed in a sport. Educators interested in exploring the essence of Mental Discipline Theory as a source of Sara's reading difficulty would gather information about the amount of reading practice in which she engages both at home and at school. If the amount of practice time were judged to be insufficient, increased reading practice would be indicated. Although Mental Discipline Theory is over 2,000 years old, many educators still view its primary premise, time on task, as a critical component of reading success.

Associationism also dates back to the work of Aristotle and the fourth century B.C. Aristotle speculated about three kinds of connections that would aid memory and learning: *contiguity* (things that occur together in time tend to become associated), *similarity* (things that are similar tend to become associated), and *contrast* (things that are opposite tend to become associated). Applying Associationism to Sara's reading problem, one would investigate the types of mental connections that Sara makes before, during, and after reading. Weaknesses in her thinking would be remediated by an intervention that focused on strengthening her mental connections before, during, and after reading. Brainstorming prior to reading is a good example of a contemporary application of Associationism that might help Sara if she were not making sufficient mental connections before reading.

The Unfoldment Theory, fostered by the writings of Rousseau, Pestalozzi, and Froebel in the period from the mid-1700s to the early 1800s, emphasized the central role of children's curiosity in learning. Applying Unfoldment Theory to Sara's reading situation, one would question whether or not the assigned reading materials were of interest to her. An educator who believed strongly in Unfoldment Theory would likely vary the reading materials given to Sara to see if her reading improved in response to texts that were of greater interest to her. Additionally, Froebel's work in Unfoldment Theory added awareness of the significant role of play in learning. Educators interested in this dimension of Unfoldment Theory would investigate the use of games and dramatic engagement in Sara's reading development.

Structuralism, a theory dating from the late 1800s to the early 1900s, sought to explain learning through the study of perceptual processes. Structuralism suggests that Sara's reading problem might be caused by factors related to print perception. Advocates of this theory would examine Sara's visual processing and create interventions based on print perception, perhaps by varying the size of the print and the type and color of the font in the texts she is assigned. Modern followers of Structuralism would probably use electronic interventions such as text-to-speech software and the digitized highlighting of text during the reading process to aid Sara's visual processing.

The theories described in Chapter 2 of this book date as far back as 2,000 years ago and even the "youngest" of them in 100 years old, yet they still have applications in the modern classroom. As has been shown, these theories provide information that can be used to understand students' reading difficulties and suggest directions for the remediation of their reading problems.

## BEHAVIORISM

Behaviorism is a theoretical perspective of learning that focuses on observable changes in behavior. From a behavioral perspective, the outcome of learning is a changed behavior. In a behavioral perspective, learning is seen as "a change in an individual caused by experience" (Slavin, 1997, p. 151). There are three major behavioral theories: Classical Conditioning Theory, created by Ivan Pavlov and John Watson; Connectionism, proposed by Edward Thorndike; and Operant Conditioning Theory, established by B. F. Skinner. All three theories are built on the earlier foundation of Associationism, presented in Chapter 2.

Classical Conditioning Theory suggests that learning occurs through the process of association. In Pavlov's famous studies, dogs began to salivate when they heard the ringing of a bell because they associated the bell with the arrival of their food dishes. Although Classical Conditioning Theory is not often used to explain the reading process or reading difficulties, Sara's distress at reading aloud during class can be viewed through a Classical Conditioning Theory lens. This perspective suggests that Sara's in-class oral reading has become associated with failure. The intervention suggested by this theory would be to pair Sara's reading efforts with success. Sara's teacher might begin by reading to Sara and building positive associations with reading in that context. Next, the teacher and Sara could take turns reading easy material to each other. When Sara is successful in this situation, her teacher could gradually increase the difficulty level of Sara's texts and giver her greater responsibility for the reading. When she is ready, Sara could then take a turn reading aloud to the class. This instructional intervention is consistent with Classical Conditioning Theory because in each step of the process the goal is to build an association between the act of reading and positive experiences and feelings for Sara.

While Pavlov and Watson were primarily interested in events that preceded actions, Edward L. Thorndike extended the study of Behaviorism by showing that "stimuli that occurred after a behavior [also] had an influence on future behaviors" (Slavin, 1998, p. 154). Thorndike created Connectionism, which posits four laws: the Law of Effect, the Law of Readiness, the Law of Identical Elements, and the Law of Exercise. The Law of Effect, also known as the Principle of Reinforcement, states that when satisfying events follow behaviors, it is likely that those behaviors will be repeated. Conversely, when unsatisfying events follow behaviors, it is unlikely that those behaviors will be repeated. The Law of Readiness states that learning is enhanced when easier tasks precede those that are related but more difficult. The Law of Identical Elements states that the more elements of one situation are identical to elements in a second situation, the greater the transfer of knowledge, and thus the easier the learning in the second situation. Finally, the Law of Exercise states that the more stimulus–response connections are practiced, the stronger the bonds between them become. The less the connections are used, the weaker the bonds.

The Laws of Effect, Readiness, Identical Elements, and Exercise can easily be applied as lenses through which to understand and provide directions for intervention for Sara's reading problems. The Law of Readiness suggests that Sara should be given easy reading material for practice and instruction prior to receiving more difficult material. The Law of Effect suggests that positive experiences should follow each reading session. The Law of Identical Elements indicates that the reading of similar types of materials containing similar vocabulary words will enhance Sara's developing skills. Last, the Law of Exercise would investigate the amount of reading practice in which Sara engages, and recommend additional practice to further strengthen her ability.

Skinner's Operant Conditioning Theory further extended Behaviorism. Skinner continued Pavlov's and Watson's work on the importance of Associationism in learning. He also continued Thorndike's work regarding the relationships between behavior and its consequences. Skinner's research focused on the use of reinforcement and punishment in changing behavior. He experimented with varying the immediacy of consequences and schedules of reinforcement. He also refined the concept of *shaping*, in which behaviors that successively approximate desired behaviors are reinforced.

Application of an Operant Conditioning Theory lens to Sara's reading problems would investigate the use of reinforcers and punishers in the learning situation. The reading task itself would be viewed as composed of isolated skills that could be individually identified and reinforced. Reading readiness skills such as knowledge of letter names and sounds would be reviewed and correct responses to each learning task would be reinforced with positive consequences such as praise, candy, points, stickers, or tokens. Using the concept of shaping, initially all reading responses would be rewarded. Gradually, however, the rewards would be used for reading behaviors that approximated more complex, mature, fluent, grade-level performance.

Theories comprising Behaviorism dominated the field of American education from 1900 to 1950. Since then, many alternative educational theories have been proposed. Behaviorism, however, has retained a place in contemporary American education. To this day, many children's educational, psychological, and reading problems are examined and treated through this lens.

## CONSTRUCTIVISM AND READING

In approximately the same time period that Behaviorism was developing and impacting the American educational system, Constructivism was also influencing American educators. Constructivism is a theory of learning that emphasizes the *active construction* of knowledge by individuals (Woolfolk, 1998). From a constructivist viewpoint, learning occurs when individuals integrate new knowledge with existing knowledge. In this theoretical perspective, the integration of new knowledge with existing knowledge can only occur when the learner is actively involved in the learning process.

John Dewey was one of the first American constructivists. His notion of learning was based on the early Unfoldment Theory as developed by Rousseau, Pestalozzi, and Froebel. Incorporating the work of these classic philosophers and educators, Dewey emphasized the growth of the individual, the importance of the environment, and the role of the teacher in students' learning. His work also emphasized the importance of problems-based learning and social collaboration. Dewey argued that to optimize learning, students needed to work together to formulate hypotheses, collect data to test hypotheses, draw conclusions, and reflect on the original problem and the thinking processes needed to solve it. Dewey's philosophy of education became known as Inquiry Learning.

The application of Dewey's Inquiry Learning to Sara's reading difficulties would consider the effects of a problems-based approach and the impact of social collaboration on Sara's reading skills. Constructivists who believe in Inquiry Learning would suggest that Sara should be given reading material in a subject area about which she is very curious, and that a problem related to the reading material should be posed for her to solve. Sara would then be required to read and write to solve the problem. Inquiry Learning also suggests that this experience should include social collaboration as part, if not all, of the lesson. For example, if Sara were interested in the topic of travel, she could be asked to choose a destination where she would like to go. After reading about the destination, she could be encouraged to create a travel brochure advertising her special place. Other students could create their own brochures or help Sara create hers.

Schema Theory is another constructivist theory. Anderson and Pearson (1984) extended Bartlett's (1932) writing on the topic. In their work, a *schema* refers to knowledge and the way it is organized in the mind. Additionally, Schema Theory includes the processes through which existing knowledge structures are modified to incorporate new information, and the ways in which schemas change across periods of time. According to Schema Theory, readers need adequate background knowledge on the subject of the reading text in order for comprehension to occur. Schema Theory states that readers must connect the material that they are reading with background knowledge on the topic that already exists in their minds.

An application of Schema Theory to Sara's reading problem would investigate the quality of her existing schemas (background knowledge) related to the reading topic and the process of reading. Schema Theory would also examine whether or not Sara was able to activate existing schemas and suggest ways to build her background knowledge if existing schemas were not sufficient. For example, if Sara were assigned a reading on the topic of the Civil War, the teacher would explore with Sara what she already knew about the Civil War. Useful instructional techniques for this activity include using a brainstorming or KWL chart. If the teacher found Sara's background schema to be insufficient, she would provide Sara with additional facts and/or active learning experiences about the Civil War prior to Sara's reading. Using instructional techniques related to Schema Theory, Sara's teacher might also teach her to pose questions prior to reading, and review the questions after reading. An example of an active learning experience that would increase background knowledge would be to create a map of the United States during the Civil War era.

Rosenblatt (1994) further extended the application of Schema Theory in the field of reading. Based on the idea that every individual is unique with regard to what constitutes his or her schema in any particular area, Rosenblatt argued that every reading experience is therefore unique to each individual as well. The notion that all readers have reading experiences that vary from one another forms the cornerstone of Rosenblatt's Transactional/Reader Response Theory. Rosenblatt's work also articulates two kinds of responses that all readers have to texts: efferent responses and aesthetic responses. *Efferent responses* are those that are factual and objective in nature; *aesthetic responses* are those that are feeling-based, personal, and subjective.

Applying Transactional/Reader Response Theory to Sara's reading difficulty, one would investigate her efferent and aesthetic responses to the reading material. The teacher might start by first reading a section of text to Sara and discussing her thoughts about the passages with Sara. The discussion would include statements and questions aimed to highlight both efferent and aesthetic responses from Sara. Gradually, Sara could be encouraged to independently take on more of the reading herself. Discussion of both efferent and aesthetic responses to the text would continue.

Psycholinguistic Theory (Goodman, 1967) is another theory that can be classified as Constructivist in nature. At the core of the Psycholinguistic Theory of reading is the assumption that reading is primarily a language process. A central component of the Psycholinguistic Theory is that readers rely on language cueing systems to help them rapidly read text. Although readers use multiple cueing systems, those most often cited in conjunction with Psycholinguistic Theory are the syntactic system, the semantic system, and the graphophonic information system. *Syntactic cues* are those related to the grammatical structure or syntax of the language that enable readers to predict the next words in the text. *Semantic cues* are those related to the meaning of the words and sentences that allow readers to predict the next words in the text. *Graphophonic* cues are those that are derived from the visual patterns of letters and words with their corresponding sounds that, again, allow readers to predict the next words in the text.

Application of Psycholinguistic Theory to Sara's reading problem would suggest that her teacher should examine her miscues (i.e., oral reading errors) to see which cueing systems Sara is and is not effectively using during reading. For example, an analysis of Sara's miscues might reveal that she is not correctly sounding out words—in other words, not making adequate use of graphophonic cues. This profile would indicate that Sara needs additional instruction in this skill area. Alternatively, Sara's miscue analysis might reveal that she is reading aloud words that do not make sense in a sentence. This profile would suggest that Sara is not adequately using her semantic cueing system, and would indicate that this area is in need of remediation. In short, the miscue analysis system of Psycholinguistic Theory will show Sara's strengths and weaknesses during reading and reveal areas for instructional intervention.

In 1971 Smith applied concepts from Psycholinguistic Theory to the teaching of reading in his highly influential book *Understanding Reading*. It was this work that laid the foundation for Whole Language Theory, a theory of literacy learning and instruction that has had a powerful impact on the field of literacy education since the 1980s. Whole Language Theory is a philosophy about how children learn to read from which educators derive strategies for teaching. Literacy learning in a Whole Language classroom is designed to be child-centered, meaningful, and functional. Additionally, literacy activities are purposefully integrated into the learning of content area subjects such as art, music, social studies, science, and math. In Whole Language Theory instruction the use of themes connects the content areas and literacy experiences. Varied genres of children's literature are the main source of reading material for instruction.

Application of a Whole Language Theory lens to Sara's reading difficulties would lead to questions about whether Sara is having adequate meaningful and functional experiences with literacy. Furthermore, this approach would examine the degree to which Sara's literacy instruction was integrated with her learning in other content areas. Interventions from a Whole Language Theory perspective would consist of creating authentic, personally meaningful literacy experiences for Sara, such as writing a letter to a favorite author about a book or researching a topic of special interest. Additionally, Sara's reading needs would be addressed during lessons in other content areas.

Metacognition is the process of thinking about one's own thinking. While studying the topic of metacognition, researchers determined that proficient readers employ a number of metacognitive strategies during reading that assist them in understanding their texts (Pressley, 2000). For example, proficient readers are aware of whether or not they comprehend what they are reading and employ "fix-up" strategies such as rereading, slowing down, or looking up word meanings when comprehension failures occur. Research consistently shows that, in contrast to the effective use of metacognitive strategies by good readers, poor readers do not possess these skills (Baker, 2002). As a result, Metacognitive Theory indicates that poor readers' comprehension can be enhanced through direct and explicit instruction of metacognitive skills. The application of Metacognitive Theory to Sara's reading difficulty would question whether or not she were employing metacognitive strategies during reading, and if she were not, would provide direct and explicit instruction in these areas to remediate her reading problems.

The constructivist theories reviewed in this book were Inquiry Learning, Schema Theory, Transactional Reader Response Theory, Psycholinguistic Theory, Whole Language Theory, and Metacognitive Theory. Constructivist theories focus extensively on the active construction of meaning by the reader. Despite this shared orientation, however, each of the theories suggests unique ways of viewing Sara's reading difficulty and unique approaches to its remediation.

## THEORIES OF LITERACY DEVELOPMENT

During the early 1900s, at about the same time that constructivist theorists such as Dewey (1916) were trying to explain the ways in which individuals create internal understanding, and behaviorist theorists such as Watson (1913) and Thorndike (1903, 1931) were trying to explain how learning could be understood in term of observable behavior, developmental theorists were trying to explain literacy growth from a longitudinal perspective. Theorists working from a developmental perspective attempt to explain the growth of specific behaviors and abilities across time.

Piaget (Piaget & Inhelder, 1969) can be considered a developmental theorist because he created the Theory of Cognitive Development that describes the ways in which the quality of children's thinking changes over time. Piaget articulated the factors that affect the quality of an individual's thinking as he or she grows, the processes that children use to adapt their thinking, and the stages through which children progress as they mature. Piaget's theory provides literacy educators with a general understanding of the ways in which children at different levels of maturity are likely to think and of the relationship between cognitive and literacy development. Applying the Theory of Cognitive Development to Sara's reading difficulty, a Piagetian would examine whether or not Sara was cognitively ready for the task of reading, which is inherently abstract. If it were determined that she was not yet cognitively mature enough to handle tasks involving abstract thinking, easier tasks would be given to her until her thinking skills matured more fully.

Maturation Theory, advocated by Morphett and Washburne (1931), supported the postponement of reading instruction until a child was developmentally old enough to be successful with the tasks of early reading. Morphett and Washburne's research indicated that the optimal time for children to begin reading instruction was 6 years and 6 months, and therefore they recommended that children not receive reading instruction until that age. The prevailing belief associated with this theory was that parents and educators would cause damage to children's reading ability if they attempted to teach reading to children who were too young. Although Maturation Theory has long been discredited, it survives in a much weakened form: many educators still believe that children should demonstrate a certain level of maturity prior to beginning formal reading instruction. Maturation Theory does not suggest additional or alternate recommendations that would be applicable to remediate Sara's reading difficulty.

In Holdaway's (1979) Theory of Literacy Development learning to read is viewed as a natural, developmental occurrence. Holdaway argues that learning to read begins in the home when children first see their parents read and have stories read to them. In this theory, parents are the models for children, and children strive to emulate what their parents do. This emulation results in children's first attempts, or approximations, at reading, which are usually quite inaccurate, or, in Holdaway's words, "gross approximations." Nonetheless, Holdaway believes that these first attempts at reading are, and should be, reinforced by parents. Gradually, according to this theory of literacy development, as more refined attempts at reading are reinforced, the child begins to actually read. Thus, in Holdaway's theory, the development of reading is natural and very much mimics children's natural development of oral language skills.

Examining Sara's reading problem from the perspective of the Theory of Literacy Development, one would investigate the quality of Sara's at-home reading situation and the degree to which Sara's teacher employs specific literacy practices. In addition to stressing the importance of a rich literacy home environment, the Theory of Literacy Development recommends a rich literacy classroom environment. Teachers can create this classroom environment by labeling key items around the room, using a classroom management style that fosters children's independence and self-regulation, and immersing children in meaningful language experiences with high-quality children's literature. Holdaway is also a strong advocate of promoting peer interaction among students. His most significant recommended instructional strategies are the use of big books and shared reading techniques. The Theory of Literacy Development suggests using all of these interventions in treating Sara's reading problem. Much of Holdaway's theory and associated practices are consistent with Emergent Literacy Theory (Clay, 1985).

Beginning in the 1980s educators interested in the development of reading ability began to propose theories regarding the stages through which readers pass as they move toward reading proficiency. Although reading development is in reality ongoing, continuous, and gradual, a stage perspective helps clarify the developmental process. Stages of reading development have been proposed by a number of reading theorists including Ehri (1991), Chall (1986), Gough, Juel, and Griffith (1992), and Frith (1985). In all of these Stage Models, readers go through a visual stage of word recognition, an alphabetic stage of word recognition, and an orthographic stage of word recognition.

Applying a Stage Model lens to Sara's reading difficulty, one would assess Sara to determine her level of development. If Sara were in the visual (logographic) stage of development, she would either be able to read whole words by sight or not be able to read them at all. For example, Sara might be able to read familiar words such as her own name and the words *mom* and *dad* but have no idea how to read the word *pad*. Since readers in the visual stage only have sight-word recognition available to them as a word recognition skill, Sara would be unable to use any other strategies to read the word *pad*. If Sara were able to begin to sound out the word *pad* using a letter-by-letter approach, she would be in the alphabetic stage. If Sara were able to decode the word *pad* by approaching it as *p-ad*, she would be in the orthographic stage in which she is able to break words apart into chunks. This is the final stage of reading development, the way in which mature readers attack unknown words. Sara's instructional intervention would be dependent on her developmental stage. For example, if she were in the visual stage of reading, she would be helped to learn the sounds of individual letters and word families to help her progress to the next level of reading.

While Stage Models have been invaluable in helping educators understand children's early reading development, this body of work has focused almost exclusively on the area of word recognition. Other theorists and researchers interested in studying early literacy development from a perspective broader than word recognition alone created what is now known as Emergent Literacy Theory. Emergent literacy theorists believe that children's development in the areas of listening, speaking, reading, and writing are all interrelated. They also believe that literacy development starts at birth and is continuous and ongoing. Since Emergent Literacy Theory holds as a basic belief the idea that children's listening, speaking, reading, and writing skills begin at birth, it also emphasizes the critical role that children's home environments have on the development of these abilities.

Followers of Emergent Literacy Theory would examine Sara's reading difficulties from a broad perspective including her abilities in the areas of listening, speaking, reading, and writing. This approach would also investigate the quality of her home literacy environment and her attitudes toward literacy learning. The Emergent Literacy Theory perspective would strive to ensure that Sara mastered concepts about books and concepts about print, in addition to the three levels of word recognition articulated by the Stage Model theorists. Teachers viewing Sara's reading problem from an Emergent Literacy Theory perspective would use many of the strategies suggested by other developmental theorists (e.g., Holdaway) to treat Sara's reading difficulty.

Family Literacy Theory, the final developmental theory presented in this text, refers to the study of the relationships between families and the development of literacy (Tracey, 1995). Research has now demonstrated that literacy-rich home environments contribute more powerfully to children's early, successful literacy development than do excellent preschool and kindergarten classrooms (Bus et al., 1995; Hart & Risley, 1999; Scarborough & Dobrich, 1994). Such homes provide reading environments that include books and other reading materials and family members who serve as models of involvement in literacy activities. In addition, parents of successful readers are usually involved with their children's schoolwork and seek information about their children's literacy development.

Using Family Literacy Theory (Taylor, 1983) to frame Sara's reading difficulties, one would focus on the quality of the literacy environment in Sara's home, including the frequency and quality of the interactions surrounding literacy she has with her family members. Interventions to help Sara from this perspective would try to both disseminate information to, and gather information from, Sara's family regarding her literacy development. Teachers might share information with Sara's parents about ways that they could help her with reading at home. Additionally, Family Literacy Theory recommends that teachers try to get parents to provide as much information as possible about Sara's literacy experiences at home. Family literacy experts view this two-way style of communication as optimal.

The developmental theories presented in this text include the Theory of Cognitive Development (Piaget, 1926), Maturation Theory (Morphett & Washburne, 1931), the Theory of Literacy Development

(Holdaway, 1979), Stage Models (Ehri, 1991; Frith, 1985; Pough et al., 1992; Chall, 1983), Emergent Literacy Theory (Clay, 1985), and Family Literacy Theory (Taylor, 1983). All of these theories present complementary ways of viewing children's early literacy development and are associated with techniques and interventions that can be used to understand and remediate Sara's reading difficulties.

## SOCIAL LEARNING PERSPECTIVES

When applied to the field of reading, the social learning perspective emphasizes the importance of social influences and social interaction on literacy learning. The first application of the social perspective to the field of reading emerged in the 1970s with Sociolinguistic Theory (Bernstein, 1972a, 1972b). Sociolinguistic Theory particularly emphasizes the role of an individual's language in reading acquisition and reading ability. According to Sociolinguistic Theory, varying patterns of social and language interactions subsequently lead to differences in individual reading skills.

The application of Sociolinguistic Theory to Sara's reading problem would be founded on an investigation of her oral language abilities. Assessments of Sara's ability to comprehend spoken language and produce oral language herself would be administered. Areas that would be examined would include Sara's comprehension and production of speech sounds, dialect, syntax (i.e., the ability to use and understand the correct order of words in sentences), and semantics (i.e., the ability to understand and produce sentences that are meaningful). If deficits were detected in any of these areas, Sociolinguistic Theory suggests that remediation of spoken language should be implemented. The use of a Language Experience Approach as an intervention for Sara would be a popular choice for a teacher using a Sociolinguistic Theory lens for reading remediation. This technique could help strengthen Sara's oral language skills while at the same time enhancing her understanding of concepts surrounding print.

Socio-Cultural Theory (Bronfenbrenner, 1979) emphasizes the roles of social, cultural, and historical factors in the human experience. Socio-Cultural Theory is similar to Sociolinguistic Theory because both emphasize the social aspect of learning, but Sociolinguistic Theory focuses more on the language aspects of these interactions while Socio-Cultural Theory focuses more on the broader concept of culture which includes, but is not limited to, language.

The application of Socio-Cultural Theory to Sara's case would start with an examination of the concentric layers of influence in her life. At the innermost and most powerful level of influence, the microsystem, Sara's home and classroom experiences would be studied to see if optimal conditions for literacy development were present. If they were not, attempts to intervene at these levels would be undertaken. Note, however, that Socio-Cultural Theory does not provide specific interventions for deficits. At the next level, the mesosystem, the quality of the relationship between Sara's home and school lives would be considered. Care would be taken to ensure that communication between Sara's teachers and parents was focused and effective. At the third and outermost level, the exosystem, factors affecting Sara's life at the community, national, and global levels would be explored. Thus, the Socio-Cultural Theory lens provides an opportunity to study the many levels by which Sara's reading development might be affected.

Social Constructivism, created by Vygotsky (1978) and also known as Socio-Historical Theory, is another social learning theory. Social Constructivism is based on the belief that "children's knowledge, ideas, attitudes, and values develop through interaction with others" (Woolfolk, 1999, p. 44). Social Constructivism also emphasizes the critical importance of the mastery of sign systems (e.g., oral language, writing, and counting) in children's development. A key concept in Social Constructivism is the *zone of proximal development*, which refers to the ideal level of task difficulty required to optimize learning. *Scaffolding*, another prominent Vygotskian idea, refers to the assistance that adults and more competent peers provide to children during educational episodes.

A Social Constructivist perspective on Sara's reading problem would study her interactions during literacy learning with her teachers, her parents, and her peers. Care would be taken to ensure that all of Sara's literacy tasks completed during social collaboration fell within her zone of proximal development and that high-quality scaffolding techniques were used by others with whom she interacted. As discussed in this text, the instructional techniques of partner, buddy, and cross-age reading would be likely choices for educators trying to address Sara's reading problems using a Social Constructivist perspective since the primary emphasis in all of these approaches is learning from one's peers.

Bandura (1969, 1977, 1986, 1997) developed Social Learning Theory, recently renamed Social Cognitive Theory. Bandura's primary reason for creating Social Learning Theory was his belief that the behavioral explanations of learning did not account for the phenomenon of vicarious learning, the notion that people learn from observing others. In fact, Bandura argued that people learn more from observing others than they do from the consequences of experiencing things themselves. In Social Learning Theory the people from whom we learn are called *models*. Similarly, *modeling* is the action performed by the model.

Social Learning Theory suggests that the models and the modeling in Sara's life would be important areas to examine regarding her reading problems. The models in Sara's life would include her family members, classroom teacher, and classmates. Social Learning Theory recommends that these models should engage in the kinds of behaviors that are desired for Sara, such as sustained silent reading of a wide variety of materials, the display of positive attitudes about reading, writing for a variety of purposes, and thoughtful discussion of materials that have been read. These modeling behaviors would be helpful in developing Sara's reading skills.

In addition to spawning Sociolinguistic Theory, Socio-Cultural Theory, Social Constructivism, and Social Learning Theory, the social learning perspective also provides the foundation for writings and investigations related to the political aspects of literacy education. Work that uses a political lens to examine literacy education falls under the umbrella of Critical Literacy Theory (Friere, 1970; Siegel & Fernandez, 2000). Critical Literacy Theory challenges the traditional belief that education is a politically neutral process designed to promote individual development. Instead, the theory argues that "teaching and the curriculum are political practices inasmuch as they produce knowledge for the purposes of social regulation" (Siegel & Fernandez, 2000, p. 141). This position asserts that one of the reasons that schools remain ineffective in low SES communities is to satisfy this country's need for workers willing to assume menial jobs (Gee, 1990). The application of Critical Literacy Theory to Sara's reading problem would question if everything possible were being done to remediate her deficits, and if not, why inadequacies in her treatment are allowed to exist.

The social learning perspective incorporates several different theories, all of which emphasize the central role of social interaction in the development of knowledge and learning. Sociolinguistic Theory, Social Constructivism, and Social Learning Theory all provide direction for explanation of and intervention for Sara's reading problems. Socio-Cultural Theory and Critical Literacy Theory provide broad viewpoints from which her reading can be understood.

## INFORMATION/COGNITIVE
## PROCESSING PERSPECTIVES

In the 1950s there was a shift in research from the study of observable behaviors related to learning to the study of unobservable cognitive behaviors related to learning. As a result, researchers in the fields of education and psychology began to investigate the underlying cognitive processes involved in reading.

Information processing theories and models represent one perspective within the cognitive theories and models orientation. According to Slavin (1997), "information processing theory is the cognitive theory of learning that describes the processing, storage, and retrieval of knowledge from the mind" (p. 185). Atkinson and Shiffrin's (1968) Information Processing Model, which suggests that information moves through different stages, or storage systems, as it is processed, reflected upon, learned, saved, and retrieved, most notably represents information processing theories. Stages in Atkinson and Shiffrin's model include the sensory register, the working memory, the articulatory loop, and long-term memory. Executive control processes organize the processing system and attention is central to its smooth and efficient operation.

If one were to apply the Information Processing Model to Sara's case, the lens would focus on the adequacy of the stages of the processing system. Care would be taken to evaluate Sara's visual perceptual system to make sure that data were being sufficiently perceived by her sensory register. Sara's short-term memory abilities would be evaluated to assess her resources for working memory, and her auditory processing skills would be examined to evaluate her abilities related to her articulatory loop. Sara's long-term memory abilities would also be measured, including her ability to organize and retrieve information from that processor. Sara's cognitive executive control processes would be investigated, as would her abilities in the area of attention. Deficits in any of these areas would be targeted during remediation, with the assumption that an improvement in Sara's overall ability to process information would be positively related to her reading ability.

Holmes's (1953) Substrata-Factor Theory of Reading was the first specific application of the cognitive processing perspective to the field of reading. Holmes identified variables and subvariables that were correlated with reading ability. In his work he used subvariables in the categories of cognitive ability, verbal ability, fine motor skills, eye movements, and personality factors to predict the speed and power of an individual's reading ability. The Substrata-Factor Theory of Reading would use these same variables to evaluate Sara's reading skills. Weaknesses in any area would be remediated in the belief that strengthening the underlying skills would lead to greater reading proficiency.

In Carver's (1977) Rauding Theory, the concept of general reading ability is referred to as "rauding efficiency level." Within rauding efficiency level are the factors "rauding accuracy level" and "rauding rate level." *Rauding accuracy level* reflects a reader's knowledge of vocabulary; *rauding rate level* refers to a reader's rate of typical reading (rauding). According to Carver (1995), research strongly supports these two subfactors as *the* critical components of standardized measures of reading comprehension. Carver's (1995) work has generated two important hypotheses that have been tested in research. The first is that reading improvement requires that readers use texts that are closely matched to their ability levels. The second is that the use of texts that are easy for readers helps them maintain an adequate reading rate. Rauding Theory suggests that Sara's reading problem indicates that the texts she is reading are too difficult for her. An intervention based on Rauding Theory would be to reduce her texts' difficulty until a comfortable rauding rate is found.

In 1972, Gough proposed a model of reading based on the information processing perspective. Early cognitive models of reading such as Gough's became known as "bottom-up" information processing models because they depicted the cognitive processing of information as proceeding from lower order to higher level stages. In Gough's model, as in the general information processing perspective, the reading process is depicted as consisting of a series of discrete stages. Gough calls his stages the scanner, the character register, the decoder, the code book, the librarian, the lexicon, the primary memory, and the TPWSGWTAU (the place where sentences go when they are understood). Gough's model was revised and renamed the Simple View in 1986, emphasizing reading comprehension as a result of two processes: decoding and language comprehension. As with Atkinson and Shiffrin's Information Processing Model, if one were to apply Gough's Model to Sara's case, the lens would focus on the adequacy of the stages of the processing system. Similarly, deficits in any of the processing areas would be targeted during remediation.

Another cognitive processing model of the reading process that emerged in the 1970s was the Automatic Information Processing Model (LaBerge & Samuels, 1974). The Automatic Information Processing Model is similar to Gough's Model (1972) in that it is linear and "bottom-up" in nature. The distinctive characteristic of LaBerge and

Samuels's model is its heavy emphasis on the importance of internal attention during the reading process. LaBerge and Samuels suggested that all readers have limited amounts of internal cognitive energy that can be used during the reading process, and that if too much of it is used for decoding not enough is left available for comprehension. This leads to reading failure.

To apply the Automatic Information Processing Model to Sara's reading case, one would review her skills related to the stages of information processing as described above, but especially focus on her decoding fluency. Sara's inability to decode fluently would be interpreted as an overuse of internal cognitive energy on decoding, which would be associated with, and lead to, comprehension deficits. The remedial solution indicated by this model would be to provide Sara with reading material at an easier level of difficulty. Easier reading materials allow for automaticity of decoding, which uses little internal attention. Sara's internal cognitive attention would then be available for her to use in comprehending the meaning of the text—the true goal of reading.

Rumelhart (1977) rejected bottom-up cognitive models of reading because they did not conceptually allow for higher level thinking (such as comprehending the meaning of a sentence) to influence lower level thinking (such as word identification). In Rumelhart's Interactive Model a variety of processors handle visual information simultaneously, rather than in a linear process. The simultaneous processing of syntactic information (word order within sentences), semantic information (message construction), orthographic information (visual input), and lexical information (vocabulary meaning) allows for higher level and lower level processes to simultaneously interact on the text. Rumelhart's Interactive Model is considered interactive rather than bottom-up because it depicts multiple processors converging on text simultaneously, rather than in a linear, sequential manner.

To apply the Interactive Model to Sara's reading problems, one would investigate the adequacy of her skills in the different processing areas: syntax, semantics, visual perception, and vocabulary. Interventions based on this model would aim to strengthen these processors while especially attending to their interactive qualities. For example, teaching Sara how to use context clues to help decipher an unknown word represents using a higher level skill (semantics) to influence a lower level skill (word recognition).

Six theoretical models based on cognitive processing that emerged between 1950 and 1970 have been reviewed in this section. All of the models attempt to explain unobservable cognitive processes that occur during the reading process. Although the models are several decades old and our understanding of cognitive processing has progressed since their publication, many of them retain value for their central components that are still relevant to practice and research today.

## INFORMATION/COGNITIVE PROCESSING
## PERSPECTIVES, CONTINUED

Stanovich (1980) extended Rumelhart's (1977) model with his idea that not only are text processors interactive and nonlinear, but they are also compensatory. By this, Stanovich meant that if one processor is not working well, or has insufficient data, the other processors compensate for it.

Stanovich's (1980) Interactive–Compensatory Model would guide Sara's remediation by providing her with explicit instruction regarding the many approaches that can be used to help her decode words and comprehend messages during reading. Teaching Sara to "read ahead" as an approach to helping her identify an unknown word is an example of teaching her to use her reading skills in a compensatory manner.

In the same year that Stanovich (1980) published the Interactive–Compensatory Model, Erhi (1980) published an article that described the ways in which the brain processes orthographic information (visual, printed text) during the reading process. She reported that print is encoded along with its phonological properties. More recently, Ehri (2000) has been stressing the importance of graphophonemic awareness, which refers to the reader's ability to connect printed text (graphemes) to sounds (phonemes). In lay language, graphophonemic awareness is the knowledge that underlies word decoding skill.

Since Ehri's (2000) research emphasizes that graphophonemic awareness is critically important to successful early reading, the application of this lens to Sara's reading difficulties suggests that her decoding skills be carefully assessed. If her graphophonemic/decoding skills were found to be deficient, this body of work suggests that effective remediation in this area would be likely to improve Sara's problems.

Perfetti's (1985) Verbal Efficiency Theory emphasizes the role of speech access in reading. The theory states that the amount of time it takes to read an isolated word aloud (vocal latency) is an indication of how well the reader knows the word. It states that faster word recognition is associated with improved reading because automatic word recognition requires less cognitive energy than decoding, thus freeing up cognitive capacity for comprehension processing (Wolf & Katzir-Cohen, 2001). The theory also argues that how well a reader can decode will determine how quickly he or she can identify words when reading isolated words.

Similar to the Orthographic Processing Perspective, the Verbal Efficiency Theory suggests that Sara's decoding ability is at the root of her reading difficulties. Specifically, the theory indicates that her decoding speed is too slow, thus impeding word identification and comprehension processing. Like the Orthographic Processing Perspective, the Verbal Efficiency Theory suggests that graphophonic intervention designed to speed word identification as the route to ameliorate Sara's reading distress.

The Construction–Integration Model (Kintsch, 1994) suggests that readers construct three levels of representations during reading: linguistic (word meaning), conceptual (sentence comprehension), and situational (message construction integrating text and background knowledge). Furthermore, the model hypothesizes that there are two primary cognitive processes in which readers engage during reading: a construction phase in which information from a variety of sources is collected, and an integration phase in which the information is synthesized. To apply the Construction–Integration Model to Sara's reading issues, one would assess her abilities in these five areas. Deficits in one or more of the areas would suggest the route(s) for intervention.

Stanovich's (1988) Phonological–Core Variable Difference Model argues that the primary difference between normal and dyslexic individuals is determined by deficits in the phonological realm of cognitive functioning. As has been described earlier, phonological capabilities refer to an individual's awareness and ability to hear and manipulate sounds within words. This model suggests that Sara's phonological skills are the likely root of her reading difficulty. It indicates that careful evaluation of her phonological abilities, and targeted intervention if deficits are revealed, is the proper treatment for her reading disorder.

## INFORMATION/COGNITIVE
## PROCESSING PERSPECTIVES: STATE OF THE ART

The final chapter of the present text offers four current prominent lenses for viewing Sara's reading difficulties.

According to the Parallel Distributed Processing Model (Rumelhart & McClelland, 1986), successful reading is dependent on a reader's abilities in four areas: automatic letter recognition, accurate phonemic processing, strong vocabulary knowledge, and the ability to construct meaningful messages during reading. The information within and between each of these processors is organized according to connectionist principles. Furthermore, the processors are all interactive and compensatory.

To apply the Parallel Distributed Processing Model to Sara's situation, one should examine her abilities in four key areas: automatic letter recognition, phonemic processing, vocabulary knowledge, and reading comprehension. As with all of the other models presented thus far, deficits in any of these areas would be seen as setting the direction for intervention. Additionally, the model suggests that rereading is a powerful remedial technique because it strengthens connections between print, sounds, and, ultimately, message construction.

In contrast to the Parallel Distributed Processing Model (Rumelhart & McClelland, 1986), the Dual-Route Cascaded Model (Coltheart, Curtis, Atkins, & Haller, 1993), has two routes for processing text input: one path for handling words that are already known to the reader, and another for handling unknown words and nonwords. The lexical route identifies a word as familiar and then processes the word as a whole, immediately providing the reader with the correct meaning and pronunciation. The second route of the Dual-Route Cascaded Model, called the nonlexical or sublexical route, is based on a letter-to-sound rule procedure.

A proponent of the Dual-Route Cascaded Model would examine Sara's reading abilities to process two kinds of words: known and unknown. Sara's knowledge of known words could be evaluated by her ability to read high-frequency words in lists or her ability to read connected text at varying levels of difficulty. Sara's knowledge of unknown words might be assessed by her skill in reading nonwords in lists because this task limits the reader to using only graphophonemic knowledge. After Sara's processing of these two types of words was evaluated, a remediation would be accordingly designed.

The Double-Deficit Hypothesis (Wolf & Bowers, 1999) is a theory used to explain the causation of reading disabilities. According to Wolf and Bowers's hypothesis, reading-disabled children fall into one of three categories: children for whom phonological deficits are the core of their reading disability, children for whom naming speed deficits are the core of their reading disability, and children for whom both phonological deficits and naming speed deficits are problematic. The children who fall into the last category, those with a "double deficit," are also those whose reading impairment is most severe. Used as a lens to view reading problems, the Double-Deficit Hypothesis would evaluate Sara's phonological skills and her naming speed ability. The outcomes of these two areas of assessment would determine the course of intervention.

The last theoretical lens described in this book is that of neuroscience, which examines patterns of brain functioning through the use of brain imaging technology (Goswami, 2004). If Sara were evaluated from this perspective, doctors would examine her using an fMRI. The assumption of this perspective is that Sara's brain functioning would differ in significant ways from the brain functioning of those who don't exhibit reading difficulties. Following the identification of neurological differences, targeted remedial programs would be implemented. Afterward, Sara would be posttested with another fMRI.

## FINAL THOUGHTS

This chapter provides a practical understanding of the ways in which the theories and models presented in this book can be used as lenses to view one student's reading difficulties. The work suggests that there are a myriad of perspectives from which Sara's reading problem can be seen, and that each perspective provides different suggestions for routes of assessment and intervention. This chapter underscores the position that there is not just one correct way to teach reading or to address a child's reading difficulty.

Overall, this text has sought to present an introduction to the theories and models that have been most influential in the field of reading. It has explained that theories and models are explanations for phenomena, and that everyone has theories that affect his or her behavior regardless of his or her level of consciousness of them. The text has suggested that a greater understanding of theories can lead to better informed decision making and more effective classroom practices by teachers, a finding supported by Pressley et al.'s (2001) study of exemplary educators. Indeed, as Pressley et al. found, highly effective, exemplary teachers are able to articulate the relationships between what they do in the classroom and their theoretical reasons for doing so.

The text has also sought to elucidate the roles of theories and models in literacy research. Theories are central to educational research because they are the concepts through which scholars explain their research. Researchers use theories to explain *why they expect something will happen* in their studies (their hypotheses) as well as *why they believe something did happen* in their studies (their discussion). Additionally, researchers turn to theories to identify variables to be investigated and the possible relationships between them. If a variable is found significant in one study framed by a particular theory, it is reasonable to assume it could be important in another study framed by the same theory. Theories and models are the vehicles through which research investigations are connected.

Perhaps most importantly, this book has argued on behalf of the value of multiple lenses for viewing literacy learning. Because no single theory can capture all the complexities of the reading experience, theories and models are best used in conjunction with each other. Educators who believe in the importance of multiple lenses assert that each theory makes a unique and valuable contribution to understanding the phenomena under examination. A metaphor of a camera lens can be used to explain the value of multiple theories to understand an educational issue. Each lens provides a unique view of the object under consideration. So too with educational theories and models that aim to explain an educational issue. Each of the theories and models provides a unique and valuable perspective on the topic. The use of multiple lenses has also been applied to the classroom activities and teaching anecdotes in this book. The ability to see the ways in which classroom practices are reflective of many theories strengthens the mind of the observer and underscores the primary premise of the text: the value of multiple perspectives in improving literacy education.

In sum, in this text we have attempted to tell a semihistorical story of the major strands of thinking that have come to be known as theories and models, and their influence on our understanding of the reading process, reading instruction, and reading research. We hope that as a result of reading this text educators better understand the full range of perspectives (theories and models) from which the reading process can be examined. It is our belief that a greater understanding of these perspectives will enhance the work of practitioners and researchers alike.

# APPENDICES

# APPENDIX A. Summary Chart: Onset of Presented Theoretical Perspectives Affecting Literacy Education

| | CA. 400 B.C. | CA. 350 B.C. | 1700s | 1870s | 1920s | 1930s |
|---|---|---|---|---|---|---|
| Early Historical Theories | Mental Discipline Theory (Plato, Historical) | Associationism (Aristotle) | Unfoldment Theory (Rousseau, Pestalozzi, Froebel) | Structuralism (Wundt, Cattell, Javal, Quantz, Dearborn) | | |
| Behaviorism | | | | | Classical Conditioning Theory (Pavlov, Watson) | |
| | | | | | Connectionism (Thorndike) | |
| Constructivism | | | | | | Inquiry Learning (Dewey) |
| | | | | | | Schema Theory (Bartlett) |
| | | | | | | Transactional/ Reader Response Theory (Rosenblatt) |
| | | | | | | |
| Theories of Literacy Development | | | | | | Theory of Cognitive Development (Piaget) |
| | | | | | | Maturation Theory (Morphett & Washburn) |
| | | | | | | |
| Social Learning Theories | | | | | | |
| | | | | | | |
| | | | | | | |
| | | | | | | |
| | | | | | | |
| Information/ Cognitive Processing Theories | | | | | | |
| | | | | | | |
| | | | | | | |
| | | | | | | |
| | | | | | | |
| | | | | | | |

| 1950s | 1960s | 1970s | 1980s | 1990s | 2000s |
|---|---|---|---|---|---|
| | | | | | |
| Operant Conditioning Theory (Skinner) | | | | | |
| | | | | | |
| | | Psycholinguistic Theory (Smith, Goodman) | | | |
| | | Whole Language Theory (Goodman) | | | |
| | | Metacognition (Flavell, Brown) | | | |
| | | Engagement Theory (Guthrie, Wigfield) | | | |
| | | Theory of Literacy Development (Holdaway) | Stage Models of Reading (Ehri, Chall, Gough, Frith) | | |
| | | | Emergent Literacy Theory (Clay) | | |
| | | | Family Literacy Theory (Taylor) | | |
| | | Sociolinguistic Theory (Bernstein) | | | |
| | | Socio-Cultural Theory (Bronfenbrenner) | | | |
| | | Social Constructivism (Vygotsky) | | | |
| | | Social Learning Theory (Bandura) | | | |
| | | Critical Literacy Theory (Freire) | | | |
| Substrata-Factor Theory of Reading (Holmes) | Information Processing Model (Atkinson & Shiffrin) | Rauding Theory (Carver) | Interactive–Compensatory Model (Stanovich) | Parallel Distributed Processing Model/Connectionism (Seidenberg & McClelland) | |
| | | Gough's Model (Gough) | Orthographic Processing Perspective (Ehri) | Dual-Route Cascaded Model (Colheart & Rastle) | |
| | | Automatic Information Processing Model (LaBerge & Samuels) | Verbal Efficiency Theory (Perfetti) | Double-Deficit Hypothesis (Wolf & Bowers) | |
| | | Interactive Model (Rumelhart) | Construction–Integration Model (Kintsch) | | |
| | | | Phonological–Core Variable Difference Model (Stanovich) | | |
| | | | | | Neuroscientific Contributions (Goswami) |

## APPENDIX B. Summary of Theories Presented and Sample Representative Instructional Practices

*Note*: Many instructional practices can be linked to multiple theories. This appendix provides only a sample of practices linked to theories. Many other pairings are possible.

### Chapter 2. Early Roots: Early Theories and Models Applicable to Reading (400 B.C.–1899)

Mental Discipline Theory
- Activities related to practicing a skill.
- Homework, time on task, and repeated reading.

Associationism
- Creating associations through webbing and brainstorming to increase comprehension (*see also* Schema Theory).

Unfoldment Theory
- Literacy center in the classroom.

Structuralism and Early Scientific Foundations of Reading
- Changing font size to improve children's reading.

### Chapter 3. Behaviorism: The Dominant Educational Theory for 50 Years (1900–1950s)

Classical Conditioning Theory
- Creating positive, success-oriented reading experiences for students to help them overcome negative associations with reading.

Connectionism
- Sequencing the presentation of literacy tasks in order of difficulty.

Operant Conditioning Theory
- Direct instruction, use of incentives.

### Chapter 4. Constructivism (1920s–Present)

Inquiry Learning
- Problem-based and collaborative learning activities.

Schema Theory
- Brainstorming and webbing before reading.

Transactional/Reader Response Theory
- Reading response activities, use of efferent and aesthetic responses.

Psycholinguistic Theory and Whole Language Theory
- Authentic, meaningful reading and writing tasks.

Metacognition

- Activities that teach students to monitor whether or not they are comprehending.
- Fix-up strategies to employ if comprehension is not occurring.

Engagement Theory
- Use of teaching strategies shown to increase student engagement: (1) the use of themes in reading instruction, (2) an emphasis on student choice for both reading texts and responses, (3) the use of hands-on activities, (4) the availability of a wide variety of text genres chosen to interest students, and (5) the integration of social collaboration into reading response activities.

## Chapter 5. Theories of Literacy Development (1930s–Present)

Theory of Cognitive Development
- Instruction sensitive to the ways in which children's cognitive development can affect reading development.

Maturation Theory
- Waiting until children reach a certain age or developmental milestone before implementing reading instruction.

Theory of Literacy Development
- Use of big books and shared reading.

Stage Models of Reading
- Use of environmental print to teach reading.

Emergent Literacy Theory
- Literacy-rich classroom environments.

Family Literacy Theory
- Teaching practices that involve parents.

## Chapter 6. Social Learning Perspectives (1960s–Present)

Sociolinguistic Theory
- Language Experience approach.

Socio-Cultural Theory
- Literature circles.

Social Constructivism
- Cross-age and buddy reading.

Social Learning Theory
- Modeling.

Critical Literacy Theory
- Teaching students about the social and political consequences of literacy achievement and illiteracy.

## Chapter 7. Information/Cognitive Processing Perspectives (1950s–1970s)

Information Processing Theories
- Diagnostic applications.

Substrata-Factor Model of Reading
- Diagnostic applications.

Rauding Theory
- Fluency training.

Gough's Model
- Letter identification and decoding instruction.

Automatic Information Processing Model
- Guided reading instruction.

Interactive Model
- Using context clues, cloze technique.

## Chapter 8. Information/Cognitive Processing Perspectives, Continued (1980s)

Interactive–Compensatory Model
- Teaching children to be flexible, strategic readers.

Orthographic Processing Perspective
- Decoding/phonics instruction.

Verbal Efficiency Theory
- Activities to strengthen children's oral language.

Construction–Integration Model
- Comprehension instruction

Phonological–Core Variable Difference Model
- Phonemic awareness development activities.

## Chapter 9. Information/Cognitive Processing Perspectives: State of the Art (1989–Present)

Parallel Distributed Processing Model
- Word families.

Dual-Route Cascaded Model
- Sight-word instruction.

Double-Deficit Hypothesis
- Diagnostic applications.

Neuroscientific Contributions
- Neuroscientific examinations to inform reading instruction.

# References

Adams, M. J. (1990). *Beginning to read*. Cambridge, MA: MIT Press.

*American Heritage Dictionary* (4th ed.). (2001). Boston: Houghton Mifflin.

Anderson, E., & Guthrie, J. T. (1996, January). Teaching with CORI: Taking the big jump. *NRRC News: A Newsletter of the National Reading Research Center*, pp. 1–3.

Anderson, R. C., & Pearson, P. D. (1984). A schema-theoretic view of basic processes in reading. In P. D. Pearson (Ed.), *Handbook of reading research* (Vol. 1, pp. 185–224). New York: Longman.

Apel, K., & Masterson, J. (2001). *Beyond baby talk: From sounds to sentences: A parent's guide to language development*. Rocklin, CA: Prima.

Armbruster, B. B., Lehr, F., & Osborn, J. (2001). *Put reading first: The research building blocks for teaching children to read*. Washington, DC: Center for Improvement of Early Reading Achievement.

Atkinson, R. C., & Shiffrin, R. M. (1968). Human memory: A proposed system and its control processes. In K. Spence & J. Spence (Eds.), *The psychology of learning and motivation* (Vol. 2, pp. 89–195). New York: Academic Press.

Au, K. H. (1980). Participation structures in a reading lesson with Hawaiian children: Analysis of a culturally appropriate instructional event. *Anthropology and Education Quarterly, 11*, 91–115.

Au, K. H. (1997). A sociocultural model of reading instruction: The Kamehameha Elementary Education Program. In S. A. Stahl & D. A. Hayes (Eds.), *Instructional models in reading* (pp. 181–202). Hillsdale, NJ: Erlbaum.

Baker, L. (2002). Metacognition in comprehension instruction. In C. C. Block & M. Pressley (Eds.), *Comprehension instruction: Research-based best practices* (pp. 77–95). New York: Guilford Press.

Bandura, A. (1969). *Principles of behavior modification*. New York: Holt.

Bandura, A. (1977). *Social learning theory.* Englewood Cliffs, NJ: Prentice Hall.

Bandura, A. (1986). *Social foundations of thought and action: A social cognitive theory.* Englewood Cliffs, NJ: Prentice-Hall.

Bandura, A. (1997). *Self-efficacy: The exercise of control.* New York: Freeman.

Bartlett, F. C. (1932). *Remembering: A study in experimental and social psychology.* Cambridge, UK: Cambridge University Press.

Bauer, P. J., & Fivush, R. (1992). Constructing event representations: Building on a foundation of variation and enabling relations. *Cognitive Development, 7,* 381–401.

Bean, T. W., & Rigoni, N. (2001). Exploring the intergenerational dialogue journal discussion of multicultural young adult novel. *Reading Research Quarterly, 36*(3), 232–248.

Bergeron, B. S. (1990). What does the term Whole Language mean?: Constructing a definition from the literature. *Journal of Reading Behavior, 22*(4), 301–329.

Bernard, H. R. (2000). *Social research methods: Qualitative and quantitative methods.* Thousand Oaks, CA: Sage.

Bernstein, B. (1972a). A sociolinguistic approach to socialization; with some reference to educability. In J. Gumperez & D. Hymes (Eds.), *Directions in sociolinguistics* (pp. 465–497). New York: Holt, Rinehart & Winston.

Bernstein, B. (1972b). Social class, language, and socialization. In P. Giglioli (Ed.), *Language and social context* (pp. 157–178). Harmondsworth, UK: Penguin Books.

Best, J. L., & Kahn, J. V. (1998). *Research in education* (8th ed). Needham Heights, MA: Allyn & Bacon.

Bigge, M. L., & Shermis, S. S. (1992). *Learning theories for teachers* (5th ed.). New York: HarperCollins.

Block, C. C., & Pressley, M. (Eds.). (2002). *Comprehension instruction: Research-based best practices.* New York: Guilford Press.

Bloom, D., & Green, J. (1984). Directions in the sociolinguistic study of reading. In P. D. Pearson, R. Barr, M. Kamil, & P. Mosemthal (Eds.), *Handbook of reading research* (pp. 395–421). New York: Longman.

Bloome, D., & Talwalker, S. (1997). Book reviews: Critical discourse analysis and the study of reading and writing. *Reading Research Quarterly, 32*(1), 104–112.

Booth, J. R., Perfetti, C. A., & MacWhinney, B. (1999). Quick, automatic, and general activation of orthographic and phonological representations in young readers. *Developmental Psychology, 35*(1), 3–19.

Bronfenbrenner, U. (1979). *The ecology of human development: Experiments by nature and design.* Cambridge, MA: Harvard University Press.

Brown, A. L. (1978). Knowing when, where, and how to remember: A problem of metacognition. In R. Glaser (Ed.), *Advances in instructional psychology* (Vol. 1, pp. 77–165). Hillsdale, NJ: Erlbaum.

Brown, R. (2002). Straddling two worlds: Self-directed comprehension instruction for middle schoolers. In C. C. Block & M. Pressley (Eds.), *Comprehen-*

sion instruction: Research-based best practices (pp. 337–350). New York: Guilford Press.

Brumbaugh, R. S., & Lawrence, N. M. (1963). *Philosophers on education: Six essays on the foundations of western thought.* Boston: Houghton Mifflin.

Brumbaugh, R. S., & Lawrence, N. M. (1985). *Philosophical themes in modern education.* Landham, MD: Houghton Mifflin

Bryant, P. (2002). Thoughts about reading and spelling. *Scientific Studies of Reading, 6*(2), 199–216.

Buchoff, R. (1995). Family stories. *The Reading Teacher, 49*(3), 230–233.

Burns, G. L., & Kondrick, P. A. (1998). Psychological behaviorism's reading therapy program: Parents as reading therapists for their children's reading disability. *Journal of Learning Disabilities, 31*(3), 278–285.

Burns, P. C., Roe, B. D., & Ross, E. P. (1999). *Teaching reading in today's elementary schools* (7th ed.). Boston: Houghton Mifflin.

Bus, A., van IJzendoorn, M., & Pellegrini, A. (1995). Joint reading makes for success in learning to read: A meta-analysis on intergenerational transmission of literacy. *Review of Educational Research, 65,* 1–21.

Byrnes, J. P. (2001). *Minds, brains, and learning: Understanding the psychological and educational relevance of neuroscientific research.* New York: Guilford Press.

Caillies, S., Denhiere, G., & Kintsch, W. (2002). The effect of prior knowledge on understanding from text: Evidence from primed recognition. *European Journal of Cognitive Psychology, 14*(2), 267–286.

Cardoso-Martins, C. (2001). The reading abilities of beginning readers of Brazilian Portuguese: Implications for a theory of reading acquisition. *Scientific Studies of Reading, 5*(4), 289–317.

Cardoso-Martins, C., & Pennington, B. F. (2004). The relationship between phoneme awareness and rapid naming skills and literacy acquisition: The role of developmental period and reading ability. *Scientific Studies of Reading, 8*(1), 27–52.

Carnine, D. W., Silbert, J., Kame'enui, E. J., & Tarver, S. G. (2004). *Direct reading instruction.* Upper Saddle River, NJ: Pearson.

Cartwright, K. B. (2002). Cognitive development and reading: The relation of multiple classification skills to reading comprehension in elementary school children. *Journal of Educational Psychology, 54,* 56–63.

Carver, R. P. (1977). Toward a theory of reading and rauding. *Reading Research Quarterly, 13,* 8–63.

Carver, R. P. (1992). Commentary: Effect of prediction activities, prior knowledge, and text type upon amount comprehended: Using rauding theory to critique schema theory research. *Reading Research Quarterly, 27*(2), 165–174.

Carver, R. P., & Leibert, R. E. (1995). The effect of reading library books at different levels of difficulty upon gain in reading ability. *Reading Research Quarterly, 30*(1), 26–48.

Cattell, J. M. (1886). The time it takes to see and name objects. *Mind, 11,* 63–65.

Cattell, J. M. (1890). Mental tests and measurement. *Mind, 15,* 373–380.

Chall, J. S. (1983). *Stages of reading development.* New York: McGraw-Hill.

Christie, J., Enz, B., & Vukelich, C. (1997). *Teaching language and literacy: Preschool through elementary grades.* New York: Longman.

Clay, M. M. (1966). *Emergent reading behavior.* Unpublished doctoral dissertation, University of Aukland, New Zealand.

Clay, M. M. (1985). *The early detection of reading difficulties* (3rd ed.). Portsmouth, NH: Heinemann.

Coltheart, M., Curtis, B., Atkins, P., & Haller, M. (1993). Models of reading aloud: Dual-route and parallel-distributed-processing approaches. *Psychological Review, 100*(4), 589–608.

Coltheart, M., & Rastle, K. (1994). Serial processing in reading aloud: Evidence for dual-route models of reading. *Journal of Experimental Psychology: Human Perception and Performance, 20*(6), 1197–1211.

Coltheart, M., Rastle, K., Perry, C., Langdon, R., & Ziegler, J. (2001). DRC: A dual-route cascaded model of visual word recognition and reading aloud. *Psychological Review, 108*(1), 204–256.

Cox, C. (1996). *Teaching language arts: A student and response centered classroom* (2nd ed.). Needham Heights, MA: Allyn & Bacon.

Creswell, J. W. (2002). *Educational research: Planning, conducting, and evaluating quantitative and qualitative research.* Upper Saddle River, NJ: Merrill Prentice Hall.

Daniels, H. (1994). *Literature circles: Voice and choice in the student-centered classroom.* York, ME: Stenhouse.

Dearborn, W. F. (1906). *Psychology of reading: An experimental study of the reading pauses and movements of the eye.* New York: Science Press.

Delgado-Gaitan, C. (1992). School matters in the Mexican American home: Socializing children to education. *American Educational Research Journal, 29,* 495–513.

Dewey, J. (1916). *Democracy and education.* New York: Macmillan.

Dixon-Krauss, L. A. (1995). Partner reading and writing: Peer social dialogue and the zone of proximal development. *Journal of Reading Behavior, 27*(10), 45–63.

Dixon-Krauss, L. A. (1996). *Vygotsky in the classroom: Mediated literacy instruction and assessment.* White Plains, NY: Longman.

Dole, J. A., Brown, K. J., & Trathen, W. (1996). The effects of strategy instruction on the comprehension performance of at-risk students. *Reading Research Quarterly, 31*(1), 62–88.

Droop, M., & Verhoeven, L. (1998). Background knowledge, linguistic complexity, and second-language reading comprehension. *Journal of Literacy Research, 30*(2), 253–271.

Duffy, G. G. (2002). The case for direct explanation of strategies. In C. C. Block & M. Pressley (Eds.), *Comprehension instruction: Research-based best practices* (pp. 28–41). New York: Guilford Press.

Dupuis, A. M. (1985). *Philosophy of education in historical perspective.* Lanham, MD: University Press of America.

Durkin, D. (1966). *Children who read early.* New York: Teachers College Press.

Durkin, D. (1978–1979). What classroom observation reveals about reading comprehension instruction. *Reading Research Quarterly, 14,* 481–533.

Edwards, P. A. (1995). Empowering low-income mothers and fathers to share books with young children. *The Reading Teacher, 48,* 558–564.

Edwards, P. A., Pleasants, H. M., & Franklin, S. H. (1999). *A path to follow: Learning to listen to parents.* Portsmouth, NH: Heinemann.

Ehri, L. C. (1980). The development of orthographic images. In V. Frith (Ed.), *Cognitive processes in spelling* (pp. 311–338). London: Academic Press.

Ehri, L. C. (1991). Development of the ability to read words. In R. Barr, M. L. Kamil, P. B. Mosenthal, & P. D. Pearson (Eds.), *Handbook of reading research* (Vol. 2, pp. 383–417). New York: Longman.

Ehri, L. C. (1992). Reconceptualizing the development of sight word reading and its relationship to recoding. In P. B. Gough, L. C. Ehri, & R. Treiman (Eds.), *Reading acquisition* (pp. 107–143). Hillsdale, NJ: Erlbaum.

Ehri, L. C. (2000). Learning to read and learning to spell: Two sides of a coin. *Topics in Language Disorders, 20*(3), 19–36.

El-Dinary, P. B. (2002). Challenges of implementing transactional strategies instruction for reading comprehension. In C. C. Block & M. Pressley (Eds.), *Comprehension instruction: Research-based best practices* (pp. 201–215). New York: Guilford Press.

Fitzgerald, J., & Noblit, G. W. (1999). About hopes, aspirations, and uncertainty: First-grade English-language learners' emergent reading. *Journal of Literacy Research, 31*(2), 133–182.

Flavell, J. H. (1976). Metacognitive aspects of problem solving. In L. B. Resnick (Ed.), *The nature of intelligence* (pp. 231–235). Hillsdale, NJ: Erlbaum.

Flood, J. (1977). Parental styles in reading episodes with young children. *Reading Teacher, 30,* 846–867.

Foorman, B. R., Francis, D. J., Fletcher, J. M., & Lynn, A. (1996). The relation of phonological and orthographic processing to early reading: Comparing two approaches to regression-based, reading-level-match designs. *Journal of Educational Psychology, 88*(4), 639–652.

Fountas, I. C., & Pinnell, G. S. (1996). *Guided reading: Good first reading for all children.* Portsmouth, NH: Heinemann.

Freire, P. (1970). *Pedagogy of the oppressed.* New York: Herder & Herder.

Freud, S. (1933). *New introductory lectures on psychoanalysis.* New York: Norton.

Frith, U. (1985). Beneath the surface of developmental dyslexia. In K. E. Patterson, J. C. Marshall, & M. Coltheart (Eds.), *Surface dyslexia* (pp. 301–330). London: Erlbaum.

Fry, E. B., Kress, J. E., & Fountoukidis, D. L. (2000). *The reading teacher's book of lists* (4th ed.). Somerset, NJ: Jossey-Bass/Wiley.

Fuchs, L. S., Fuchs, D., Hosp, M. K., & Jenkins, J. R. (2001). Oral reading fluency as an indicator of reading competence: A theoretical, empirical, and historical analysis. *Scientific Studies of Reading, 5*(3), 239–256.

Gaffney, J. S., & Anderson, R. C. (2000). Trends in reading research in the United States: Changing intellectual currents over three decades. In M. L. Kamil, P. B. Mosenthal, P. D. Pearson, & R. Barr (Eds.), *Handbook of reading research* (Vol. 3, pp. 53–74). Mahwah, NJ: Erlbaum.

Gambrell, L. B., & Almasi, J. E. (Eds.). (1996). *Lively discussions!: Fostering engaged reading.* Newark, DE: International Reading Association.

Gee, J. (1990). *Social linguistics and literacies.* London: Falmer Press.

Ginsburgh, H. P. (1985). Piaget and education. In N. Entwistle (Ed.), *New directions in educational psychology: Vol. 1. Learning and teaching* (pp. 45–60). Philadelphia: Farmer Press/Taylor & Francis.

Goodman, K. S. (1967). Reading: A psycholinguistic guessing game. *Journal of the Reading Specialist, 6,* 126–135.

Goswami, U. (1998). The role of analogies in the development of word recognition. In J. L. Metsala & L. C. Ehri (Eds.), *Word recognition in beginning literacy* (pp. 41–63). Mahwah, NJ: Erlbaum.

Goswami, U. (2004). Neuroscience and education. *British Journal of Educational Psychology, 74,* 1–14.

Gough, P. B., Juel, C., & Griffith, P. (1992). Reading, spelling, and the orthographic cipher. In P. B. Gough, L. C. Ehri, & R. Treiman (Eds.), *Reading acquisition* (pp. 35–48). Hillsdale, NJ: Erlbaum.

Gough, P. B., & Tunmer, W. E. (1986). Decoding, reading, and reading disability. *Remedial and Special Education, 7,* 6–10.

Greeno, J. G., Collins, A. M., & Resnick, L. B. (1996). Cognition and learning. In D. C. Berliner & R. C. Calfee (Eds.), *Handbook of educational psychology* (pp. 15–46). New York: Macmillan.

Gunning, T. G. (1996). *Creating reading instruction for all children* (2nd ed.). Needham Heights, MA: Allyn & Bacon.

Gunning, T. G. (2003). *Creating literacy instruction for all children* (4th ed.). Boston: Pearson Education.

Gutek, G. L. (1972). *A history of the Western educational experience.* Prospect Heights, IL: Waveland Press.

Guthrie, J. T. (2004). Teaching for literacy engagement. *Journal of Literacy Research, 36*(1), 1–29.

Guthrie, J. T., Schafer, W. D., & Huang, C. W. (2001). Benefits of opportunity to read and balanced instruction on the NAEP. *Journal of Educational Research, 94,* 145–162.

Guthrie, J. T., & Wigfield, A. (Eds.). (1997). *Reading engagement: Motivating readers through integrated instruction.* Newark, DE: International Reading Association.

Guthrie, J. T., & Wigfield, A. (2000). Engagement and motivation in reading. In M. L. Kamil, P. B. Mosenthal, P. D. Pearson, & R. Barr (Eds.), *Handbook of reading research* (Vol. 3, pp. 403–422). Mahwah, NJ: Erlbaum.

Halliday, M. A. K. (1975). *Learning how to mean: Explorations in the development of language.* London: Arnold.

Hart, B., & Risley, T. R. (1995). *Meaningful differences in the everyday experience of young American children.* Baltimore: Brookes.

Hart, B., & Risley, T. R. (1999). *The social world of children: Learning to talk.* Baltimore: Brookes.

Hart, B., & Risley, T. R. (2003). The early catastrophe: The 30 million word gap. *American Educator, 27*(1), 4–9.

Hayes, D. A. (1997). Models of professional practice in teacher thinking. In S. Stahl & D. A. Hayes (Eds.), *Instructional models in reading* (pp. 31–58). Mahwah, NJ: Erlbaum.

Heath, S. B. (1982). What no bedtime story means: Narrative skills at home and school. *Language and Society, 11*, 49–76.

Heilman, A. W., Blair, T. R., & Rupley, W. H. (1986). *Principles and practices of teaching reading* (6th ed.). Columbus, OH: Merrill.

Heim, S., Eulitz, C., & Elbert, T. (2003). Altered hemispheric asymmetry of auditory P100m in dyslexia. *European Journal of Neuroscience, 17*, 1715–1722.

Hennings, D. G. (2000). *Communication in action: Teaching literature-based language arts.* Boston: Houghton-Mifflin.

Hiebert, E. H., & Raphael, T. E. (1996). Psychological perspectives on literacy and extensions to educational practice. In D. C. Berliner & R. C. Calfee (Eds.), *Handbook of educational psychology* (pp. 550–602). New York: Simon & Schuster Macmillan.

Hogaboam, T. W., & Perfetti, C. A. (1978). Reading skill and the role of verbal experience in decoding. *Journal of Educational Psychology, 70*, 717–729.

Holdaway, D. (1979). *The foundations of literacy.* Sydney, Australia: Ashton Scholastic.

Holdaway, D. (1989). Shared book experience: Teaching reading using favorite books. In G. Manning & M. Manning (Eds.), *Whole language : Beliefs and practices, K–8* (pp. 137–150). Washington, DC: National Education Association.

Holmes, J. A. (1953). *The Substrata-Factor Theory of reading.* Berkeley, CA: California Book Press.

Hudson, J., & Nelson, K. (1983). Effects of script structure on children's story recall. *Developmental Psychology, 19*, 625–635.

Huey, E. B. (1968). *The psychology and pedagogy of reading.* Cambridge, MA: MIT Press. (Original work published 1908)

Iser, W. (1978). *The act of reading.* Baltimore: Johns Hopkins University Press.

Jimenez, R. T., Smith, P. H., & Martinez-León, N. (2003). Freedom and form: The language and literacy practices of two Mexican schools. *Reading Research Quarterly, 38*(4), 488–508.

Jordan, G. E., Snow, C. E., & Porche, M. V. (2000). Project EASE: The effect of a family literacy project on kindergarten students' early literacy skills. *Reading Research Quarterly, 35*(4), 524–546.

Juel, C. (1991). Beginning reading. In R. Barr, M. L. Kamil, P. B. Mosenthal, & P. D. Pearson (Eds.), *Handbook of reading research* (Vol. 2, pp. 759–788). New York: Longman.

Kame'enui, E. J., Simmons, D. C., Chard, D., & Dickson, S. (1997). Direct reading instruction. In S. A. Stahl & D. A. Hayes (Eds.), *Instructional models in reading* (pp. 59–84). Mahwah, NJ: Erlbaum.

Katz, I. C. (1980). *The effects of instructional methods on reading acquisition systems.* Unpublished doctoral dissertation, University of California, Riverside.

Kintsch, W. (1994). The role of knowledge in discourse comprehension: A construction–integration model. In R. B. Ruddell, M. R. Ruddell, & H. Singer (Eds.), *Theoretical models and processes of reading* (4th ed., pp. 951–995). Newark, DE: International Reading Association.

Korkeamaki, R., & Dreher, M. J. (1996). Trying something new: Meaning-based reading instruction in a Finnish first-grade classroom. *Journal of Literacy Research, 28*(1), 9–34.

Koskinen, P. S. (1993). Motivating independent reading and writing in the primary grades through social cooperative literacy experiences. *The Reading Teacher, 47*(2), 162–164.

Kuhara-Kojima, K., Hatano, G., Saito, H., & Haebara, T. (1996). Vocalization latencies of skilled and less skilled comprehenders for words written in hiragana and kanji. *Reading Research Quarterly, 31*(2), 158–171.

LaBerge, D., & Samuels, S. J. (1974). Toward a theory of automatic information processing in reading. *Cognitive Psychology, 6,* 293–323.

Langer, J. (1995). *Envisioning literature: Literacy understanding and literature instruction.* New York: Teachers College Press.

Leseman, P., & DeJong, P. F. (1998). Home literacy: Opportunity, instruction, cooperation, and social–emotional quality predicting early reading achievement. *Reading Research Quarterly, 33*(3), 294–319.

McCarthey, S. J. (1997). Connecting home and school literacy practices in classrooms with diverse populations. *Journal of Literacy Research, 29*(2), 145–182.

McGee, L. M. (1996). Response-centered talk: Windows on children's thinking. In L. B. Gambrell & J. F. Almasi (Eds.), *Lively discussions!: Fostering engaged reading* (pp. 194–207). Newark, DE: International Reading Association.

Moll, L. C. (1992). Literacy research in community and classrooms: A sociocultural approach. In R. Beach, J. Green, M. Kamil, & T. Shanahan (Eds.), *Multidisciplinary perspectives on literacy research* (pp. 179–207). Urbana, IL: National Council of Teachers of English.

Moll, L. C. (1994). Literacy research in community and classrooms: A sociocultural approach. In R. B. Ruddell, M. R. Ruddell, & H. Singer (Eds.), *Theoretical models and processes of reading* (4th ed., pp. 179–207). Newark, DE: International Reading Association.

Moll, L. C., & Greenberg, J. (1990). Creating zones of possibilities: Combining social contexts for instruction. In L. C. Moll (Ed.), *Vygotsky and education* (pp. 319–348). New York: Cambridge University Press.

Montare, A. (1988). Classical conditioning of beginning reading responses. *Perceptual and Motor Skills, 67*(2), 611–621.

Morphett, M. V., & Washburne, C. (1931). When should children begin to read? *The Elementary School Journal, 31,* 496–508.

Morrow, L. M. (Ed.). (1995). *Family literacy: Connections in schools and communities.* Newark, DE: International Reading Association.

Morrow, L. M. (2001). *Literacy development in the early years* (4th ed.). Boston: Allyn & Bacon.

Morrow, L. M. (2002). *The literacy center: Contexts for reading and writing* (2nd ed.). Portland, ME: Stenhouse.

Morrow, L. M. (2005). *Literacy development in the early years: Helping children read and write* (5th ed.). Pearson: Boston.

Neuman, S. B. (1995). Toward a collaborative approach to parent involvement in early education: A study of teenage mothers in an African-American community. *American Educational Research Journal, 32*(4), 801–827.

Orellana, M. F., Reynolds, J., Dormer, L., & Meza, M. (2003). In other words: Translating or "para phrasing" as a family literacy practice in immigrant households. *Reading Research Quarterly, 38*(1), 12–34.

Paratore, J. R. (1993). An intergenerational approach to literacy: Effects on the literacy learning of adults and on the practice of family literacy. In D. J. Leu & C. K. Kinzer (Eds.), *Examining central issues in literacy research, theory, and practice* (Forty-second Yearbook of the National Reading Conference, pp. 83–92). Chicago: National Reading Conference.

Paratore, J. R. (2001). *Opening doors, opening opportunities: Family literacy in an urban community.* Needham Heights, MA: Allyn & Bacon.

Pearson, P. D., Barr, R., Kamil, M. L., & Mosenthal, P. (Eds.). (1984). *Handbook of reading research.* New York: Longman.

Pemberton, M. A. (1993). Modeling theory and composing process models. *College Composition and Communication, 44,* 40–58.

Perfetti, C. A. (1985). *Reading ability.* New York: Oxford University Press.

Piaget, J., & Inhelder, B. (1969). *The psychology of the child* (H. Weaver, Trans.). New York: Basic Books.

Plaut, D. C., & McClelland, J. L. (1993). Generalization with componential attractors: Word and nonword reading in an attractor network. In *Proceedings of the Fifteenth Annual Conference of the Cognitive Science Society* (pp. 824–820). Hillsdale, NJ: Erlbaum.

Posner, M. I., & Snyder, C. R. R. (1975a). Attention and cognitive control. In R. Soiso (Ed.), *Information processing and cognition: The Loyola Symposium* (pp. 55–85). Hillside, NJ: Erlbaum.

Posner, M. I., & Snyder, C. R. R. (1975b). Facilitation and inhibition in the processing of signals. In P. M. A. Rabbitt & S. Dornic (Eds.), *Attention and performance* (Vol. 5, pp. 669–682). New York: Academic Press.

Pressley, M. (2000). What should comprehension instruction be the comprehension of? In M. L. Kamil, P. B. Mosenthal, P. D. Pearson, & R. Barr (Eds.), *Handbook of reading research* (Vol. 3, pp. 545–561). Mahwah, NJ: Erlbaum.

Pressley, M., Allington, R. L., Wharton-McDonald, R., Block, C. C., & Morrow, L. M. (2001). *Learning to read: Lessons from exemplary first-grade classrooms.* New York: Guilford Press.

Pressley, M., & McCormick, C. B. (1995). *Advanced educational psychology for educators, researchers, and policymakers.* New York: HarperCollins.

Pugh, K. R., Mencl, W. E., Jenner, A. R., Katz, L., Frost, S. J., Lee, J. R., et al. (2001). Neurobiological studies of reading and reading disability. *Journal of Communication Disorders, 34,* 479–492.

Purcell-Gates, V. (1995). *Other people's words: The cycle of low literacy.* Cambridge, MA: Harvard University Press.

Purcell-Gates, V. (1996). Stories, coupons, and the *T.V. Guide*: Relationships between home literacy experiences and emergent literacy knowledge. *Reading Research Quarterly, 31*(4), 406–428.

Purves, A. (1975). Research in the teaching of English. *Language Arts, 52,* 463–466.

Quantz, J. O. (1897). Problems in the psychology of reading. *Psychological Monographs, 2*(1, Whole No. 5). (Summary in *Psychological Review,* 1898, 434–436)

Reutzel, D. R., & Cooter, R. B. (1996). *Teaching children to read: From basals to books* (2nd ed.). Englewood, NJ: Merrill.

Reutzel, D. R., Hollingsworth, P. M., & Eldredge, J. L. (1994). Oral reading instruction: The impact on student reading development. *Reading Research Quarterly, 23*(1), 40–62.

Rosenblatt, L. M. (1978). *The reader, the text, the poem: The transactional theory of literacy work.* Carbondale, IL: Southern Illinois University Press.

Rosenblatt, L. M. (1994). The transactional theory of reading and writing. In R. B. Ruddell, M. R. Ruddell, & H. Singer (Eds.), *Theoretical models and processes of reading* (4th ed., pp. 1057–1092). Newark, DE: International Reading Association.

Ruddell, R. B., & Ruddell, M. R. (1995). *Teaching children to read and write: Becoming an influential teacher.* Needham Heights, MA: Allyn & Bacon.

Ruddell, R. B., Ruddell, M. R., & Singer, H. (Eds.). (1994). *Theoretical models and processes of reading* (4th ed.). Newark, DE: International Reading Association.

Rumelhart, D. E. (1994). Toward an interactive model of reading. In R. B. Ruddell, M. R. Ruddell, & H. Singer (Eds.), *Theoretical models and processes of reading* (4th ed., pp. 864–894). Newark, DE: International Reading Association.

Rumelhart, D. E. (1989). The architecture of mind: A connectionist approach. In M. I. Posner (Ed.), *Foundations of cognitive science* (pp. 133–159). Cambridge, MA: MIT Press.

Rumelhart, D. E. (1977). Toward an interactive model of reading. In S. Dornic (Ed.), *Attention and performance VI* (Vol. 6, pp. 573–603). Hillsdale, NJ: Erlbaum.

Rumelhart, D. E., & McClelland, J. L. (Eds.). (1986). *Parallel distributed processing: Vol. 1. Foundations.* Cambridge, MA: MIT Press.

Samuels, S. J. (1994). Toward a theory of automatic information processing in reading, revisited. In R. B. Ruddell, M. R. Ruddell, & H. Singer (Eds.),

*Theoretical models and processes of reading* (4th ed., pp. 816–837). Newark, DE: International Reading Association.

Samuels, S. J., & Kamil, M. L. (1984). Models of the reading process. In P. D. Pearson, R. Barr, M. L. Kamil, & P. Mosenthal (Eds.), *Handbook of reading research* (pp. 185–224). New York: Longman.

Santa Barbara Discourse Group. (1994). Constructing literacy in classrooms: Literate action as social accomplishment. In R. B. Ruddell, M. R. Ruddell, & H. Singer (Eds.), *Theoretical models and processes of reading* (4th ed., pp. 124–154). Newark, DE: International Reading Association.

Scarborough, H. S., & Dobrich, W. (1994). On the efficacy of reading to preschoolers. *Developmental Review, 14,* 245–302.

Schraw, G. (1996). Interactive, compensatory reading strategies. *Journal of Literacy Research, 28*(1), 55–70.

Schwartz, B., & Reisberg, D. (1991). *Learning and memory.* New York: Norton.

Schwartz, B., & Robbins, S. J. (1995). *Psychology of learning and behavior* (4th ed.). New York: Norton & Company.

Seefeldt, C., & Barbour, N. (1994). *Early childhood education: An introduction* (3rd ed.). New York: Macmillan.

Seidenberg, M. S., & McClelland, J. L. (1989). A distributed, developmental model of word recognition and naming. *Psychological Review, 96,* 523–568.

Seidenberg, M. S., Plaut, D. C., Petersen, A. S., McClelland, J. L., & McRae, K. (1994). Nonword pronunciation and models of word recognition. *Journal of Experimental Psychology: Human Perception and Performance, 20*(6), 1177–1196.

Senechal, M., LeFerve, J., Thomas, E. M., & Daley, K. E. (1998). Differential effects of home literacy experiences on the development of oral and written language. *Reading Research Quarterly, 33*(1), 96–116.

Shanahan, T., Mulhern, M., & Rodriguez-Brown, F. (1995). Project FLAME: Lessons learned from a family literacy program for linguistic minority families. *The Reading Teacher, 48*(7), 586–593.

Shannon, P. (1990). *The struggle to continue: Progressive reading instruction in the United States.* Portsmouth, NH: Heinemann.

Shaywitz, B. A., Pugh, K. R., Jenner, A. R., Fulbright, R. K., Fletcher, J. M., Gore, J. C., et al. (2000). The neurobiology of reading and reading disability (dyslexia). In M. L. Kamil, P. B. Mosenthal, P. D. Pearson, & R. Barr (Eds.), *Handbook of reading research* (Vol. 3, pp. 229–249). Mahwah, NJ: Erlbaum.

Shaywitz, B. A., Shaywitz, S. E., Blachman, B. A., Pugh, K. R., Fulbright, R. K., Skudlarski, P., et al. (2004). Development of left occipitotemporal systems for skilled reading in children after a phonologically-based intervention. *Biological Psychiatry, 55*(9), 926–933.

Shaywitz, B., Shaywitz, S., Pugh, K., Mencl, W., Fulbright, R., Skudlarski, P., et al. (2002). Disruption of posterior brain systems for reading in children with developmental dyslexia. *Biological Psychiatry, 52,* 101–110.

Siegel, M., & Fernandez, S. L. (2000). Critical approaches. In M. L. Kamil, P. B. Mosenthal, P. D. Pearson, & R. Barr (Eds.), *Handbook of reading research* (Vol. 3, pp. 141–151). Mahwah, NJ: Erlbaum.

Simos, P. G., Fletcher, J. M., Bergman, E., Breier, J. I., Foorman, B. R., Castillo, E. M., et al. (2002). Dyslexia-specific brain activation profile becomes normal following successful remedial reading. *Neurology, 58,* 1203–1213.

Singer, H. (1983). A critique of Jack Holmes's study: The substrata-factor theory of reading and its history and conceptual relationship to interaction theory. In L. M. Gentile, M. L. Kamil, & J. S. Blanchard (Eds.), *Reading research revisited.* Columbus, OH: Merrill.

Singer, H. (1994). The Substrata-Factor Theory of reading. In R. B. Ruddell, M. R. Ruddell, & H. Singer (Eds.), *Theoretical models and processes of reading* (4th ed., pp. 895–927). Newark, DE: International Reading Association.

Skinner, B. F. (1953). *Science and human behavior.* New York: Free Press.

Skinner, B. F. (1954). The science of learning and the art of teaching. *Harvard Educational Review, 24,* 86–97.

Skinner, B. F. (1965). Reflections on a decade of teaching machines. In R. Glaser (Ed.), *Teaching machines and programmed learning: 2. Data and directions* (pp. 5–20). Washington, DC: National Education Association.

Slavin, R. E. (1997). *Educational psychology: Theory and practice (5th ed.).* Needham Heights, MA: Allyn & Bacon.

Smith, F. (1971). *Understanding reading: A psycholinguistic analysis of reading and learning to read.* New York: Holt, Rinehart, & Winston.

Smith, N. B. (1986). *American reading instruction.* Newark, DE: International Reading Association.

Snow, C. E. (1983). Literacy and language: Relationships during the preschool years. *Harvard Educational Review, 53,* 165–189.

Snow, C. E., Barnes, W. S., Chandler, J., Goodman, I. F., & Hemphill, L. (1991). *Unfulfilled expectations: Home and school influences on literacy.* Cambridge, MA: Harvard University Press.

Snow, C. E., Burns, S. M., & Griffin, P. (Eds.). (1998). *Preventing reading difficulties in young children.* Washington, DC: National Academy Press.

Sperling, G. (1967). Successive approximations to a model for short-term memory. *Acta Psychologica, 27,* 285–292.

Stahl, S. A., & Murray, B. (1998). Issues involved in defining phonological awareness and its relation to early reading. In J. L. Metsala & L. C. Ehri (Eds.), *Word recognition in beginning literacy* (pp. 65–87). Mahwah, NJ: Erlbaum.

Stanovich, K. E. (1980). Toward an interactive–compensatory model of individual differences in the development of reading fluency. *Reading Research Quarterly, 16,* 32–71.

Stanovich, K. E. (1986). Matthew effects in reading: Some consequences of individual differences in the acquisition of literacy. *Reading Research Quarterly, 21,* 360–407.

Stanovich, K. E. (1988). Explaining the differences between the dyslexic and the garden-variety poor reader: The phonological–core variable-difference model. *Journal of Learning Disabilities, 21,* 590–612.

Stanovich, K. E. (1992). *How to think straight about psychology* (3rd ed.). Glenview, IL: Scott, Foresman.

Stanovich, K. E. (2000). *Progress in understanding reading: Scientific foundations and new frontiers.* New York: Guilford Press.

Stanovich, K. E., & Siegel, L. S. (1994). The phenotypic performance profile of reading-disabled children: A regression-based test of the phonological–core variable-difference model. *Journal of Educational Psychology, 86,* 24–53.

Sternberg, R. J. (1996). *Cognitive psychology.* Fort Worth, TX: Holt, Rinehart, & Winston.

Taylor, D. (1983). *Family literacy.* Exeter, NH: Heinemann Educational Books.

Taylor, R. D. (1995). Functional uses of reading and shared literacy activities in Icelandic homes: A monograph in family literacy. *Reading Research Quarterly, 30*(2), 194–219.

Teale, W. H., & Sulzby, E. (1986). *Emergent literacy: Writing and reading.* Norwood, NJ: Ablex.

Theios, J. (1973). Reaction time measurements in the study of memory processes: Theory and data. In G. Bower (Ed.), *The psychology of learning and motivation: Advances in research and theory* (Vol. 7, pp. 43–85). New York: Academic Press.

Thomas, R. M. (1996). *Comparing theories of child development* (4th ed.). Pacific Grove, CA: Brooks/Cole.

Thorndike, E. L. (1903). *Educational psychology.* New York: Lemcke & Buechner.

Thorndike, E. L. (1931). *Human learning.* New York: Century.

Tierney, R. J. (1994). Dissensions, tensions, and the models of literacy. In R. B. Ruddell, M. R. Ruddell, & H. Singer (Eds.), *Theoretical models and processes of reading* (4th ed., pp. 1162–1182). Newark, DE: International Reading Association.

Tracey, D. H. (1995). Family literacy: Overview and synthesis of an ERIC search. In K. A. Hinchman, D. J. Leu, & C. K. Kinzer (Eds.), *Perspectives on literacy research and practice: Forty-fourth yearbook of the National Reading Conference* (pp. 280–288). Chicago: National Reading Conference.

Tracey, D. H., & Morrow, L. M. (2002). Preparing young learners for successful reading comprehension: Laying the foundation. In M. Pressley & C. C. Block (Eds.), *Reading comprehension instruction* (pp. 219–233). New York: Guilford Press.

Tracey, D. H., & Young, J. W. (2002). Mothers' helping behaviors during children's at-home oral reading practice: Effects of children's reading ability, children's gender, and mothers' educational level. *Journal of Educational Psychology, 94*(4), 729–737.

Venezky, R. L. (1984). The history of reading research. In P. D. Pearson, R. Barr,

M. Kamil, & P. Mosenthal (Eds.), *Handbook of reading research* (Vol. 2, pp. 46–67). New York: Longman.

Viise, N. N. (1996). A study of the spelling development of adult literacy learners compared with that of classroom children. *Journal of Literacy Research, 28*(4), 561–587.

Vygotsky, L. S. (1978). *Mind in society: The development of higher psychological processes.* Cambridge, MA: MIT Press.

Vygotsky, L. S. (1986). *Thought and language.* Cambridge, MA: MIT Press. (Original work published 1962)

Vygotsky, L. S. (1987). *Problems of general psychology.* New York: Plenum Press.

Vygotsky, L. S. (1993). *The collected works of L. S. Vygotsky: Vol. 2* (J. Knox & C. Stevens, Trans.). New York: Plenum Press.

Walton, P. D., & Walton, L. M. (2002). Beginning reading by teaching in rime analogy: Effects on phonological skills, letter–sound knowledge, working memory, and word-reading strategies. *Scientific Studies of Reading, 6*(1), 79–115.

Watson, J. B. (1913). Psychology as a behaviorist views it. *Psychological Review, 20*(2), 158–177.

Widmayer, S. A. (2004). *Schema theory: An introduction.* Retrieved December 26, 2004, from chd.gse.edu/immersion/knowledgebase/strategies/cognitivism/SchemaTheory.htm.

Wiederholt, J. L., & Bryant, B. R. (1986). *Gray Oral Reading Tests—Revised.* Los Angeles: Western Psychological Services.

Wolf, M., & Bowers, P. (1999). The "double-deficit hypothesis" for the developmental dyslexias. *Journal of Educational Psychology, 91*(3), 1–24.

Wolf, M., & Katzir-Cohen, T. (2001). Reading fluency and its intervention. *Scientific Studies of Reading, 5*(3), 211–238.

Wolf, M., Miller, L., & Donnelly, K. (2000). Retrieval, Automaticity, Vocabulary Elaboration, Orthography (RAVE-O): A comprehensive fluency-based reading intervention program. *Journal of Learning Disabilities, 33,* 375–386.

Woodcock, R. W. (1987). *Woodcock Reading Mastery Tests—Revised.* Circle Pines, MN: American Guidance Service.

Woolfolk, A. E. (1998). *Educational psychology* (7th ed.). Boston: Allyn & Bacon.

Yaden, D. B., Rowe, D. W., & McGillivray, L. (2000). Emergent literacy: A matter (polyphony) of perspectives. In M. L. Kamil, P. B. Mosenthal, P. D. Pearson, & R. Barr (Ed.), *Handbook of reading research* (Vol. 3, pp. 425–454). Mahwah, NJ: Erlbaum.

Yopp, H. K., & Yopp, R. H. (2002). Supporting phonemic awareness development in the classroom. In International Reading Association (Eds.), *Evidence-based reading instruction: Putting the National Reading Panel Report into practice* (pp. 3–18). Newark, DE: International Reading Association.

# Author Index

Adams, M. J., 84, 165, 166, 167, 176
Allington, R. L., 6, 204
Almasi, J. E., 121
*American Heritage Dictionary*, 2
Anderson, E., 65
Anderson, R. C., 48, 52, 66, 74, 121, 188
Apel, K., 101
Arbruster, B. B., 25
Atkins, P., 169, 176, 178, 181, 182, 203
Atkinson, R. C., 126, 127, 146, 148, 198
Au, K. H., 100, 105, 106, 109, 122, 123

**B**

Baker, L., 61, 62, 63, 190
Bandura, A., 100, 111, 124, 196
Barbour, N., 21, 49, 77
Barnes, W. S., 88, 122
Barr, R., 133, 135, 139
Bartlett, F. C., 48, 52, 66, 74, 188
Bauer, P. J., 29
Bean, T. W., 73
Bergeron, B. S., 59
Bergman, E., 174

Bernard, H. R., 10
Bernstein, B., 101, 123, 195
Best, J. L., 7, 10
Bigge, M. L., 5, 6, 15, 16, 18
Blachman, B. A., 156, 180
Blair, T. R., 58
Block, C. C., 6, 64, 204
Bloom, D., 100, 101, 102
Bloome, D., 114
Booth, J. R., 159, 160
Bowers, P., 171, 177, 181, 182, 203
Breier, J. I., 174
Bronfenbrenner, U., 100, 105, 123, 195
Brown, A. L., 48, 61
Brown, K. J., 73
Brown, R., 62
Brumbaugh, R. S., 6, 11, 15, 16, 18, 20, 37, 38, 77
Bryant, B. R., 44
Bryant, P., 96
Buchoff, R., 95
Burns, G. L., 44
Burns, P. C., 81
Burns, S. M., 28, 85, 101
Bus, A., 88, 121, 194
Byrnes, J. P., 165, 167

227

**C**

Caillies, S., 161
Cardoso-Martins, C., 97, 145, 179, 180
Carnine, D. W., 40, 41, 102, 176, 177
Carver, R. P., 131, 144, 147, 148, 199
Castillo, E. M., 174
Cattell, J. M., 23, 30
Chall, J. S., 77, 83, 99, 193, 195
Chandler, J., 88, 122
Chard, D., 40, 44, 45
Christie, J., 47
Clay, M. M., 77, 85, 99, 193, 195
Collins, A. M., 33
Coltheart, M., 169, 170, 176, 178, 181, 182, 203
Cooter, R. B., 91
Cox, C., 67
Creswell, J. W., 7
Curtis, B., 169, 176, 178, 181, 182, 203


**D**

Daley, K. E., 88
Dearborn, W. F., 23, 30
DeJong, P. F., 88, 121
Denhiere, G., 161
Dewey, J., 48, 71, 74, 76, 191
Dickson, S., 40, 44, 45
Dixon-Krauss, L. A., 108, 120
Dobrich, W., 88, 194
Dole, J. A., 73
Donnelly, K., 177, 178
Dormer, L., 122
Dreher, M. J., 96
Droop, M., 72
Duffy, G. G., 61, 62
Dupuis, A. M., 19
Durkin, D., 61, 88


**E**

Edwards, P. A., 88
Ehri, L. C., 83, 99, 148, 151, 160, 162, 193, 195, 201
El-Dinary, P. B., 62, 64

Elbert, T., 175
Eldredge, J. L., 92
Enz, B., 47
Eulitz, C., 175


**F**

Fernandez, S. L., 100, 114, 197
Fitzgerald, J., 98
Fivush, R., 29
Flavell, J. H., 48, 61
Fletcher, J. M., 30, 160, 174
Flood, J., 89
Foorman, B. R., 160, 174
Fountas, I. C., 143
Fountoukidis, D. L., 93, 177
Francis, D. J., 160
Franklin, S. H., 88
Freire, P., 100, 114, 124, 197
Freud, S., 32
Frith, U., 77, 83, 99, 193, 195
Frost, S. J., 174
Fry, E. B., 93, 177
Fuchs, D., 145
Fuchs, L. S., 145
Fulbright, R. K., 30, 156, 174, 180


**G**

Gaffney, J. S., 121
Gambrell, L. B., 121
Gee, J., 100, 114, 124, 197
Ginsburgh, H. P., 78
Goodman, I. F., 88, 122
Goodman, K. S., 48, 57, 59, 149, 189
Gore, J. C., 30
Goswami, U., 82, 173, 174, 175, 181, 182, 204
Gough, P. B., 83, 193
Green, J., 100, 101, 102
Greenberg, J., 121, 122
Greeno, J. G., 33
Griffin, P., 28, 85, 101
Griffith, P., 83, 193
Gunning, T. G., 82, 86
Gutek, G. L., 15, 16, 18, 19, 20, 49
Guthrie, J. T., 48, 64, 65

**H**

Haebara, T., 152, 153, 160
Haller, M., 169, 176, 178, 181, 182, 203
Halliday, M. A. K., 101, 123
Hart, B., 88, 102, 194
Hatano, G., 152, 153, 160
Hayes, D. A., 5
Heath, S. B., 100, 102, 123
Heilman, A. W., 58
Heim, S., 175
Hemphill, L., 88, 122
Hennings, D. G., 55, 78, 90
Hiebert, E. H., 10, 23, 35, 39, 52, 125
Hogaboam, T. W., 152
Holdaway, D., 77, 80, 81, 88, 90, 91, 97, 99, 192, 195
Hollingsworth, P. M., 92
Holmes, J. A., 129, 131, 147, 148, 198
Hosp, M. K., 145
Huang, C. W., 65
Hudson, J., 29
Huey, E. B., 23, 30, 129

**I**

Inhelder, B., 76, 90, 96, 98, 191

**J**

Jenkins, J. R., 145
Jenner, A. R., 30, 174
Jimenez, R. T., 123
Jordan, G. E., 88, 98, 122
Juel, C., 83, 158, 193

**K**

Kahn, J. V., 7, 10
Kame'enui, E. J., 40, 41, 44, 45, 102, 176, 177
Kamil, M. L., 132, 133, 135, 139
Katz, I. C., 144
Katz, L., 174
Katzir-Cohen, T., 135, 143, 146, 152, 177, 201

Kintsch, W., 148, 154, 161, 162, 163, 202
Kondrick, P. A., 44
Korkeamaki, R., 96
Koskinen, P. S., 44
Kress, J. E., 93, 177
Kuhara-Kojima, K., 152, 153, 160

**L**

LaBerge, D., 134, 135, 138, 146, 147, 148, 149, 168, 199
Langdon, R., 170
Langer, J., 55
Lawrence, N. M., 6, 11, 15, 16, 18, 20, 37, 38, 77
Lee, J. R., 174
LeFerve, J., 88
Lehr, F., 25
Leibert, R. E., 131, 144
Leseman, P., 88, 121
Lynn, A., 160

**M**

McCarthey, S. J., 88
McClelland, J. L., 164, 169, 178, 181, 202, 203
McCormick, C. B., 11
McGee, L. M., 56
McGillivray, L., 97
McRae, K., 178
MacWhinney, B., 159, 160
Martinez-Léon, N., 123
Masterson, J., 101
Mencl, W. E., 174
Meza, M., 122
Miller, L., 177, 178
Moll, L. C., 100, 106, 121, 122
Montare, A., 43
Morphett, M. V., 77, 79, 90, 98, 192, 195
Morrow, L. M., 6, 20, 21, 25, 26, 27, 29, 48, 69, 85, 86, 87, 89, 90, 92, 94, 99, 121, 158, 204
Mosenthal, P., 133, 135, 139
Mulhern, M., 88
Murray, B., 83

**N**

Nelson, K., 29
Neuman, S. B., 88
Noblit, G. W., 98

**O**

Orellana, M. F., 122
Osborn, J., 25

**P**

Paratore, J. R., 88, 95
Pearson, P. D., 48, 52, 66, 74, 133, 135, 139, 188
Pellegrini, A., 88, 121, 194
Pemberton, M. A., 7
Pennington, B. F., 145, 179, 180
Perfetti, C. A., 148, 152, 159, 160, 162, 201
Perry, C., 170
Petersen, A. S., 178
Piaget, J., 76, 90, 96, 98, 191
Pinnell, G. S., 143
Plaut, D. C., 164, 178
Pleasants, H. M., 88
Porche, M. V., 88, 98, 122
Pressley, M., 6, 11, 29, 48, 62, 64, 204
Pugh, K. R., 30, 156, 174, 180
Purcell-Gates, V., 88
Purves, A., 78

**Q**

Quantz, J. O., 23, 30

**R**

Raphael, T. E., 10, 23, 35, 39, 52, 125
Rastle, K., 170, 176, 181, 182
Reisberg, D., 126
Resnick, L. B., 33
Reutzel, D. R., 91, 92
Reynolds, J., 122
Rigoni, N., 73
Risley, T. R., 88, 102, 194
Robbins, S. J., 15

Roe, B. D., 81
Rogriguez-Brown, F., 88
Rosenblatt, L. M., 9, 48, 54, 56, 66, 67, 74, 101, 123, 188
Ross, E. P., 81
Rowe, D. W., 97
Ruddell, M. R., 8, 9, 48
Ruddell, R. B., 8, 9, 48
Rumelhart, D. E., 132, 138, 139, 147, 148, 149, 150, 162, 164, 168, 181, 200, 201, 202, 203
Rupley, W. H., 58

**S**

Saito, H., 152, 153, 160
Samuels, S. J., 132, 134, 135, 136, 137, 138, 146, 147, 148, 149, 168, 199
Santa Barbara Discourse Group, 121, 122
Scarborough, H. S., 88, 194
Schafer, W. D., 65
Schraw, G., 159
Schwartz, B., 15, 126
Seefeldt, C., 21, 49, 77
Seidenberg, M. S., 164, 169, 178, 181
Senechal, M., 88
Shanahan, T., 88
Shannon, P., 20, 42, 57, 79, 100, 114, 124
Shaywitz, B. A., 30, 156, 174, 180
Shaywitz, S. E., 156, 174, 180
Shermis, S. S., 5, 6, 15, 16, 18
Shiffrin, R. M., 126, 127, 146, 148, 198
Siegel, L. S., 161, 162
Siegel, M., 100, 114, 197
Silbert, J., 40, 41, 102, 176, 177
Simmons, D. C., 40, 44, 45
Simos, P. G., 174
Singer, H., 8, 9, 129, 144
Skinner, B. F., 39
Skudlarski, P., 156, 174, 180
Slavin, R. E., 34, 77, 78, 108, 109, 111, 126, 127, 128, 185, 198
Smith, F., 47, 59, 149, 190
Smith, N. B., 21, 28, 48, 49, 57
Smith, P. H., 123
Snow, C. E., 28, 85, 88, 98, 101, 121, 122
Stahl, S., 83
Stanovich, K. E., 73, 126, 132, 148, 149, 150, 151, 153, 155, 156, 158, 161, 162, 163, 168, 171, 201, 202

Sternberg, R. J., 15, 17, 18, 19, 22, 34
Sulzby, E., 85

**T**

Talwalker, S., 114
Tarver, S. G., 40, 41, 102, 176, 177
Taylor, D., 77, 87, 88, 99, 173, 195
Taylor, R. D., 88
Teale, W. H., 85
Thomas, E. M., 88
Thomas, R. M., 2, 9, 10, 11, 12, 32, 33, 37, 39
Thorndike, E. L., 35, 76, 191
Tierney, R. J., 9, 10
Tracey, D. H., 8, 87, 88, 89, 194
Trathen, W., 73

**V**

van IJzendoorn, M., 88, 121, 194
Venezky, R. L., 8, 22, 23, 24, 32, 125
Verhoeven, L., 72
Viise, N. N., 96
Vukelich, C., 47
Vygotsky, L. S., 100, 108, 124, 196

**W**

Walton, L. M., 45
Walton, P. D., 45
Washburne, C., 77, 79, 90, 98, 192, 195
Watson, J. B., 33, 76, 191
Wharton-McDonald, R., 6, 204
Widmayer, S. A., 52
Wiederholt, J. L., 44
Wigfield, A., 64
Wolf, M., 135, 143, 146, 152, 171, 177, 178, 181, 182, 201, 203
Woodcock, R. W., 44, 180
Woolfolk, A. E., 11, 32, 36, 37, 39, 47, 49, 77, 78, 104, 108, 126, 127, 128, 187, 196

**Y**

Yaden, D. B., 97
Yopp, H. K., 159
Yopp, R. H., 159
Young, J. W., 8, 88

**Z**

Ziegler, J., 170

# Subject Index

Accretation, 52
Activity Curriculum, 49–50
Aesthetic responses, 55
*American Reading Instruction,* 21
Aristotle, 16, 17
  connections that would aid memory/
    learning, 184
Associationism, 17–19, 184. *See also*
    Schema Theory
  in classroom practice, 25
    brainstorming, 25
    *literacy education,* 25
    webbing activities, 25
  research applications, 28–29
    foundation for cognitive psychology
      and Behaviorism, 28–29
  teacher's anecdote, 19
*Attention* (A), 136
  alertness/selectivity/limited capacity,
    136
Automatic Information Processing Model,
    134–137, 135f, 199–200
  classroom applications, 141
  components, 134
  research applications, 14–146
  teacher's anecdote, 138

**B**

Bandura, Albert
  Social Learning Theory/Social Cognitive
    Theory, 111–113, 196–197
  stages of observational learning, 111
  *vicarious learning* (observations about),
    111
Bartlett, F. C., 52
Behaviorism, 33, 45–46, 185–187. *See
    also* Classical Conditioning
    Theory; Connectionism; Operant
    Conditioning Theory
  classroom applications, 38–42
    chaining, 39
    educational software development, 39
    programmed learning/programmed
      instruction, 38
    shaping, 38
  educators as "scientific managers," 42
  historical importance of, 32–33
  vs. Maturation Theory, 79
  reading applications, 39
    direct instruction, 40–41
    reading readiness, 41–42
    subskills approach, 39–40

research applications, 43–45
roots in Associationism, 28–29
Big books, 90–91
"Bottom-up" models of reading process,
      132, 134, 137, 149
Brainstorming, 25, 66–67
a web (perspectives on), 12, 67
Bronfrenbrenner, U.
   concentric levels of influence concept,
      105
   Ecological Model of human
      development, 105


C

Carver, R. P., 131–132
   identification of cognitive skills in
      reading, 131
Cattell, J. M., 23
Chaining, 39
Character register, 132
Classical Conditioning Theory, 33–34, 185
   and research, 43
Clay, Marie, 85
Code book, 132
Cognitive Development Theory, 77–78,
      191
   classroom applications, 90
   research applications, 96
   stages of cognitive development
      (Piaget), 78
Cognitive neuroscience, 173
Cognitive processing theoretical
      orientation to reading, 23–24
   general characteristics, 126, 148
   and specific phonological deficit
      hypothesis, 30
Cognitive processing theoretical
      orientation to reading (1950s to
      1970s), 125, 146–148, 198–201.
      See also Automatic Information
      Processing Model; Gough's Model;
      Information Processing Model;
      Interactive Model; Rauding
      Theory; Substrata-Factor Theory
      of Reading
   classroom applications, 140–143
   information processing theories, 126–
      128
   research applications, 143–146

Cognitive processing theoretical
      orientation to reading (1980s),
      148, 162–163, 201–202. See also
      Construction–Integration Model;
      Interactive–Compensatory Model;
      Orthographic processing
      perspective; Phonological–Core
      Variable Difference Model; Verbal
      Efficiency Theory
   classroom applications, 157–159
   research applications, 159–162
Cognitive processing theoretical orientation
      to reading (1989–present), 181–
      182, 202–204. See also Double-
      Deficit Hypothesis; Dual-Route
      Cascaded Model; Neuroscience
      and education; Parallel Distributed
      Processing Model
   classroom applications, 175–178
   research applications, 178–181
Cognitive psychology, roots in
      Associationism, 28–29
Concept-Oriented Reading Instruction
      (CORI), 65
Connectionism, 34–36, 164–165
   laws, 35
   and research, 43
   teacher's anecdote, 36
Construction–Integration Model, 153–
      155, 202
   levels of representation during reading,
      154
   processes during reading, 154–155
   research applications, 161
Constructivism, 47–48, 74–75. See also
      Dewey, John; Engagement Theory;
      Inquiry learning; Metacognition;
      Psycholinguistic Theory; Schema
      Theory; Social Constructivism;
      Whole Language Theory
   classroom applications, 65–71
      Dewey's influence, 66
      Metacognition, 70–71
      Psycholinguistic Theory, 68
      Schema Theory, 66–67
      Transactional/Reader Response
         Theory, 67–68
      Whole Language Theory, 69–70
   and reading, 187–191
   research applications, 71–74
Contiguity concept (Associationism), 17

*Contrast* concept (Associationism), 18
Creationism, 3
Critical Literacy Theory, 113–115, 197
  research applications, 123


**D**

D.E.A.R. time (Drop Everything and
  Read time), 113
*Decoder,* 132
Deficit perspective vs. "funds of
  knowledge," 106–107
Dewey, John, 21, 48–50, 187
  "Activity Curriculum," 49
  influence/classroom applications, 66
  research applications, 71–72
Differentiated instruction, 110
Direct instruction, 40–41
  research, 44–45
Double-Deficit Hypothesis, 171–172,
  203–204
  categorization of reading-disabled
    children, 171
  classroom applications, 177–178
  research applications, 179–180
  teacher's anecdote, 172–173
Dual-Route Cascaded Model, 169–170, 203
  classroom applications, 176–177
  *lexical route,* 170
  *nonlexical/sublexical route,* 170
  research applications, 178–179
  teacher's anecdote, 171
Dyslexic readers, identification of, 155–156


**E**

Ecological Model of human development,
  105
Educational practice and theory. *See*
  Classroom applications of theory
Educational research. *See also* Research
  applications of theory
  "fishing expeditions" (without theory), 8
  importance of theories in, 6–9, 14
Educational software, 27–28, 39
Efferent responses, 55
Emergent Literacy Theory, 42, 84–87,
  193–194
  classroom applications, 94–95
  and literacy-rich home environments, 86

modeling and observational learning
  (importance of), 112–113
  research applications, 97–98
  teacher's anecdote, 87
*Emile,* 20
Engagement Theory, 64–65
*Episodic memory* (EM), 136
Event-related potentials (ERPs), 174
*Exosystem* level of influence, 105
Expectancy Theory, influence on
  Interactive Model, 138
Explicit instruction, 62
Eye–voice span concept, 23


**F**

Family Literacy Theory, 87–89, 99, 194
  classroom applications, 95–96
  research applications, 98–99
  teacher's anecdote, 89
"Fan-spread effects," 156
Freire, P., 114
  "pedagogy of oppression" argument, 114
Freud, S., 32
Froebel, F., 21, 184
Functional magnetic resonance imaging
  (fMRI), 174
"Funds of knowledge" vs. deficit
  perspective, 106–107


**G**

Gough's Model, 132, 133f, 134, 199
  classroom applications, 140–141
  research applications, 145
  teacher's anecdote, 134
Graphophonemic awareness, 151–152
Graphophonic cues, 58, 189
Guided reading, 141–142
  and assessment, 142–143


**H**

Heath, Shirley Brice, reading research
  perspective, 102
High-frequency words/lists, 177
Holdaway, D., 80–82, 192–193. *See also*
  Literacy Development Theory
Holmes, Jack, 129

## I

*Iconic image,* 132
Inferencing, 48
Information Processing Model, 126–128, 127f, 198
 *articulatory loop,* 128
 classroom applications, 140
 *decay,* 128
 *executive control processes,* 127
 *long-term memory,* 128
 *perception,* 127
 research applications, 143–144
 *schemas,* 128
 *sensory register/memory,* 127
 teacher's anecdote, 128–129
 *working/short-term memory,* 127
Information/cognitive processing perspectives. *See* Cognitive processing theoretical orientation to reading
Inquiry learning, 49–50, 187–188
 research applications, 71–72
 teacher's anecdote, 50–51
Instructional approaches
 aligning practice with theory, 6
 and underlying theories, 2, 4–5
Integrated language arts instruction, 44
Intellitalk, 28
Interactive Model, 138–139, 139f, 200. *See also* Parallel Distributed Processing Model
 research applications, 146
 teacher's anecdote, 139–140
Interactive models of reading, 149–150
Interactive–Compensatory Model, 149–150, 201
 classroom applications, 157–158
 research applications, 159
 teacher's anecdote, 150–151

## J

Javal, E., 23

## K

*Kindergarten,* 21
KWL approach, 67

## L

LaBerge–Samuels Model. *See* Automatic Information Processing Model
Language experience chart, 115–116
Law of Effect, 35, 185–186
Law of Identical Elements, 35, 43, 186
Law of Readiness, 186
Learning
 Contructivism perspective on, 47–48
 Inquiry learning, 49–50
*Librarian/lexicon,* 134
Linguistic cueing systems, 57–58
*Literacy center,* 25–26
 implementation of, 26–27
 integrated language arts investigation, 44
 research in, 29
 theoretical support for, 26
Literacy Development Theory, 76–77, 80–82, 191–195. *See also* Cognitive Development Theory; Emergent Literacy Theory; Family Literacy Theory; Maturation Theory; Stage Models of Reading
 classroom applications, 90–96
 reading as a natural process, 81
 research applications, 97
 teacher's anecdote, 82
Literacy growth promotion issues, 1
Literature circles, 117
 implementation, 118–119
 roles
  artist, 118
  connector, 118
  discussion director, 117
  investigator, 118
  passage master, 117–118
  summarizer, 118
  vocabulary enricher, 118
Locke, John, 18
Logographic reading, 83

## M

Manipulatives, 20
Materials available to teachers, 1
"Matthew Effects in Reading," 156
Maturation Theory, 79, 192
 classroom applications, 90
 research applications, 96–97
 teacher's anecdote, 80

Mental Discipline Theory, 16, 183–184
  classroom applications, 24–25
    *repeated reading* practice, 25
  in research applications, 28
  teacher's anecdote, 17
Mentalism, 32–33
*Merlin,* 134
*Mesosystem* level of influence, 105
Metacognition, 61–63, 190–191
  classroom applications, 70–71
  effectiveness of metacognitive
    instruction, 64
  and explicit instruction, 62
  research applications, 73–74
  teacher's anecdote, 63–64
*Microsystem* level of influence, 105
Miscues, 59, 68
Model
  importance of understanding, 10
  and modeling, 112
  vs. theory, 9–10
Montare, A., 43
Morning message technique, 117


N

Neuroimaging, 173–174
Neuroscience and education, 173–175, 204
  research applications, 180–181
  teacher's anecdote, 175


O

Observational learning stages, 111
Operant Conditioning Theory, 36–37,
    186–187. *See also* Behaviorism/
    classroom applications
  research, 44
Orthographic processing perspective, 151–
    152
  research applications, 159–160
Orthographic stage of reading, 83–84


P

Parallel Distributed Processing Model,
    146, 164–168, 202–203
  classroom applications, 175–176
  connectionist theory, 164

four processors, 165, 165f
  context processor, 168
  meaning processor, 167
  orthographic processor (print
    recognition), 165–167
  phonological processor, 167–168
  research applications, 178–179
  teacher's anecdote, 169
Pavlov, Ivan, 33, 185. *See also* Classical
    Conditioning Theory
Perspective/lenses, value of multiple views,
    10–12
Pestalozzi, J. H., 20, 184
"Phonemic awareness," 158–159
*Phonemic tape,* 132
*Phonological memory* (PM), 136
Phonological recoding stage of reading,
    83–84, 93–94
Phonological–Core Variable Difference
    Model, 155–156, 202
  classroom applications, 158–159
  research application, 161–162
  teacher's anecdote, 157
Piaget, Jean, 77, 191. *See also* Cognitive
    Development Theory
  four factors affecting thinking, 77–78
  stages of cognitive development, 78
  vs. Vygotsky, 109
Plato, 16, 183
Political aspects of literacy education. *See*
    Critical Literacy Theory
Positron emission tomography (PET),
    174
*Primary memory,* 134
Principles of Reinforcement (Law of
    Effect), 35, 185–186
Programmed learning/programmed
    instruction, 38
Progressive education, and Rousseau, 20
Psychoanalytic Theory, 32. *See also*
    Mentalism
Psycholinguistic Theory, 57–59, 189–
    190. *See also* Whole Language
    Theory
  and classroom applications, 68
  multiple cueing systems, 57–58
  research applications, 73
  teacher's anecdote, 60–61
  as "top-down" model example, 149
  use of prediction and hypotheses
    during reading, 58
Psychology of reading, 23

**R**

Rauding Theory, 131–132, 199
  research applications, 144
RAVE-O program, 143–144, 178
Reading process
  perspectives about, 2
    Schema Theory perspectives, 52–53
Reading readiness, 41–42. *See also*
    Emergent Literacy Theory
Reading Recovery, 157
Reading research, 31
  early history of, 22–23
  structuralist framework, 22
Reading specialists, as resource for
    classroom teachers, 2
*Repeated reading* practice, 25
Research applications of theory, 6–9
  Associationism, 28–29
  Behaviorism, 43–45
  Connectionism, 43
  Mental Discipline Theory, 28
  Schema Theory, 29
  Structuralism, 30
  Unfoldment Theory, 29
Restructuring, 52
Rosenblatt, Louise, 54, 188–189
Rousseau, J. J., 20, 184
Rumelhart's Model. *See* Interactive Model

**S**

Saccade, 23
Scaffolding, 109
Schema Theory, 29, 51–53, 188. *See also*
    Transactional/Reader Response
    Theory
  accretion, 52
  classroom applications, 66–67
  and reading process, 52, 188–189
  research applications, 72–73
  restructuring, 52
  teacher's anecdote, 53–54
  tuning, 52
*Schemas* (Information Processing Model), 128
Self-efficacy, 112
Semantic cues, 58, 189
*Semantic memory* (SM), 136
"Semiotic mediation," 109
Shaping, 38
Shared reading technique, 91–92

*Sign systems,* 108–109
*Similarity* concept (Associationism), 17
Skinner, B. F., 33, 186. *See also* Operant
    Conditioning Theory
Smith, F., 59
Social Cognitive Theory. *See* Social
    Learning Theory/Social Cognitive
    Theory
Social Constructivism/Socio-Historical
    Theory, 8, 108–109, 196
  classroom applications
    buddy reading, 121
    partner reading, 119–120
    teacher's anecdote, 110–111
Social learning perspective, 100–101, 123–
    124, 195–197. *See also* Critical
    Literacy Theory; Social Construc-
    tivism/Socio-Historical Theory;
    Social Learning Theory/Social
    Cognitive Theory; Socio-Cultural
    Theory; Sociolinguistic Theory
  classroom applications, 115–121
  research applications, 121–123
Social Learning Theory/Social Cognitive
    Theory, 111–113, 196–197
  teacher's anecdote, 113
Socio-Cultural Theory, 104–107, 195–196
  classroom applications, literature
    circles, 117–119
  emphasis on culture and social nature
    of learning, 106
  research applications, 122–123
  teachers' anecdotes, 107–108
Sociolinguistic Theory, 101–103, 195
  anthropological/linguistic/literary
    analysis roots, 101
  classroom applications, 115–116
    language experience chart, 115–116
    morning message technique, 116
  research studies, 121–122
  teacher's anecdote, 103–104
Software (educational), 27–28, 39
Specific phonological deficit hypothesis, 30
Stage Models of Reading, 82–84, 193
  alphabetic/phonetic cue stage, 83
  classroom applications, 92–94
  phonological recoding stage/
    orthographic stage/cipher reading,
    83–84
  research applications, 97–98
  teacher's anecdote, 84
  visual cue reading/logographic stage, 83

Structuralism, 22–24, 184. *See also*
    Cognitive processing theoretical
    orientation to reading
  in classroom practices, 27
  and educational software, 27–28
  and research applications, 30
    reading research advances, 23–24
  teacher's anecdote, 24
Subskills approach, 39–40
Substrata-Factor Theory of Reading, 129–
    130, 198–199
  classroom applications, 140–141
  research applications, 144
  teachers' anecdotes, 130
Syntactic cues, 57–58, 189
*Syntactic and semantic rules processor,* 134


**T**

Tabula Rasa Theory, 18
Thematic instruction, 69–70
Theory, 2–3, 13, 30–31, 204–205. *See
    also* Associationism; Classroom
    applications of theory;
    Constructivism; Literacy
    Development Theories; Mental
    Discipline Theory; Perspective/
    lenses; Research applications of
    theory; Social learning perspective;
    Structuralism; Unfoldment Theory
  associations about, 2
  consciousness/unconsciousness about,
    3–4, 5–6
  definition for education, 4
  and educational practice, 4–5
  and educational research, 6–9
  as lens, 3, 10–12, 205
  vs. model, 9–10
Thorndike, Edward, 33, 185–186. *See
    also* Connectionism
  laws, 35
"Top-down" models of reading process,
    149
*TPWSGWTAU* (the place where sentences
    go when they are understood), 134
Transactional/Reader Response Theory,
    54–56, 188–189
  aesthetic responses, 55
  classroom applications, 67–68
  efferent responses, 55

research applications, 73
  teacher's anecdote, 56–57
Tuning, 52


*Understanding Reading,* 59
Unfoldment Theory, 19–21, 184
  in classroom practice, 25–26
    *literacy center,* 25
  influence on Dewey, 49
  influence on Whole Language Theory,
    60
  research applications, 29
  teacher's anecdote, 21–22
*Unitization,* 135


**V**

Variables (in research), 7–8
Verbal Efficiency Theory, 152–153, 201–
    202
  classroom applications, 158
  research applications, 160
  teacher's anecdote, 153
Vicarious learning, 111
*Visual memory* (VM), 134–135
Vygotsky, Lev Semionovich, 108–109,
    196
  learning and social interactions, 108
    sign systems, 108–109
  vs. Piaget, 109
  scaffolding, 109
  zone of proximal development, 109


**W**

Watson, J. B., 33, 185
Webbing activities, 25, 53, 54, 67
  KWL approach, 67
Whole Language Theory, 59–60, 190
  classroom applications, 69–70
    instructional strategies, 69
  teacher's anecdote, 60–61
*Word families,* 176
Wundt, Wilhelm, 23


**Z**

Zone of proximal development, 109